How Things Work

It is beyond trite to say that technology is prevalent in our daily lives. However, many of us remain clueless as to how much of it works. Unfortunately, even for the curious among us, the Web is not always the best vehicle to acquire such knowledge: Information appears in fragments, some of it is incorrect or dated, and much of it serves as jargon-laden discussions intended for professionals.

How Things Work: The Technology Edition (HTW) will serve as a compendium of tutorials. Each section will focus on one technology or concept and provide the reader with a thorough understanding of the subject matter. After finishing the book, readers will understand the inner workings of the technologies they use every day and, more importantly, they will learn how they can make these tools work for them. In addition, the book will also inform readers about the darker side of modern technology: Security and privacy concerns, malware, and threats from the dark web.

How Things Work
Series Editor: Charles F. Bowman

How Things Work: The Computer Science Edition
Charles F. Bowman

For more information about this series please visit:
https://www.routledge.com/How-Things-Work/book-series/HTW

How Things Work
The Technology Edition

Charles F. Bowman

CRC Press
Taylor & Francis Group
Boca Raton London New York

CRC Press is an imprint of the
Taylor & Francis Group, an **informa** business

A CHAPMAN & HALL BOOK

First edition published 2023
by CRC Press
4 Park Square, Milton Park, Abingdon, Oxon, OX14 4RN

and by CRC Press
6000 Broken Sound Parkway NW, Suite 300, Boca Raton, FL 33487-2742

British Library Cataloguing-in-Publication Data
A catalogue record for this book is available from the British Library

---

Library of Congress Cataloging-in-Publication Data

Names: Bowman, Charles F., author.
Title: How things work : The technology edition / Charles F. Bowman.
Description: First edition. | Boca Raton ; London : CRC Press, 2023. |
    Includes bibliographical references and index. | Contents: How do cell
    phones work? — How does GPS work? — How does computer hardware
    work? — What is software? — How do computers communicate? — How does the
    Internet work? — How do cryptocurrencies work? — What is artificial
    intelligence? — What is quantum computng? — What's next? |
Identifiers: LCCN 2022028339 | ISBN 9780367698270 (hbk) |
    ISBN 9780367697259 (pbk) | ISBN 9781003143437 (ebk)
Subjects: LCSH: Telecommunication—Popular works. | Computer
    science—Popular works. | Explanation—Popular works.
Classification: LCC TK5101 .B66 2023 | DDC 621.382—dc23/eng/20221018
LC record available at https://lccn.loc.gov/2022028339

ISBN: 978-0-367-69827-0 (hbk)
ISBN: 978-0-367-69725-9 (pbk)
ISBN: 978-1-003-14343-7 (ebk)

DOI: 10.1201/9781003143437

Typeset in Minion
by KnowledgeWorks Global Ltd.

Other Books by Charles F. Bowman

Algorithms & Data Structures: An Approach in C
Objectifying Motif
Broadway: The New X Windows System
How Things Work: The Computer Science Edition

As Editor
The Wisdom of the Gurus

This one is for Ro Ro.

Contents

Acknowledgments

Although only one name appears on the cover of a book, a project of this magnitude requires the contributions of many dedicated professionals.

First, I'd like to thank my Editor, Randi Cohen, for making authoring a book as pleasant as possible.

During its development, a manuscript undergoes many reviews and critiques. The suggestions of the following reviewers made this book a better read. I can't thank them enough.

- Emily Riederer

- My friends and business partners Joseph Cerasani and Michael Bardash

That said, any errors or omissions are the sole responsibility of the author.

I am also grateful to the excellent staff at CRC Press, who shepherded the manuscript through all production phases. Their dedicated professionalism is evident in the quality of the book. It was a pleasure to work with them.

Finally, I'd like to thank my family for their support and Maria for always being there when I need her.

Charles F. Bowman
August 2022

CHAPTER 1

Introduction

> Technology is the knack of so arranging the world [so] that we don't have to experience it.
>
> MAX FRISCH

TECHNOLOGY: AN OVERVIEW

When we encounter the word "technology," most of us conjure images of computers and electronic devices—but such a mindset is far too limiting. From automobiles to Zambonis, BMX bikes to hay balers, and 3D printers to ingestible chips embedded into caplets, technology is at the heart of almost everything we do and use.

DEFINITION 1

Technology is the purposeful adaptation of science and knowledge by human beings to benefit other human beings.

Since the advent of tools, humans have been adapting their understanding of nature in ways to improve living conditions (e.g., antibiotics), overcome earthly limitations (e.g., flight), and expand our imaginations (e.g., 3D goggles).

Look around you right now. Unless you're sitting naked and alone in the middle of a forest, you'll likely see technology in every direction. It's inescapable. It's knitted and interwoven into the fabric of our daily existence (see Figure 1.1).

FIGURE 1.1   Technology on the move.

DOI: 10.1201/9781003143437-1

1

Can We Ignore Technology?

There is a better way to phrase this question: Can we engage in daily activities without considering the technology we use?

The answer is yes—to a limited degree. For example, we rarely think about how electricity works when turning lights on and off. However, we'd better know something about how it functions if we intend to replace some wiring. And most of us don't consider the complexities of combustion engines when we drive to the grocery store. Yet, we'd likely extend our automobile's life expectancy if we had some understanding of how cars work and how to maintain them.

How Much Knowledge is Enough?

Well, that often depends on need. For example, consider your smartphone. Yes, we can use it to make calls without knowing how it functions. However, with just a bit of effort, we can become familiar enough with its features so it can metaphorically bring the world to our fingertips. A slightly deeper insight would allow us to customize its functionality. A more extensive study would enable us to alter its underlying programming in ways that might surprise the original designers.

Which Technologies are Important Study?

This is the trickier question, and its answer also depends on your needs—and interests. Are you a photographer? Then an understanding of lens technology would benefit your images. Are you a writer? Then a broad knowledge of the features provided by your favorite word processor would surely boost your productivity. Do you like to bake? Then appreciating the chemistry of leavening ingredients would allow you to create custom cakes.

So, What are the Objectives of This Book?

I'm sure most of you are not looking to become computer scientists, aeronautical engineers, or biochemists—you'd be perusing different types of books. Nonetheless, if you are reading this one, you are interested in acquiring a deeper appreciation of the technologies you encounter in your daily life.

Alas, no single book can discuss all the current technologies—such a tome would become prohibitively long. That said, this book addresses both questions posed in the prior section: It presents a selection of the most common, essential, and pervasive technologies we use every day and describes them in sufficient detail to allow readers to form a conceptual understanding of their design and functionality.

ORGANIZATION

Chapters present one technology in its entirety. Each is self-contained, and the subject matter doesn't depend on prior material; thus, feel free to "jump around" if you'd like.

Every chapter also includes an Advanced Section for those readers who'd like to dive a bit deeper into a particular topic.

To simplify our discussions, we'll use everyday language throughout the text. Nonetheless, understanding technology does require familiarity with terminology. Thus, whenever jargon is unavoidable, we'll introduce it gently and explain it thoroughly. In addition, we have included a glossary at the end of the text.

FORMATTING CONVENTIONS

To simplify the presentation of this material, we've adopted the following formatting conventions.

- When first introduced, technical jargon will appear in *italics*

- Computer-related terms will appear in THIS FONT

- We'll highlight formal definitions using centered text highlighted in gray

This is an example of a formal definition.

- We will highlight program listings in gray, number their lines, and present the code in THIS FONT

```
001  // THIS IS A SAMPLE CODE LISTING
002  #INCLUDE <STDIO.H>
003  MAIN()
004  {
005       PRINTF( "HELLO WORLD\N" );
006  }
```

SUMMARY

Contrary to this chapter's opening quotation, I believe it's essential that we experience reality as it is. Moreover, because technology has become an integral part of modern life, we shouldn't avoid it. Instead, we should welcome it, understand it, and harness it to enhance our experience of the world.

So, find your favorite reading spot, kick back, and join me on an enjoyable journey of discovery.

CHAPTER 2

How Do Cell Phones Work?

Email, instant messaging, and cell phones give us fabulous communication ability, but because we live and work in our own little worlds, that communication is totally disorganized.

MARILYN VOS SAVANT

INTRODUCTION

Throughout the chronicles of human history, there have been epochal moments we can look back on and declare that life fundamentally changed: The discovery of fire, the development of tools, the advent of flight, etc.

Regarding the subject matter of this chapter, some notable moments include the following:

- On March 10, 1876, Alexander Graham Bell uttered the words "Mr. Watson, come here. I want to see you"[1] into the first telephone and ushered in the era of telecommunications.

- In 1977, Apple, Radio Shack, and Commodore introduced mass-market computers, kick-starting the age of personal computing.

- On April 3, 1973, Martin Cooper, a Motorola engineer, completed the first hand-held cellular phone call[2] while walking along the Avenue of the Americas in New York City.

- In 1992, IBM unveiled the Simon Personal Communicator, which ushered in the smartphone era. Although clumsy and clunky by today's standards, this device established a baseline of functionality for all future smartphones.

---

[1] There are disagreements among historians about the actual phrase Mr. Bell spoke. There were also lawsuits alleging that Mr. Bell may not have invented the telephone.

[2] Legend has it that Mr. Cooper called his rival, Mr. Joel Engel, at Bell Laboratories to inform him that Motorola had beaten Bell Labs to the punch.

DOI: 10.1201/9781003143437-2

- In 2007, Apple debuted the inaugural version of the iPhone. This device was as sleek as it was powerful, and for the first time, telecommunications and the Internet became fully integrated into the palm of a user's hand.

The rest, as they say, is history.

CELL PHONE DEVELOPMENT

Before we describe how they work, let's begin our discussion of cell phones with some definitions and a brief overview of their development.

What is a Cell Phone?

A cell phone is a portable communication device that uses radio signals to communicate with a cell provider's network. Once connected, a cell phone allows users to initiate and receive calls from any other telephone (mobile, landline, or Voice over Internet Protocol [VoIP][3]).

What is a Smartphone?

As depicted in Figure 2.1, a smartphone is a mobile electric device that provides functionality beyond basic cell phone capabilities. Examples include email, movie streaming, videoconferencing, interactive games, and payment services.

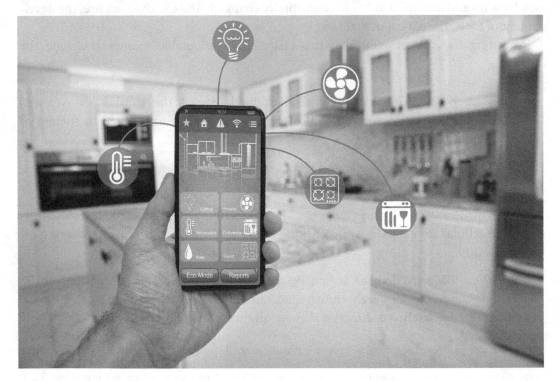

FIGURE 2.1   Smartphone features.

---

[3] This technology supports voice communications via the Internet.

Smartphones and Modern Life

When smartphones became commonplace, the genie bolted from its bottle, and it was never returning. Businesses and consumers quickly understood the power and convenience of these devices, and the world shrunk to the point where we could now hold it in our hands.

Let's briefly look at how this technology changed modern life in just a few years.

Communication	We routinely call, text, and email friends, family, and colleagues using just a thumb or our voice. In addition, we can have books read to us while we jog or watch movies while we relax on the beach.
Information	Modern society demands instant gratification. So, if we have a question, we *google* the answer. If we need to know how our investments are doing, we open a portfolio analyzer. If we want to see how our children are doing in nursery school, we launch a camera app.
Commerce	From frozen corn to electric cars, we can buy almost anything "on the Web." But that convenience doesn't come without a price. Advertisers blast our inboxes with spam and "exclusive offers." Worse,[4] retailers can direct targeted messages to individual customers as they stroll past storefronts or browse through specific aisles while inside a store. And most insidiously, marketers garner and sell our personal information via "free" apps. Alas, privacy was something our grandparents enjoyed.
Culture	Being the blessing and bane of modern life, social media platforms influence opinions, disseminate information (from factual to subjective to wholly inaccurate), and create unrealistic expectations and unattainable goals. Everybody's life is perfect on social media.

The above notwithstanding, smartphones are here to stay. Indeed, they will become even more powerful and pervasive and will increasingly inflict their influence on our lives.

Cell Phone Network Evolution

Along with advances in smartphone technology, cell phone networks have undergone a series of evolutionary improvements, each denoted by a "generation" label. (That's what the "G" represents in 1G, 2G, 3G, etc.)

However, before we cannonball into the deep end of the pool, let's begin with a few definitions.

---

[4] At least in my opinion.

In IT, we define a network as follows:

DEFINITION 1

A network comprises two or more systems (called *nodes* in network terminology) that exchange data via wired or wireless communication technologies.

And we define a cell phone (cellular) network as follows:

DEFINITION 2

A cellular network is a set of interconnected stations (called *cells*) that use radio-based technologies (i.e., wireless connectivity) to communicate with mobile phones.

These definitions will suffice for the moment. So, let's resume our discussion of the history of this technology.

In the beginning, there was 1G. Introduced in the 1980s, this standard supported only analog-based communications.

DEFINITION 3

Analog communication[5] uses a continuous signal that varies in frequency or amplitude. The human voice is an excellent example of an analog signal.

Though revolutionary for its time, 1G phones lacked the call quality and battery life we've come to expect today. Also absent were data channels (which allow you to surf the Web) and any semblance of security (to protect your privacy).

The next evolutionary step, 2G, began rolling out in the early 1990s and moved cell phones into the digital age.

We define digital information as follows:

DEFINITION 4

Digital information[6] is data that we can represent as a series of 1s and 0s. So, for example, every file on your smartphone or computer—emails, songs, pictures, etc.—contains only 1s and 0s.

2G also increased transmission speeds, reduced "dropped calls,"[7] and introduced communication features such as text messaging[8] and encryption.

---

[5] We will compare that with digital communication later in the text.
[6] We will expand on this topic later in the text.
[7] "Can you hear me now?"
[8] Short Message Service (SMS) and Multimedia Messaging Service (MMS).

Introduced in the late 1990s, 3G improved data transmission rates even more. Cell phone users could now participate in video calls and hold the Internet in their hands.

The year 2008 saw the initial rollout of 4G networks. This generation's performance improvements allowed users to participate in video conferences, watch HD movies, and experience 3D entertainment.

As is often the case, products can become victims of their success. Mobile phones are a perfect example. As their power and functionality increased, so did the demand. To meet that ever-increasing need, carriers began rolling out the fifth generation (5G) of mobile technology in 2019. 5G ensures considerable increases in bandwidth while further reducing call and data latency. In addition, the performance improvements may allow consumers to ditch their Internet Service Providers (ISPs) and replace all their in-home wired connections (e.g., cable TV, Internet) with a wireless 5G router.

CELL PHONE TECHNOLOGY OVERVIEW

Earlier in this chapter, I provided a brief description of a cell phone. It's now time to get a bit more formal.

> **DEFINITION 5**
>
> A cell phone is a portable device that allows users to connect to the traditional, public (switched) telephone network[9] to initiate and receive calls.

As depicted in Figure 2.2, cell phones are essentially two-way radios. They connect to base stations using radio waves.[10] Base stations, in turn, connect to Mobile Switching Centers, which provide seamless integration into the traditional telephony infrastructure.

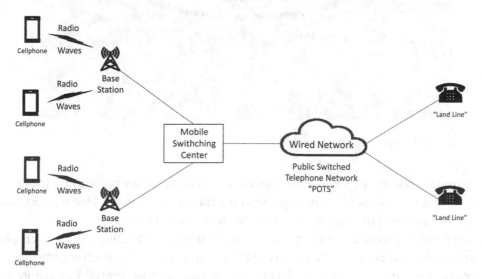

FIGURE 2.2   Simplified cell network.

---

[9] The term "traditional telephone network" (also called "POTS" which stands for Plain Old Telephone System) refers to the copper and fiber-based infrastructure that serves as the backbone of our public, circuit-switched telephone network (i.e., "landlines").

[10] Discussed later in this chapter.

As we'll see, it's a tad more complicated than I just described. Nonetheless, in the sections that follow, we'll peel away the layers of this onion so that you'll acquire a thorough understanding of how this extraordinary technology functions.

What are Radio Waves?

As mentioned in the prior section, cell phones rely on radio waves to send and receive signals to/from base stations. Radio waves are a form of energy generated by *electromagnetic radiation*; we can understand how they work by relating them to more familiar examples of energy propagation: Mechanical waves.

For example, all of us have dropped pebbles into a lake or pond and watched waves emanate from the point of impact. Similarly, when we press a key on a piano, a "hammer" strikes a string[11] and causes the surrounding air to vibrate, which transmits the waves to our eardrums, allowing us to "hear" the note. In both instances, a *medium*—water and air, respectively—propagates the energy (Figure 2.3).

FIGURE 2.3   Energy propagation in water.

Electromagnetic waves are like mechanical waves in that they radiate energy. The difference is that they do not require a physical medium to propagate. That is, electromagnetic waves can travel through matter, air, and the vacuum of space.

As depicted in Figure 2.4, a cell phone sends audio signals received by its microphone to a *transmitter* that converts them into electrical impulses. (A *transmitter* comprises several subcomponents: *Oscillator*, *modulator*, and *amplifier*; however, we can ignore these for this discussion.)

---

[11] For the sake of completeness, I should note that many piano keys contain more than one string.

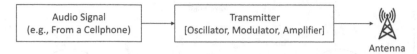

FIGURE 2.4 Simplified example of radio transmission.

Antennas are the components that send and receive signals. When transmitting, antennas convert electrical impulses into radio (electromagnetic) waves. When serving as receivers, they perform the complement operation (i.e., convert electromagnetic waves into electrical signals). Most modern smartphones ship with multiple antennas to support various connections such as cellular, Wi-Fi, and Bluetooth.

Antennas transmit radio signals omnidirectionally (Figure 2.5). However, electromagnetic waves might not arrive at a receiving antenna because surrounding objects[12] (buildings, mountains, etc.) can absorb and reflect their energy. Consequently, this may prevent signals from reaching the intended cell tower. (This is one of the reasons why you might find yourself saying, "Can you hear me now?")

FIGURE 2.5 Radio waves.

Frequencies and Channels

Radio waves propagate at the speed of light (approximately 186,000 miles per second or 300,000 kilometers per second).[13] Like all waves, electromagnetic radiation has several measurable properties, including *wavelength*, *amplitude*, and *frequency*.

Let's define each of these attributes.

---

[12] Please note that the term "surrounding object" includes your own head when you're holding the phone to your ear.

[13] For the sake of accuracy, I should note that this is the speed light travels through a vacuum, which scientists commonly represent using the letter *C*. (Think: $E = MC^2$.) Light travels more slowly through other mediums (e.g., air and glass).

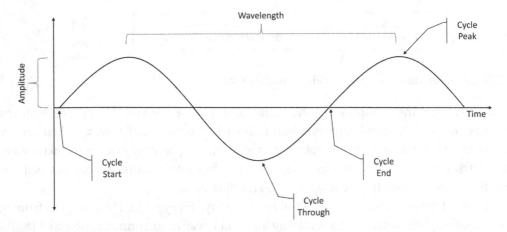

FIGURE 2.6   Anatomy of a wave.

As depicted in Figure 2.6, *amplitude* measures a wave's energy: The greater the amplitude, the greater the energy. For example, we experience amplitude as volume or loudness for sound waves: The greater the amplitude, the louder the volume.[14]

We define *wavelength* as the distance between two successive peaks in a wave, and each repetition of a wave is a *cycle*. Thus, the wavelength is the length of one *cycle*. We define *frequency* as the number of cycles per second, and we express them in units called *Hertz* (Hz).[15]

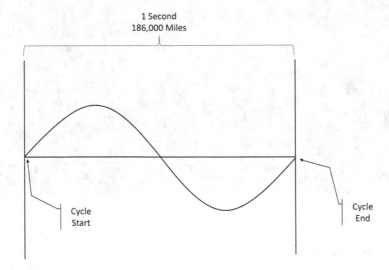

FIGURE 2.7   A 1 Hz wave.

As depicted in Figure 2.7, the frequency of a wave that completes one cycle every second is 1 Hz. Thus, based on a wave's velocity (i.e., the speed of light or *C*), a 1 Hz wave will travel 186,000 miles during each cycle.

---

[14] "These go to eleven." Forgive me, this is an obscure reference for fans of the movie, "This is Spinal Tap."
[15] Named in honor of the German physicist Heinrich Rudolf Hertz.

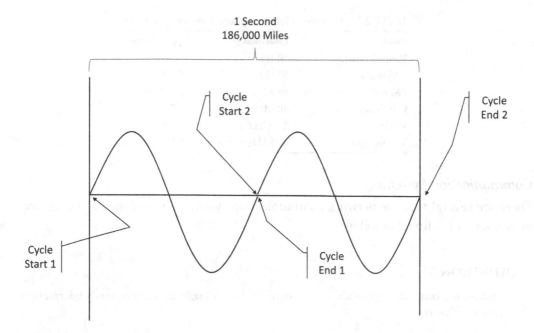

FIGURE 2.8   A 2 Hz wave.

Figure 2.8 depicts a 2 Hz wave. Note that in this example, the wave propagates 93,000 miles with the completion of each half-second cycle.

We define a *frequency band* (or simply *band*) as a predefined range of frequencies with specific upper and lower bounds. We typically use the phrase to refer to a named group of frequencies, such as in AM, FM, and Wi-Fi. For example, by design, the AM radio in your car can only receive frequencies in the range of 535 kilohertz (kHz)[16]–1.7 megahertz (MHz).[17]

A *channel* is a specific frequency within a *band*. Transmitters and receivers don't select arbitrary frequencies within a band to communicate. Instead, they use predefined *channels*. So, for example, when you want to listen to a New York Yankee's broadcast, you tune your radio to a specific frequency (i.e., 660 kHz)[18] within the AM band.

On average, humans can hear frequencies between 20 Hz and 20,000 Hz (or 20 GHz[19]). Sounds below 20 Hz are inaudible to most of us. That's why you can sometimes *feel* a piece of music (because of ultralow bass sounds) but not hear it.

Sounds above 20,000 Hz (20 kHz) are also inaudible for humans. However, dogs can hear frequencies between 40 Hz and 60,000 Hz (60 kHz). So that's how dog whistles work: they generate frequencies within the range of 23–54 kHz, which dogs can hear but we cannot.

Some examples of standard frequency bands appear in Table 2.1.

---

[16] A kilohertz is 1,000 cycles (Hertz) per second.
[17] A megahertz is one million cycles (Hertz) per second.
[18] If you're in the New York City area and you happen to be a Yankee fan—like me.
[19] A gigahertz is one billion cycles (Hertz) per second.

TABLE 2.1 Common Electromagnetic Frequency Bands

Band	Lower Range	Upper Range
Human hearing	20 Hz	20 kHz
AM radio	535 kHz	1.7 MHz
FM radio	88 MHz	108 MHz
Cordless phones	40 MHz	50 MHz
Wi-Fi	2.4 GHz	5 GHz
Visible light	400 THz[20]	790 THz

Communication Systems

There are several types of network communication systems. One of the most common is *broadcast*. We define it as follows:

> **DEFINITION 6**
>
> *Broadcast* is a one-way communication system wherein a single transmitter sends information to many recipients.

Broadcast is how over-the-air (radio and TV) and cable systems work. Each network transmits its signal, and recipients (viewers/listeners) tune to the appropriate frequency (i.e., channel) to watch/listen to their favorite programs.

However, as I'm sure you could imagine, broadcast communication would be impractical for cell phones. Telephone calls are private—we only want specific recipients to receive our transmissions. In addition, we'd usually want the other party to take part in the conversation as well.

In contrast to broadcast, *duplex communication* allows for bidirectional transmissions.

> **DEFINITION 7**
>
> Duplex communication systems allow communicating parties to exchange messages in both directions.

There are two ways in which duplex systems allow bidirectional communication: *Half duplex* and *full duplex*.

In *half-duplex* systems, communicating entities share the same channel. Thus, to ensure that messages are not "garbled," only one party can transmit at any moment in time. A common example of this approach is using walkie-talkies. When finished speaking, each party signals the end of their message by saying "over." Upon hearing this phrase, the other party knows they can begin speaking (transmitting).

Although a step in the right direction, a walkie-talkie-type verbal protocol would certainly frustrate cell phone users. Thus, cell networks employ *full-duplex* communication, wherein

---

[20] A terahertz is one trillion cycles (Hertz) per second.

each communicating entity uses two channels: One for sending and one for receiving. That's why you can simultaneously hear all the grunts and groans of customer service representatives while you're so eloquently expressing your dissatisfaction about one of their products.

WHAT IS A CELL NETWORK?

As mentioned previously, cell phones initiate and receive calls by connecting to cell sites (sometimes called base stations). Each cell site comprises a tower (hosting the antennas) and a small structure or building that hosts the necessary electronics enabling the site to connect to the mobile carrier's network.

Each cell "covers" a geographical region. That is, it maintains connections for all the cell phones within the range of its antennas. (We'll elaborate on this shortly.)

A cell network (or cellular network or mobile network) comprises a set of cell sites spanning a broad geographic area (e.g., a city). In addition to communicating with cell phones within its coverage areas, cell sites exchange data with neighboring sites to negotiate "handoffs" as cell phones move from one coverage area to another. (We'll see how this works later in this chapter.)

As you travel (i.e., as the cell phone moves), you may encounter regions where your cell phone cannot communicate with any nearby base station. We refer to that area as a "dead spot." (Another cause of the "Can you hear me now?" issue.)

The coverage range of individual cells may vary. For example, in densely populated areas, cells will cover a radius of 1–10 kilometers (or about 6.2 miles). However, in rural areas, the coverage area may extend up to 50 kilometers (or about 31 miles).

As depicted in Figure 2.9, you can envision a cell's coverage area as a circle with the transceiver tower positioned in the center. Broadcasting omnidirectionally,[21] each cell communicates using a subset of frequencies assigned to the carrier. As also highlighted in Figure 2.9, note that providers may reuse frequency groups in nonadjacent cells.

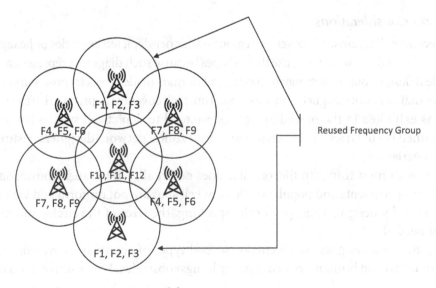

FIGURE 2.9   Circular coverage area and frequencies.

---

[21] i.e., 360 degrees.

However, most modern cell sites employ directional antennas. Thus, we tend to depict coverage areas as a set of broadcast towers located at three corners of a honeycombed group of hexagonal transmission zones.

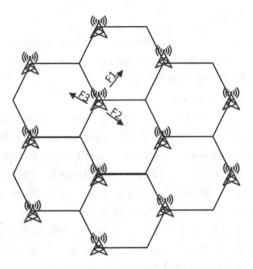

FIGURE 2.10   Hexagonal coverage areas.

As depicted in Figure 2.10, towers use three directional antennas angled 120 degrees apart. (Combined, they cover 360 degrees or a full circle.) Thus, each transmitter sends/receives signals to/from three different cells increasing the probability that a cell phone will connect with a tower when passing through a given geographic region. Regardless of how we depict them, the point to note is that each cell's coverage area overlaps with adjacent cells.

Real-World Considerations

In the preceding diagrams, cell coverage regions—whether depicted as circles or hexagons[22]—appear regular and consistent. We use these shapes because such diagrams represent a conceptual or ideal design. But unfortunately, nature and human-made issues impose some practical challenges that network designers must address. Thus, cell coverage in practice isn't so uniform.

First, as exhibited in the preceding figures, we tend to depict cell sites as having crisp, clearly defined boundaries. However, to avoid dead zones, network designers ensure coverage areas overlap.

Next, as with most things in life, one size does not fit all. Due to such considerations as geographic impediments and population density, cell sites are not uniform and vary in their coverage area (by design). Thus, practically speaking, the sizes of the circles and hexagons change as needed.

Finally, network designers often employ several types of antennas to overcome natural (e.g., mountains) and human-created (e.g., buildings) obstacles. For example, a small tower

---

[22] We tend to use hexagons to represent "perfect" cells because their shape allows them to combine in a manner such that they can cover a plane (i.e., a flat surface) without any gaps or overlaps. In mathematics, we refer to this attribute as *tessellation*.

may broadcast omnidirectionally for a limited range. However, when addressing large geographic areas, designers may use directional antennas to subdivide the coverage area into sectors (three is most common). In addition, carriers often employ multiple frequencies within a cell to minimize dead zones.

Network Protocols

For entities to communicate—computers, cell phones, or people—they need a set of procedures to govern their interaction. We call such conventions *protocols*. This concept is not new, nor is it the exclusive province of the world of technology.

For example, consider the sequence of events that transpire during a typical telephone conversation. When answering a call, most people begin with a curt, "Hello." Or, if it is a business call, they might start the conversation with a phrase such as, "Hello, this is John Smith." At that point, callers usually identify themselves using responses such as, "Hi, it's Jane." Or "Hello, my name is Jane Jones, and I'm with the Acme Marketing Company." In addition, there are usually clear signals indicating when one party should speak and the other should listen during the ensuing conversation.[23]

The point is that regardless of whether we're conscious of it, we use such social protocols to simplify and organize interpersonal communication.

In IT, *network protocols* govern the interaction of communicating electronic devices. However, because digital components are not as intelligent or adaptable as humans, network protocols require significantly more structure and formality.

DEFINITION 8

A *network protocol* establishes the rules, procedures, and formats that allow electronic components to exchange data securely, efficiently, and reliably.

In the world of electronic communication, protocols allow us to send emails (e.g., POP3, SMTP), stream movies (e.g., RTMP, MP4), display web pages (e.g., HTTP, HTTPS), download files (e.g., FTP, SFTP)—the list is quite extensive. Nonetheless, despite their variety, every one of these protocols must minimally define the following communication requirements:

- How to establish a connection

- How to exchange messages

- How to structure and format messages

- How to respond to errors

- How to terminate a connection

---

[23] Assuming a reasonable level of civility.

Absent such "rules of engagement," electronic communication would be impossible.

The same rules apply in mobile networks: Protocols establish frameworks within which cell phones and base stations communicate and exchange data.

In older cell phones (i.e., before 4G and 5G), two radio protocols dominated the market: Global System for Mobile Communication (GSM) and Code Division Multiple Access (CDMA).

Although the technical specifications of these two protocols are beyond the scope of this book, they both served as the framework for early cell phone communication. Nonetheless, the existence of two standards caused confusion and compatibility difficulties for consumers. For example, there was a time when it wasn't always possible to keep your existing cell phone when changing carriers.

Despite their initial success, technology evolved beyond these early standards. As a result, cell phone carriers began phasing out these early protocols as they rolled out their LTE, 4G, and 5G offerings. Indeed, 5G holds the promise of worldwide compatibility.

ESN and SID Codes

During its manufacture, every cell phone receives an individual identity known as Electronic Serial Number (ESN) for CDMA-based cell phones or an International Mobile Equipment Identity (IMEI) for GSM-based devices. This number ensures that carriers can uniquely identify every cell phone that connects to their network. (Moving forward, we will refer to these device identifiers generically as ESNs.)

Mobile Identification Numbers

As I'm sure you're already aware, cell phones are associated with a "home" carrier (e.g., AT&T, Verizon, and T-Mobile). In addition, they may connect to other "approved" service providers when "roaming" (i.e., when the cell phone's location is outside its home coverage area). Consequently, cell phones need some way to identify carriers when connecting to a network.

To accomplish this, each service provider identifies itself using a System Identification Number (SID). Originally assigned and administered by the Federal Communications Commission (FCC),[24] each SID uniquely identifies a single network.

Whenever you purchase a cell phone (or change carriers), in addition to assigning a telephone number,[25] the activation process stores your carrier's SID and the SIDs for the provider's approved roaming partners in your device.

When powered up, your cell phone searches for a network signal. If it doesn't find one, it displays a "no service" indication. If it does receive a network signal, your cell phone compares the SID with those stored in its memory. Based on the values, the phone "knows" whether it's on its "home" network or it's currently "roaming." (We'll discuss this in more detail shortly.)

---

[24] In many countries, an organization called iFAST, Ltd. assigns and maintains SIDs.
[25] In cell phone parlance, this is a mobile identification number or MIN.

ANATOMY OF A CELL PHONE CALL

Thus far, we've discussed the technologies and standards that support cell phones at a conceptual level. Now it's time to get practical and understand how these pieces work together to allow you to hold an extended telephone conversation while on the move.

Connecting to a Network

After a power-up or a reboot, cell phones must connect to a network. To accomplish this, they search for SIDs broadcasted by nearby base stations on a predefined frequency called a *control channel*. As we'll see below, control channels allow cell phones to complete many administrative tasks such as logging onto the network, call management, and voice channel assignment.

When a cell phone identifies a SID, it compares it to the SIDs stored in its memory as part of the activation process. When it finds a match, the cell phone "registers" with the base station, determines whether it's on its home network or roaming, and then presents an appropriate screen icon. Cell phones display a "no service" message if they fail to identify a valid SID.

The initial base station stores the cell phone's current location in a central database as part of the registration process. Then, as the cell phone "moves," cells track location changes and update the database, thus ensuring that the network "knows" the controlling location for every connected cell phone.

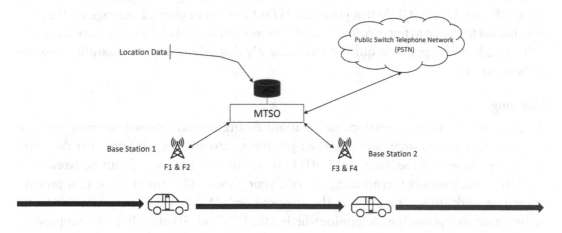

FIGURE 2.11   Cell phone location tracking.

For example, a cell phone traveling in the car depicted in Figure 2.11 registers with Base Station 1 when it enters its coverage area. Base Station 1 sends the registration data to a Mobile Telephone Switching Office (MTSO), which hosts the location database.

As the car continues traveling, the cell phone eventually leaves Base Station 1's coverage area and enters Base Station 2's coverage area. At that point, Base Station 2 sends a location update to the MTSO.

Receiving a Call

When someone calls you (whether it's from a landline or another cell phone), the MTSO looks up your location record in its database. Once it determines your cell phone's currently assigned base station, it selects two available voice channels for the call.[26]

Then, using the control channel, the MTSO informs both the base station and your cell phone which frequencies to use. After the devices switch to the newly assigned channels, the connection completes, and your conversation can commence.

Maintaining a Call

If a cell phone remains connected to the same base station for the entire call (e.g., you're using your cell phone while at home), the network has little to do until one of the parties terminates the connection. However, cell phones are designed to be mobile; thus, networks must constantly monitor a device's location to maintain seamless connectivity.

Let's see how this works.

While a call is in progress, all nearby base stations monitor signal strength. As a cell phone moves, the base station currently responsible for the connection sees the signal strength decreasing while the base station the phone is approaching sees the signal strength increasing. At this point, the two base stations must coordinate a "handoff."

For example, let's return to the call state depicted in Figure 2.11. While moving within the coverage area of Base Station 1, the cell phone uses frequencies F1 and F2. As the car approaches the boundary between the two cells, the two base stations exchange messages and coordinate a "handoff" (via the MTSO). At that point, the MTSO sends your phone a message via the control channel to switch to frequencies F3 and F4 and assigns control of the call to Base Station 2.

This exchange happens so quickly and efficiently that callers remain blissfully unaware of its occurrence.

Roaming

As described in the prior section, base stations ensure smooth transitions from one cell to another. However, what happens when you move into an area your provider does not cover? That is, what if the "next" cell's SID indicates that it's not part of your network?

In this case, instead of terminating the call, your phone will connect to the new provider's cell network. To accomplish this, the new provider's MTSO will query your provider to authenticate your phone (i.e., determine whether the ESN and SID are valid). Once approved, the call continues uninterrupted. That said, you should be aware that roaming charges may be applicable for this service.

Network Integration

One of the most remarkable aspects of mobile communication networks is their ability to integrate with the existing telephony infrastructure. For example, cell phone users can call traditional analog phones (landlines) or VoIP devices without a second thought.

Figure 2.12 provides a conceptual view of the complete telephony network.

---

[26] Please recall that full-duplex communication requires two channels.

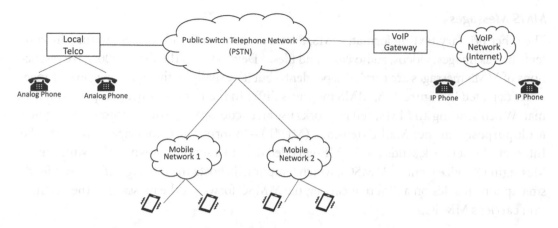

FIGURE 2.12   Telephony network—Conceptual overview.

ADVANCED SECTION

Sending Texts and Multimedia Messages

One of the most convenient features of smartphones is their ability to send and receive *text messages*. It's become cliché to say that a given technology has "revolutionized life on the planet." Nonetheless, this statement is not an exaggeration regarding cell phones in general and texting specifically.

This "fire and forget" technology is fast becoming the preferred way to communicate. Indeed, more and more smartphone users don't even activate voicemail services to "encourage" family and friends to send them texts rather than recorded voice messages.

Although it's not often apparent to users, texting comes in two *flavors*: Short Message Service (SMS) and Multimedia Messaging Service (MMS). Let's discuss each in turn.

SMS Messages

The basic service, called SMS, allows users to send and receive short text messages. Developed and standardized in the mid-to-late 1980s, it remains the most pervasive and widely used form of texting. Let's look at the details.

A single SMS message may not exceed 160 characters.[27] If a user sends a text larger than that, the network subdivides the message into 160-character segments and sends each one in sequence. Then, the receiving phone aggregates the "chunks" and displays them in the original order as one message.

The SMS infrastructure uses control channels to send and receive texts. (For information on control channels, please see the "Connecting to a Network" section.) Specifically, the design approach leverages the otherwise unused bandwidth when control channels are idle. Although this approach allows transmitting data with minimal network impact, it requires that text messages conform to the control channel's protocol formats. (That's why SMS messages cannot exceed 160 bytes.)

---

[27] Note that this limitation includes spaces (blank characters).

MMS Messages

The other primary texting format, MMS, allows users to send and receive multimedia content such as images, videos, audio clips, and files.[28] Developed in the early 2000s, size restrictions of MMS messages are carrier-dependent—but it's usually in the multi-megabyte range.

As depicted in Figure 2.13, MMS messages differ in their communication path and format. When sending an MMS, cell networks use an encoding employed by browsers—called Multipurpose Internet Mail Extensions (MIME)—to format text messages. Then, via the Internet, the network sends the MIME-encoded data to a server known as the Multimedia Messaging Service Center (MMSC), which temporarily hosts the message. If the recipient's smartphone resides on a different carrier, the MMSC forwards the message to the destination carrier's MMSC.

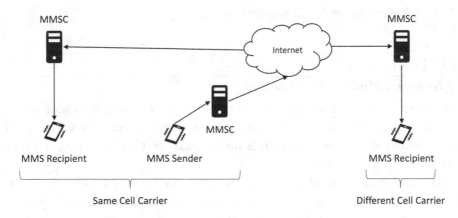

FIGURE 2.13   Simplified MMS message flow diagram.

Unlike SMS texts, MMS messages don't contain actual content. Instead, the destination smartphone receives a control message that includes a "pointer" to where the content resides.

The pointers are usually in the form of a uniform resource locator or URL and are like the "web addresses" you use when directing your browser to a web page. For example, www.nasa.gov.

When it receives an MMS control message, the recipient's smartphone uses the URL information to download and display its content.

Sending Texts via Email

On occasion, you may find sending a text message from your smartphone difficult or tedious. For example, while "working" emails on your desktop computer, you might want to text a colleague the contents of an important message you just received.

You have two choices.

You could retype the entire message into the text app on your smartphone. Or, more simply, you could forward it directly as a text message using your email app.

---

[28] Smartphones must be MMS-enabled to receive MMS messages; most are these days.

To "email" a text message to someone, you need to construct the "to" address as follows:

<TEN-DIGIT PHONE NUMBER>@<SERVICE PROVIDER'S GATEWAY>

The first segment (the part appearing to the left of the "@" sign) is the phone number (including area code) of the individual you want to text. The second (to the right of the "@" sign) is the *domain address* of the recipient's service provider's texting gateway.

For example, to send a text message to a friend who uses the AT&T cellular service and whose telephone number is: 212-555-0136,[29] you would construct the email address as follows:

2125550136@MMS.ATT.NET

Now, simply complete your email message (i.e., type in a subject, body, and add an attachment if desired) and press SEND. In short order, your colleague's phone will sound an alert indicating the arrival of an incoming text.

SUMMARY

This chapter introduced electromagnetic radiation and described how frequencies combine into bands and channels. It then described how cell phones are two-way radios that use two channels simultaneously to support full-duplex transmission.

The chapter went on to discuss how, via control channels, base stations monitor call traffic and assign frequencies as cell phones move through coverage areas. Finally, the Advanced Section examined text messaging and the difference between SMS and MMS.

---

[29] Please note that this is a BOGUS telephone number generated by a web-based service that creates bogus telephone numbers. Nonetheless, please DO NOT call it.

CHAPTER 3

How Does GPS Work?

It finally happened. I got the GPS lady so confused, she said, "In one-quarter mile, make a legal stop and ask directions."

ROBERT BREAULT

INTRODUCTION

I'm sure most readers have used the Global Positioning System (GPS) to guide their journeys using various means of transportation: Pedestrian, automobile, public transit, biking, etc. It's convenient and powerful and has simplified our lives to the point that we no longer ask for directions, just an address. In addition, we rely less on traffic reports broadcast on the radio because most navigation systems integrate real-time road conditions and automatically reroute us as appropriate.

This chapter will discuss how GPS works. We'll begin our journey with a brief history of this powerful technology and show examples of how it provides benefits far beyond ensuring that we arrive at grandma's house on time for Thanksgiving dinner. Following that, we'll describe how it serves as the foundation for the mapping software and turn-by-turn navigation systems we commonly use in our cars and cell phones.

Let's get started.

HISTORY OF GPS

Military Roots

From walkie-talkies to digital cameras, drones to virtual reality, and canned foods to duct tape, many everyday products owe their inception and development to the United States Military. We can number GPS among them.

The origins of GPS date back to the early satellite era in the 1950s.[1] At that time, scientists used shifts[2] in a satellite's radio signals to track its orbit. Then, in the mid-1960s, the United States Navy began experimenting with satellite-based navigation. Using six

---

[1] The former Soviet Union launched the first artificial satellite, called Sputnik 1, on October 4, 1957.
[2] These shifts are known as the *Doppler effect*.

DOI: 10.1201/9781003143437-3

satellites that orbited the poles, United States nuclear submarines could track their position with a high degree of accuracy.

In the 1970s, the United States Department of Defense (DoD) wanted a highly robust and accurate navigation system for military use. Thus, it launched its first Navigation System with Timing and Ranging (NAVSTAR) satellite in 1978. Requiring 24 satellites,[3] it took until 1993 for NAVSTAR to become fully operational.

Civilian Use

In the late 1990s, the United States government announced plans to make GPS available for civilian use (especially for the airline industry). The United States Congress formally approved the proposal in 2000.

Today, the United States Air Force maintains a satellite-based GPS providing two levels of service: Standard Positioning Service (SPS) and Precise Positioning Service (PPS). SPS is freely available worldwide for civilian use. However, the United States government restricts the use of PPS to the United States Armed Forces and selected allies.

Uses of GPS

Most of us are acquainted with the common uses of GPS, such as route navigation and self-driving vehicles. However, below are some additional—less common—applications of this remarkable technology.

Fleet tracking	Transportation firms—not to mention local landscapers and delivery companies—use GPS to track the location of their vehicles.
Surveying	Surveyors use GPS to confirm property lines, which can resolve land disputes.
Theft prevention	Vehicle owners, art dealers, pharmaceutical companies, etc., can embed GPS trackers in their products to thwart theft.
Wildlife tracking	Scientists use diverse types of GPS-based tracking devices (collars, implants, and backpacks) to track the migratory and feeding habits of wildlife.

GPS INFRASTRUCTURE

GPS is an integrated system comprising three main elements: *Satellites, ground stations,* and *receivers.* In the sections that follow, we'll introduce each component and describe its role in computing precise locations on planet Earth.

Satellite Network

As mentioned previously, the United States government manages a nexus of at least 24 satellites that collectively form the space-based component of the GPS. As depicted in Figure 3.1,

---

[3] To be accurate, the program deployed 27 satellites. where 3 served as spares.

each GPS satellite resides in one of six orbital planes inclined 55° from the equator in Medium Earth Orbit (MEO) at an altitude of approximately 12,550 miles (or 20,200 kilometers). Each satellite completes an orbit every 12 hours.

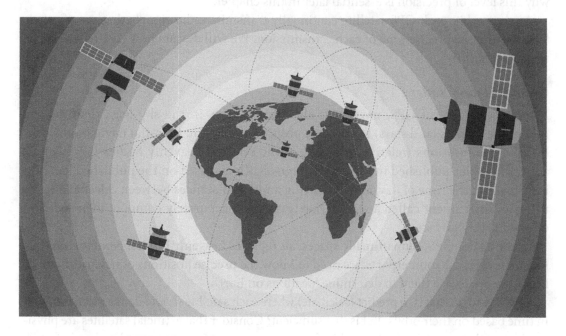

FIGURE 3.1   GPS satellite orbits.

The orbits of GPS satellites align such that at least four are "visible" from every point on the Earth's surface at any moment in time. In this context, "visible" means that their radio signals can reach GPS devices on the ground or in the air; you cannot see the satellites with the naked eye. Figure 3.2 provides an example.

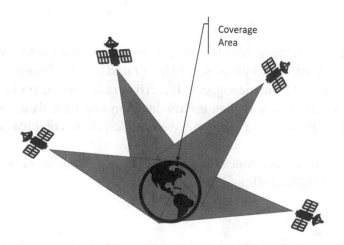

Coverage Area

FIGURE 3.2   GPS satellite coverage.

GPS satellites contain *atomic clocks* to calculate time as accurately as possible. Atomic clocks measure time by tracking the oscillation of atoms. Though not perfect, they are accurate to an error of approximately 1 second every 100 million years! We'll understand why this level of precision is essential later in this chapter.

As they orbit, each GPS satellite continually transmits radio signals that specify their location and the precise time of each transmission. We will discuss how GPS receivers use these data shortly.

Ground Station Radar

Before the advent of GPS, navigators also used objects in the sky (e.g., the Sun, the Moon, the planets, and stars) to compute positions on Earth. Celestial navigation works because the locations (relative to Earth) of the selected heavenly bodies (57 in total) appear in tables published in *Nautical Almanacs*. Thus, based on the published location information, the time of day, and measuring angular distances between celestial objects using an instrument called a *sextant*, navigators can accurately compute their location on the Earth's surface.

In the age of GPS, human-made spacecraft replaces heavenly bodies. Nonetheless, just like their celestial counterparts, we need to know the precise positions of navigation satellites if we are to use them to determine locations on Earth.

One way to do that is to predict (calculate) where each satellite *should be* at a given moment in time based on their orbits. But is that sufficient? Consider that artificial satellites are physical devices that may vary in their orbits for many reasons. Moreover, as we've already stated, navigation requires a high degree of precision. Thus, we can't *estimate* a satellite's location— we must *know* it.

To ensure and maintain computational accuracy, GPS uses ground station radar to determine the exact locations of satellites. The GPS Ground Segment (the collective name for the ground-based radar stations) continually tracks the position of all orbiting GPS components. In addition, the Ground Segment also transmits data and commands to satellites as required.

GPS Receivers

Whether it's part of a factory-installed navigation system in an automobile, a battery-operated handheld device used by hikers, or an integrated feature of modern smartphones,[4] a *GPS receiver* does what its name suggests: It receives radio signals transmitted by orbiting GPS satellites. GPS receivers then use the location and time data encoded in those signals to calculate distance and location. (We'll review those computations in the next section.)

Please note that this communication is unidirectional. That is, GPS receivers never transmit messages to GPS satellites.

---

[4] Technically, most smartphones employ Assisted Global Positioning System (A-GPS) to compute location. See the subsection entitled "Assisted Global Positioning System."

GPS POSITION CALCULATION

Although GPS technology is sufficiently advanced that it seems like magic,[5] it's easy to understand in concept.

At its core, GPS uses a process called *trilateration*[6] to determine locations.

> **DEFINITION 1**
>
> *Trilateration* is a process that relies on the geometry of triangles, circles, and spheres to compute a specific location based on measuring distances from known points.

The best way to explain this definition is by way of example. So, let's begin simply and explain two-dimensional trilateration.

2D Trilateration

Let's say you're participating in a treasure hunt, and to win, you must unearth a prize buried in a field. As a participant, you receive a copy of a "map" outlining the search area as depicted in Figure 3.3.

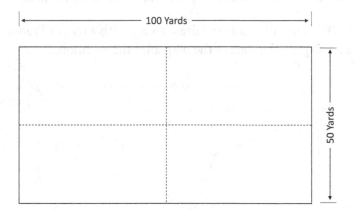

FIGURE 3.3   Treasure hunt field.

Once the hunt begins, you receive a series of clues specifying the location of the buried treasure. The first one reads as follows:

The treasure lies twenty yards from the center of the field.

After a moment's thought, you realize that the prize must lie somewhere on the circumference of a circle originating at the center of the field, having a radius of twenty yards.

---

[5] I took the liberty of paraphrasing a quote from the author Arthur C. Clarke. The original is as follows: *Any sufficiently advanced technology is indistinguishable from magic.*

[6] *Trilateration* is like *triangulation*, except that it uses distances, not angles, to compute positions.

Thus, let's label the center point "A" and update the map as depicted in Figure 3.4.

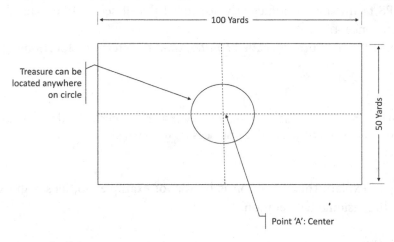

FIGURE 3.4   Map with clue 1.

The next clue arrives and states as follows:

The treasure lies sixty yards from the top righthand corner of the field.

So, let's add Point "B" to our diagram and draw an arc with a 60-yard radius originating at that spot. Figure 3.5 depicts the state of the map after the addition.

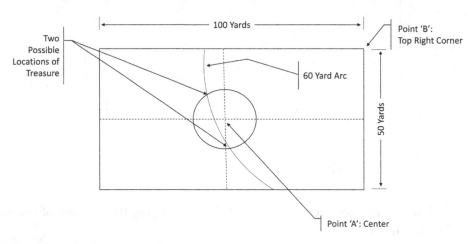

FIGURE 3.5   Map with clues 1 and 2.

Unfortunately, even after adding the second clue to our map, we realize that we can't begin digging because there are two possible points beneath which the treasure may lie. So, we still need more information.

Happily, the third clue arrives as follows:

The treasure resides forty yards from a point that lies at the center of the left side of the field.

Let's label that point "C" and add it to our map. (Figure 3.6 depicts the result.) We now know precisely where to dig for the treasure because we have three points.

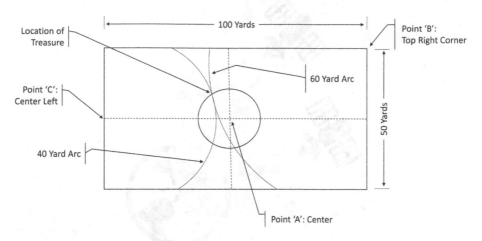

FIGURE 3.6 Location of buried treasure.

3D Trilateration

The 2D trilateration example discussed in the prior section relied on the fact that the geography was flat. That is, all the coordinates assumed a two-dimensional plane.

Three-dimensional (satellite-based) trilateration works in much the same way, except that the underlying geometry relies on spheres and cones instead of arcs and circles.

Why? Because the Earth is round, not flat.[7]

In addition, if we want precise east-west (longitude and latitude) coordinates, the computations must also address altitude.

Let's see how this works.

As depicted in Figure 3.7, you can envision a satellite's coverage area as a cone. Thus, its signal is "visible" to a large area of the planet.

FIGURE 3.7 Single satellite coverage area.

---

[7] My apologies to all the "flat-earthers."

When we add a second satellite, the coverage area narrows a bit (Figure 3.8).

FIGURE 3.8   Two satellite coverage areas.

In Figure 3.9, we narrow the location to two points when adding a third satellite.

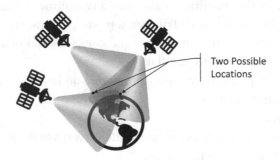

FIGURE 3.9   Three satellite coverage areas.

Finally, as presented in Figure 3.10, we converge on a single point when we include location data from the fourth satellite.

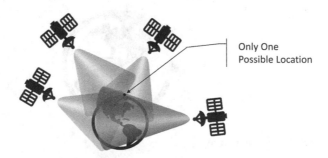

FIGURE 3.10   Four satellite coverage areas.

To simplify the representation, Figure 3.11 depicts the four satellite coverage areas using circles (rather than cones) in a 2D illustration like the diagrams used in the prior section.

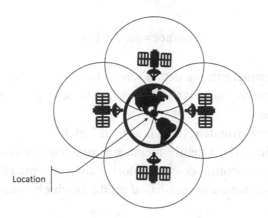

FIGURE 3.11   Four satellite coverage area redux.

Global Positioning

GPS positioning is like 3D trilateration, but it computes distances using time. Time, you say? Yes.

Let's see how this works.

In concept, GPS positioning is a straightforward process: A GPS receiver determines its distance from four (or more satellites) and, using trilateration, computes its location on Earth's surface.

But how do GPS receivers determine exact distances from each satellite?

As mentioned previously, GPS satellites contain highly accurate atomic clocks to time-stamp every message they transmit. As a result, GPS receivers can compute the travel time of messages arriving from each satellite (using their own internal clocks). Then, based on the speed at which the satellite's radio signals travel toward Earth (i.e., the speed of light—approximately 186,000 miles per second), GPS receivers can compute distances from each satellite.

However, to compute the distance from any object, we need to know its precise position. The locations of satellites appear in publications called *ephemerides*.

DEFINITION 2

An *ephemeris*[8] is a compilation of tables (often called an *astronomical almanac*) that specify the orbits of satellites (both natural and artificial).

GPS satellites continually broadcast ephemeris data.

---

[8] In the US, the National Oceanic and Atmospheric Administration (NOAA) publishes GPS positioning data.

As you may recall from elementary physics, computing distance is a straightforward calculation:

Equation 1

$$Distance = Rate \times Time$$

As noted in the prior paragraph, we define *rate* as the speed of light (usually represented as the letter "C" in formulas). *Time* is the duration that messages travel from GPS satellites to Earth-bound receivers.

Easy as pie, right? Unfortunately, there is a small "catch."

We noted earlier that GPS satellite message times remain synchronized and accurate because they employ atomic clocks. Unfortunately, atomic clocks are prohibitively expensive—far too costly for consumer-based products which must use more economical quartz clocks.

Consequently, it's likely that the clocks in GPS receivers will not align with those in the orbiting satellites. Therefore, distance calculations based on time could be highly inaccurate.

So how does GPS address this?

Unfortunately, a discussion of the complete, rigorous mathematical solution is well beyond this book's scope. However, we can describe it conceptually as follows.

GPS receivers must somehow synchronize their clocks with those of the satellites. At first blush, this seems like a *Catch-22*[9]: A GPS receiver either needs the exact time (based on an atomic clock) to compute the distance to satellites or the precise distance to satellites to compute the precise time.

The resolution to this problem relies on the fact that GPS receivers use *four* satellites to compute location.

Please recall from our description of 3D trilateration that one satellite establishes a location as a sphere. Adding a second satellite narrows the area to the intersection of the two spheres. The third satellite identifies two possible points. Finally, the fourth determines your exact location (one of the two points.)

Unfortunately, the four measurements may not converge to a single point because the GPS receiver's clock isn't synchronized with those in the GPS satellites. Thus, because the calculations are imprecise, the distance computation for the fourth satellite will not align with either of the two points previously determined using data from the first three satellites.

Nonetheless, it will be closer to one of the two points.

Therefore, a GPS receiver can resolve any time discrepancy by adjusting its clock such that the fourth satellite's distance aligns with the closer of the two previously computed points. As a result, the GPS receiver not only computes your location but, as part of the process, it also gets its time adjusted to atomic-clock precision.

---

[9] The "Catch-22" is a conflicting rule that prevents a solution. The usage derives from the satirical war novel *Catch-22*, written by Joseph Heller.

Assisted GPS

Despite the power of GPS technology, it's not perfect. (What technology is?) This section will discuss some of its shortcomings and how designers have overcome them.

As mentioned above, GPS receivers require "visibility" (we call this "line of sight") to at least four GPS satellites. However, in most environments, obstructions such as skyscrapers and mountains can interfere with a receiver's ability to acquire a signal from one or more satellites. Moreover, because GPS receivers are mobile, line-of-sight issues can vary over time.

During power-up, another issue arises because GPS receivers must determine an initial position. We call this a "fix."[10] This process can take anywhere from 20 seconds to over 2 minutes based on the type of start-up procedure (see below), the device's location, and the number of obstructions preventing the receiver from acquiring satellite signals.

Manufacturers rate GPS receivers based on how quickly they can compute an initial fix. We call this process *Time to First Fix* (TTFF).

DEFINITION 3

Time to First Fix is the time a GPS receiver requires to calculate an initial fix.

In general, GPS devices support three TTFF options:

Cold/Factory In this scenario, the user powers on a GPS receiver for the first time or initiates a "factory reset." TTFF could take over 10 minutes to complete because the device must acquire and store current satellite position and ephemeris data.

Warm/Normal This is the typical scenario. The device has not been without power long enough for its satellite data to have become "stale". As a result, TTFF would typically require less than a minute for most GPS receivers.

Hot/Standby In this case, the GPS receiver has been without power for less than a few hours, and its satellite data are "current." As a result, TTFF should take less than 15 seconds to complete.[11]

As you might expect, signal interference due to obstructions complicates acquiring satellite data, and the complexity of computing an initial fix requires a significant amount of processing. These issues could negatively affect your interactions with a GPS system. For example, you wouldn't want to wait minutes before a navigation app could begin issuing guidance instructions. And you might find it seriously inconvenient if the TTFF computations drained your GPS device's battery so quickly that you had to cut short your long-awaited hiking trip. So obviously, any improvements that reduced power consumption and processing time would be of great benefit.

---

[10] This also called a *position solution*.
[11] This is often called Time to Subsequent Fix (TTSF).

To address these concerns, many cellular providers equip their base stations[12] with components that continually receive, store, and compute GPS information. Called Assisted GPS[13] or A-GPS, this precomputed data are available to their subscriber's smartphone navigation systems.

Figure 3.12 depicts the data flow for this process.

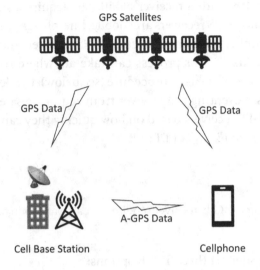

FIGURE 3.12   A-GPS data flow.

Not all smartphones leverage A-GPS data. But those that do:

- Can complete a precision fix very quickly

- Ensure a high degree of location accuracy

- Reduce the number of required "visible" satellites to two

GEOGRAPHICAL INFORMATION SYSTEMS

The development of maps is among the most significant achievements in human history. The oldest known maps—dating back thousands of years—depicted the stars. Eventually, as humans discovered the power of cartography for use in commerce and combat, surveying techniques only became more rigorous, and maps became more detailed and accurate.

GIS Data

Printed maps are visual representations of the world around us. For example, they may depict streets, property boundaries, and land elevations. Nostalgically, some readers might

---

[12] See Chapter 2.
[13] This feature is also called *Augment GPS*.

remember buying paper road maps at gas stations only to find it impossible to refold them correctly after each use. It was very frustrating!

As we entered the age of automation, software engineers needed to develop cartographic data formats suitable for processing by computers. Specifically, electronic devices can only manipulate data represented as a series of 0s and 1s. We call the process of transforming data into this format *digitization*.[14]

DEFINITION 4

Digitization is the process of converting data into a representation that consists solely of 0s and 1s. We refer to the 0s and 1s as *binary digits*.

Figure 3.13 depicts the digitization process when taking photographs. First, light reflects off the subject and enters the lens on a digital camera. Then, hardware and software components in the camera convert the light into a series of picture elements called *pixels*. Finally, the camera stores each pixel, represented by values expressed as a series of 0s and 1s, in a file that image-editing software can modify, print, and email.

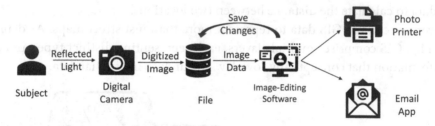

FIGURE 3.13   Example of image digitization process.

That said, endless strings of 0s and 1s would be highly unmanageable—even for computers. Thus, we need to impose structure on digital data to bring some order to the chaos.

Before continuing, I'd like to take a moment to point out that structuring data is not a new concept. For example, consider the names "Glen" and "John" written as "Glen John." In that arrangement, we might think that this is a random individual with a first name of "Glen" and a family name of "John." However, consider the effect of adding a comma, as in, "Glen, John." Having imposed some "structure" on the data, we now know we're likely referring to the famous astronaut.

In the digital world, structuring data is *de rigueur*. For example, I'm sure most readers are familiar with image (e.g., SOME-PHOTO.PNG), music (e.g., SOME-SONG.MP3), and video (e.g., SOME-MOVIE.MOV) files.[15] All three file types contain only 0s and 1s. However, each uses a different internal format and structure so that their respective display/playback software can interpret the data correctly.

---

[14] Chapter 4 discusses this topic in much more detail.

[15] File name extensions (e.g., ".PNG," ".MP3," and ".MOV") are one way to indicate the internal format of the data.

This approach holds true for cartography data. That is, we need to structure the 0s and 1s that represent geographic information in ways that allow mapping and navigation software to interpret data correctly.

There are many ways to represent cartographic data digitally. One of the most common is Geographic Information System (GIS).

GIS Data Representation

As mentioned in the prior section, the essential element of all digitization is its structure. Specifically, all software applications—and the IT professionals who develop them—must understand the underlying data formats.

To support mapping software, the industry uses a structure called a GIS.

> **DEFINITION 5**
>
> A *Geographic Information System* (GIS) functions as a data framework that allows computer-based applications to store, retrieve, and otherwise manipulate spatial and geographic-related information.

As noted in the definition, GIS represents spatial data in a digital format. Thus, you could use GIS data to calculate the distance between two locations.

However, we can use GIS data to represent more than just street maps. As depicted in Figure 3.14, a GIS comprises multiple layers, each representing distinct types and categories of information that conceptually "overlay" the underlying spatial data.

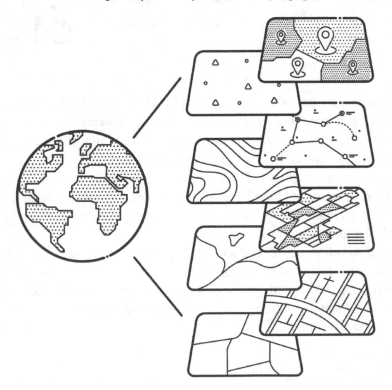

FIGURE 3.14   GIS layers.

For example, the base layer might depict streets and thoroughfares, the next layer might define municipal boundaries, and then the one above that might identify land ownership.

Note that every example layer discussed in the previous paragraph is a form of spatial data. However, because GIS formats are so flexible, we can use them to represent more than location information. For instance, you could add layers that represent demographics (e.g., economic wealth), weather (e.g., annual rainfall), and terrain (e.g., elevation).

As the previous examples demonstrate, GIS can represent any information that specifies or is related to geographic locations. To accommodate such diversity, GIS supports two major classes of data: *spatial* and *attribute*.[16]

Spatial data	There are several subclasses of *spatial data*. For our purposes, we can focus on *vector data* that represent spatial information using elements such as *points*, *lines*, and *polygons*. Using data such as longitude and latitude, *points* identify specific locations (e.g., a town center). *Lines* connect points and can thus represent such elements as roads, rivers, and railway tracks. *Polygons* comprise a series of lines and thus can represent elements such as lakes and property boundaries.
Attribute data	*Attribute data* associate nonspatial information to *points*. For example, we can associate census, rainfall, and climate information to specific geographic locations.

However, none of this information is useful until it's digitized. To that end, we can use various methods to capture and record data for use in a GIS. For example, we can incorporate the results of physical surveys, scan and trace existing paper maps, and integrate satellite imagery.

Once digitized and stored in a database, computer software can manipulate GIS data in many ways. One of the most common is the creation and display of digital maps.

Digital Maps

With the aid of computer software, we can display GIS data in graphical form as *digital maps*. As depicted in Figure 3.15, they seem remarkably like their paper predecessors. However, after a moment's interaction with one of them, the differences become abundantly clear.

Digital maps represent a quantum leap over their printed counterparts. Their advantages include the following:

Custom displays	Digital mapping software can merge multiple GIS layers to create composite images and custom displays. For example, you could combine terrain and landfall layers when researching weather patterns.
Timeliness	Software applications can display digital maps in real time. For example, if you type this link into your browser, HTTPS://PROJECT.WNYC.ORG/TRAFFIC-MAP/, you can monitor New York City's traffic conditions.

---

[16] There is a third category, called *Metadata*, which is beyond the scope of this book.

FIGURE 3.15   Digital street map.

Accuracy   GIS data are just that: data. Curators[17] continually update spatial and attribute data if it's found to be incorrect or incomplete. Thus, you always receive the most current version of a GIS data set when you query it. In other words, you don't have to wait for the next printing of a paper map or a new edition of an atlas to have accurate information.

Range   GIS systems continually evolve and incorporate new and expanded data sets.

Portability   Using a navigation system or a smartphone, you can "take" GIS data anywhere. That is, via the Internet, you can display many types of maps for almost any region of the world—usually for free. Yes, traditional maps can also travel—but you'd need scores of them if you want worldwide coverage. (There's also another advantage: There's no refolding required when using digital maps!) In effect, digital maps can place distant, exotic, and foreign lands in the palm of your hand.

ADVANCED SECTION

Route Navigation

Whether it was hiking, driving, or sailing, at one time or another, you've used a map to calculate a route to get from "here to there." The process is intuitive for most of us: We grab a hiking map, a road atlas, or a nautical chart and get to work.

Nonetheless, regardless of the technologies involved (stars, paper maps, etc.), there are several elements required to compute a route:

- Position fixes for both the beginning and ending locations;

- Cartographic renderings that display the available travel options; and

- A process by which we can calculate an optimal course. (We'll discuss what "optimal" means below.)

---

[17] Data *curators* are the professionals who ensure the accuracy and integrity of the data sets they manage.

This section will illustrate how your car or smartphone navigation system does this electronically. However, before we begin, I need to share one caveat. There are many ways to compute routes. The discussion that follows explains one approach *conceptually*.

Thus, it isn't likely that any popular products you might be familiar with (e.g., Waze, Garmin, TomTom, and Google Maps) work precisely in the manner described below. The calculations are far more intricate, the data are far more voluminous, and the constraints (cost, speed, performance, etc.) are far more, well, constraining. Moreover, there are many practical considerations that software designers and application developers must address when creating consumer-based navigation products. (See the section entitled *Real-World Considerations* below.)

That said, the discussions below will offer a representative overview of how navigation technology works.

Data Structures

Before discussing navigation systems, we need a better understanding of how software programmers organize data. In the GIS section above, we noted that computers could not use information in its natural form. Consequently, using a process called *digitization*, we must convert data into a series of 0s and 1s.

In addition, we learned that software could not process random sequences of binary digits; designers must structure the underlying data so that applications can interpret the 0s and 1s correctly.

And lastly, we noted that structuring data is not exclusive to the world of computers. As another example, consider the following sequence of digits:

  2005557890

Is this a telephone number? A bank account? A poor choice for a password string? As it stands, it's unclear.

However, let's add structure to the data as follows:

  (200) 555-7890

We can now be reasonably confident that this represents a telephone number.[18]

In computer science, we call such formats *data structures*.

DEFINITION 6

A *data structure* is a formalized arrangement of binary digits (0s and 1s).

Game Trees

Depending on the need, software developers may employ several types of data structures. For example, when writing interactive games such as Chess, Checkers, or Go,

---

[18] Please, there is NO need to call this number. At the time I wrote this, I confirmed that "200" is an inactive area code.

programmers might organize data into *trees*, where each node represents a "move" for either the "computer" or the "player."

We refer to this type of data structure as a *game tree*. See Figure 3.16 for an example.

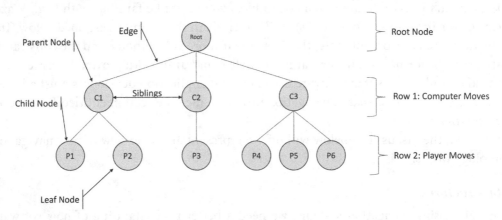

FIGURE 3.16   Example of game tree.

We call each circle a *node*, and we group nodes into *rows*.[19] Although it's counterintuitive, we draw the *root node* at the top (as a notational convenience). Then, extending the metaphor, we refer to each node residing on the bottom row as *leaf nodes*.

The lines that connect *nodes* are *edges*, and a sequence of *edges* forms a *path*. Referring again to Figure 3.16, the series of *edges* beginning at the *root* and extending to the node labeled "P6" forms the following *path*:

$$ROOT \; \text{->} \; C3 \; \text{->} \; P6$$

In gaming apps, each *node* represents a "move." *Rows* alternately represent moves for either the computer or the player. For example, when it's the computer's turn, the software examines all its choices as enumerated by all the *nodes* residing in *row* 1. As part of its "analysis," the program can also anticipate potential counter moves by the player as indicated by *row* 2 *nodes*.

Depending on time constraints (e.g., chess clocks limit player "think time") and system limitations (computers, smartphones, etc., have a finite amount of memory and processing power available to store and calculate choices), gaming software can generate row after row of successive moves, making many game apps challenging to beat.

Graphs

Another common data structure used by computer scientists is called a *graph*. Like *trees*, *graphs* have *nodes*[20] and *edges*. However, unlike *trees*, *graphs* don't require a *root node*. (Nonetheless, we can—and often do—define a starting point.). More importantly, *graphs* allow *paths* to form *cycles*.

---

[19] Rows are also called *levels*.
[20] *Nodes* are also called *vertices* in graphs.

As an example, Figure 3.17 contains two *cycles*: Nodes 3, 4, and 5 form one, and nodes 1, 3, and 4 comprise another.

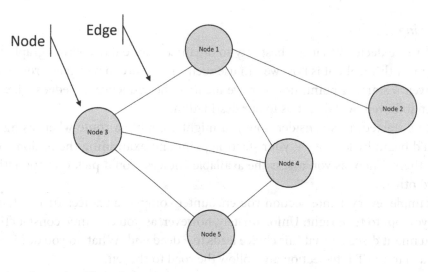

FIGURE 3.17   A graph with cycle.

Because roadways form *cycles* (i.e., you can keep making right turns until you arrive back at your starting location), *graphs* are an excellent way to represent maps. As an example, consider the street map of New York City presented in Figure 3.18.

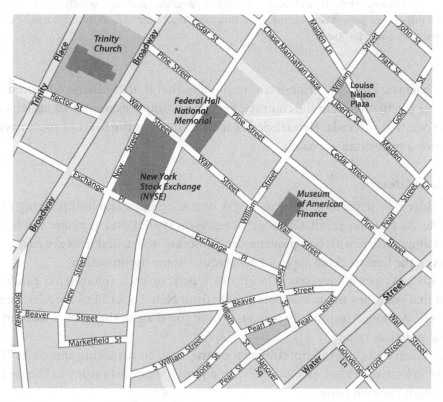

FIGURE 3.18   Street map of Lower Manhattan.

We can easily represent this map as a graph: *Nodes* represent intersections, and *edges* correspond to streets.

Backtracking

Now that we've decided that the best way to organize map data is with a graph, the next thing we must think about is how we can use such a structure to navigate a route. In other words, given a starting point, how can we identify the sequence of "edges" (i.e., streets) that, when followed, will direct us to our destination?

To get us started, let's consider how you might compute a route when using a paper map. You'd begin by looking at your starting point and examining the options originating from there. Then, as you assess the available choices, you'd pick one and either save or discard others.

For example, every T-intersection you encounter compels a choice: Turn left, or right? Let's say you opt to turn right. Unfortunately, however, as you continue constructing your route, you might discover that this choice leads to a dead end. What do you do? Intuitively, you'd return to the T-intersection and follow the road to the left.

In computer terminology, we refer to this process as *backtracking*.

DEFINITION 7

Backtracking is a programming method whereby processing continues along a given "path" in search of a solution. At each "fork in the road," the program "guesses" which "path" it should follow. If this choice proves unsuccessful, the program "backs up" (i.e., returns to) a prior choice and selects an alternate "path."

Note that backtracking is a "brute-force" technique. That is, there are no advanced formulas or clever calculations. On the contrary, a program simply examines all options until it discovers one that succeeds. Nevertheless, backtracking is at the heart of route navigation despite such a pedestrian approach.

Route Calculation

Let's consider how navigation software might leverage graphs and backtracking to calculate a route. As you may recall, GIS systems represent spatial data as *points* and *lines*. This approach aligns nicely with our *graph* model: *Points* are *nodes*, and *lines* are *edges*.

However, the backtracking approach will require some optimization.

First, we can't permit programs to choose a path at each intersection randomly. If designed that way, they might compute a route from New York to Los Angeles using only local streets! Although technically correct, I think you'd agree that such a solution would be of little practical value.

This concern leads us to an improvement on the basic backtracking approach: The software must prioritize its choices. Optimally, we'd want the navigation app to choose the *best* option at each decision point.

But here's the rub: If the program doesn't know the best route beforehand, how can it determine the best choice at a given intersection?

Moreover, we also need to specify what we mean by "best." For now, let's define *best* as "the option that creates the shortest route to the destination." (We'll return to this point shortly.)

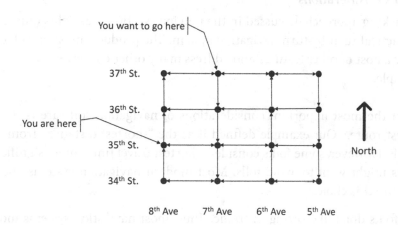

FIGURE 3.19 Graph of Midtown Manhattan.

An example is the easiest way to describe how navigation software works and addresses the above concerns. Let's begin by reviewing Figure 3.19, which depicts a section of a Midtown Manhattan Street map represented as a graph. The *nodes* designate intersections; the *arrows* (*edges*) correspond to streets and indicate the direction of traffic flow. [21]

Suppose you want to drive from 35th Street and 8th Avenue to 37th Street and 7th Avenue. After querying the GIS data, the navigation software determines there are two options: travel east on 35th Street or head north on 8th Avenue. Let's say the program arbitrarily selects the first option and "turns right" on 35th Street. However, in the event it must backtrack, the algorithm saves the other alternative—traveling north on 8th Avenue—before proceeding to the next step.

Having made its first choice, the navigation software again queries the GIS data and determines its next choices: Turn southbound on 7th Avenue or continue heading east on 35th Street. (Note that turning north on 7th Avenue is not an option because traffic may only travel in a southbound direction.)

After analyzing these options, the program determines that both alternatives lead away from the intended destination. Therefore, it discards both choices and instead elects to *backtrack* to its original option and travel north on 8th Avenue.

Processing continues in this manner until the software arrives at the optimal route: Travel north on 8th Avenue and turn right on 37th Street.

Note that the program could have avoided the first (incorrect) choice if it could have determined which of the two initial options was optimal. One way navigation systems

---

[21] Technically, because the arrows indicate traffic flow, we call this a *directed graph*.

prioritize alternatives is by computing "line-of-sight" distances to the destination. Though not perfect, this approach eliminates many "wrong turns." Returning to our example, if our program had computed the line-of-sight distance from our starting point, it would have selected traveling north on 8th Avenue at the outset.

Real-World Considerations

The backtracking approach discussed in the previous section highlights only a small portion of a practical turn-by-turn navigation system. The products most of us have come to rely on offer a host of other features and address many other concerns.

For example:

- One of the most important considerations of navigation software is the definition of "best route." Our example defined it as the "shortest distance" from point A to point B. However, some folks consider "shortest travel time" more significant. Other drivers might want to avoid tolls. Most modern navigation systems allow users to configure this choice.

- Most folks don't like sitting in traffic. Thus, most navigation systems monitor electronic traffic reports and compute alternative routes to minimize unexpected delays.

- Navigation systems can't evaluate every possible route—particularly when the trip involves long distances. The number of potential solutions and the computational costs would be prohibitive. Thus, most navigation systems rely on GIS data that classify roadways from local side streets to interstate highways. Navigation algorithms use these data to prioritize route choices when computing long-distance travel options.

Privacy Issues

I'm sure most of you are familiar with another famous quote by Joseph Heller from his book *Catch-22*, "Just because your paranoid doesn't mean they aren't after you." Despite its humorous side, this is a profound warning for all of us who live in this digital age: Permanent paranoia is a proper and healthy state of mind when concerned about protecting personal information.

Such concerns might lead many readers to wonder whether GPS technology somehow invades our privacy. Unfortunately, the answer is a bit ambiguous.

The good news first: GPS satellites only *broadcast* data. They serve as 21st-century orbiting lighthouses that transmit reference data to modern-day navigation devices. And although they do accept control information from ground stations, they don't collect any data from GPS receivers. Thus, they can't—and don't—track your movements.

Moreover, GPS receivers and navigation equipment don't transmit location data and are therefore not subject to tracking. Thus, despite how much they might want to, governments, police departments, or any other nefarious organizations can't use these devices to monitor your movements.

Now for the unwelcome news: Cellular providers can track cell phones. In addition, your smartphone can store GPS and location data that third parties might be able to retrieve—possibly without your knowledge and consent.

Thus, unfortunately, it's another clear case of *caveat emptor*. As a consumer of these devices, you must remain hypervigilant: Research products before you purchase them, read the Terms of Service (ToS), and take the time and effort to configure devices to minimize the amount of personal information they may garner and expose.

The prevention of future problems is well worth the effort.

SUMMARY

This chapter began with a discussion of the history and uses of GPS. We then described how the GPS infrastructure and 3D trilateration enable us to determine our exact position on this wondrous planet.

We also reviewed how GIS systems represent geographical data and how digital maps use and process that information. Finally, we fit all the pieces together in the Advanced Section and demonstrated how software-based, turn-by-turn navigation systems work.

How Does Computer Hardware Work?

If computers get too powerful, we can organize them into committees. That'll show 'em.

AUTHOR UNKNOWN

INTRODUCTION

Computers are everywhere: In our cars, thermostats, phones, smart devices—the list is endless. Moreover, given their impact, it's hard to believe that computers as we know them have only been around since the 1940s. And personal computers are even younger; they made their way into our lives in the 1970s.

Like any other tool we use, the more you learn about computers, the better they can serve your needs. But unfortunately, many individuals view digital devices as "closed boxes" that cause only frustration and confusion. Indeed, it's often the case that users are totally amazed at one moment, and then find themselves pounding their keyboards a few seconds later.

Well, the next few chapters are going to change that. Specifically, we will "open the cover" of these marvelous machines and "poke around under the hood." After reading this material, you'll have a complete—albeit conceptual—view of how computers work.

For our purposes, we will divide our discussion of computers into three fundamental areas: How computer hardware works (the material covered in this chapter), how computer software works (Chapter 5), how computers communicate (Chapter 6), and the Internet (Chapter 7).

However, before we can begin our discussions, we need to understand how computers acquire and process data.

WHAT IS DIGITIZATION?

For those who might have missed the discussion in Chapter 3, we reintroduce the topic of *digitization* in this section and then describe how it applies to computing in general.

DOI: 10.1201/9781003143437-4

As noted earlier, computers don't possess our senses or cognitive abilities. Specifically, computers don't "see" or "hear" as humans do. Thus, we need to transform information into a format suitable for electronic processing.

The language of computers is *digital*: Only 1s and 0s. (We'll understand the reason for this shortly.) This is true regardless of the application. So, for example, the Oscar-winning movie you streamed the other night, the vacation photographs you downloaded from your phone last month, and the podcast you listened to this morning while jogging all share one common attribute: The underlying data format was digital: A series of 1s and 0s.

However, we don't live in a digital world. Therefore, to be of any value to computers, we must somehow convert and represent data as a series of 1s and 0s. We call this process *digitization*.

DEFINITION 1

Digitization is the process of converting data into a binary representation that consists solely of 1s and 0s.

That's a great definition, but what does it mean?

Keyboard Characters

Let's start simply. A computer keyboard transmits every character you type not as a letter but as a unique numeric value. For simplification, the computer industry has standardized these codes into *character tables*, the most common of which is the American Standard Code for Information Interchange (ASCII, pronounced "AS-KEY").

For example, the ASCII representation of a lowercase "a" is the value "97"; a capital "A" has the value "65."[1] Thus, when you press the "a" key, your keyboard transmits the value "97" to the computer. Similarly, when you simultaneously press the "shift" and "a" keys (to denote a capital "A"), your keyboard transmits the value "65."

ASCII encoding supports the displaying and printing of characters as well. For example, for the letter "A" to appear on a printout, the computer must transmit the value "65" to the printer.

Digitized Images

As a more complex example, let's discuss how computers process graphics (images). We can gain some insights into this processing by reviewing how humans see.

When we focus on an image, like a beautiful landscape, light rays reflecting from the objects enter our eyes through a lens called the *cornea*. The cornea's primary function is to focus light before it passes through the rest of the eyeball.

The focused light eventually falls on the *retina*, which processes the incoming light using a layer of cells called *photoreceptors*. The photoreceptors decompose the light into a

---

[1] Although its values might appear arbitrary, I assure you there was considerable deliberation in the design of the ASCII character set.

series of "points" (or "dots") based on characteristics such as color and intensity. The retina forwards this information to the brain (via the *optic nerve*); the brain then interprets it and creates (reconstructs) the images that our minds "see."

Like the way our eyes function, we represent images in the digital world as an array of *picture elements*, called *pixels*, each of which represents the color and intensity of a particular "dot" of the image.

For example, when it takes a picture, a digital camera converts the light it receives through its lens into a series of pixels and stores them in a file in a known format (e.g., JPEG, GIF, PNG) (Figure 4.1). Regardless of the underlying structure, cameras record the value of each pixel as a series of 1s and 0s. Later, when you view the image, display software copies the pixels contained in the image file onto your screen or directs them to a printer.

FIGURE 4.1   Pixels in an image.

In addition to capturing the image (in pixels), some of the formats noted above also "compress" the data to save space. However, as is usually the case, there is a compromise: The more you compress the image, the more it may affect image quality.

Digitized Sound

I'm sure you're familiar with music CDs and audio formats such as MP3 and WAV files. But have you ever considered how computers process sound?

In nature, sound exists as waves that continuously change values. Thus, like images, we need to transform audio data into 0s and 1s. To perform this conversion, we use a component called an Analog-to-Digital Converter (ADC) that continuously "samples" (i.e., determines the value of) an audio signal (e.g., music) and converts each sample into a numerical value.

For example, to create a digital version of a song for inclusion on a CD, an ADC samples the audio signal 44,100 times per second. Thus, for every second of music, there are 44,100 individual values (stored as a series of 1s and 0s) recorded onto the CD.

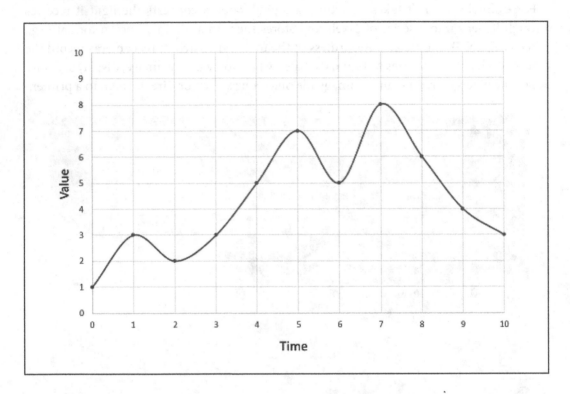

FIGURE 4.2   Sound sampling.

Figure 4.2 illustrates this process. The horizontal ("X") axis represents time; the vertical ("Y") axis represents the signal's value at a given moment. The line depicts the sound wave of the song we're playing. The ADC samples the audio signal at specific points in time (labeled 1–10 in the figure) and records each value. Thus, at time 1, the signal's value is 3; at time 7, the value is 8.

To "play" a CD or MP3 file, computers must reverse this process and create an analog signal (i.e., a sound wave) from a digital (numeric) representation. To perform this processing, we use a Digital-to-Analog Converter (DAC) to read previously sampled values and transform them back into an analog signal suitable for playback through an amplifier and speakers.

The crucial point is that electronic devices process audio signals using a digital representation. Thus, that MP3 file you emailed to a friend the other day does not contain "sound waves" but a series of 1s and 0s.

Other Examples of Digitization

As we've already noted, digital data are the *lingua franca* of computers. (That's why we refer to them as *digital devices*.) However, as computers extend into other facets of our lives (for good or ill), more data types need conversion into digital formats.

Some examples include the following:

- Medical instruments (e.g., CAT scans, MRIs, automated blood pressure cuffs)

- Biometric identification (e.g., fingerprint and facial recognition)

- Virtual reality (e.g., digital games)

- Augmented reality (e.g., Google Glass)

- Art (e.g., digital drawings)

- Voice recognition (e.g., Siri or Alexa)

- Speech synthesis (e.g., Siri or Alexa)

- GPS data (navigation information—See Chapter 3)

As this list might suggest, computers can benefit any field of endeavor once there is a way to digitize the underlying data.

That leads us to the primary subject matter of this chapter: Computer hardware.

WHAT'S INSIDE A COMPUTER?

Throughout the remainder of this chapter, we'll decompose computer hardware into its constituent components and provide an understanding of each of them. There is one caveat, however. The discussion will present a "conceptual" design of a modern digital computer. Specifically, due to the sophisticated technology and manufacturing techniques employed today, you'll not likely find any system (be it a laptop, smartphone, tablet, smartwatch, etc.) designed exactly as described below.

Basic Hardware

If we were to remove the outer casing from a computer or smartphone, we would see such items as *chips* (self-contained semiconductor components), cables, disk drives, fans, and slots to hold expansion cards. Figure 4.3 provides an example.

Despite the apparent complexity, much of the hardware displayed in Figure 4.3 is not directly involved in computing, *per se*. Instead, many of these components provide supplementary services such as power, cooling, and connectivity. Therefore, we'll ignore the ancillary hardware for the moment and focus specifically on computing components.

Let's begin with the *motherboard*.

FIGURE 4.3   Inside a PC.

Overview of Motherboard Components

The *motherboard* is the primary piece of circuitry for most electronic devices. It hosts most of the major components that make a computer function like, well, a computer.

See Figure 4.4 for an example.

FIGURE 4.4   Image of a motherboard.

Instead of decomposing each of the physical elements depicted in Figure 4.4, let's adopt a more conceptual approach. Figure 4.5 provides a simplified, logical representation of a motherboard's major components.

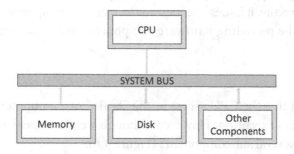

FIGURE 4.5   Motherboard: Conceptual view.

The discussions below briefly introduce each component. In subsequent sections, we'll explain the functionality of each element in detail.

Central Processing Unit

Central Processing Unit (CPU) serves as the "brain" of the computer in that it executes most instructions and manages the operation of other devices. A single CPU can execute one instruction at a time. However, many—if not most—modern computers ship with multiple CPUs, allowing them to execute more than one instruction concurrently.[2]

As an aside, you may have run across terms like *multicore, dual-core*, and *quad-core* when buying a computer. Such language refers to the modern design approach of integrating multiple CPUs into a single component.

Memory

Computer *memory* is the primary storage location[3] for all instructions and data currently executing within a computer. Specifically, a CPU cannot run a program until all its instructions and data reside in its main memory.

Generally speaking, there are two types of computer memory: RAM and ROM. RAM, or *random-access memory*, is volatile—it loses its state when the computer loses power. Most of the programs and apps you run reside in RAM while executing. (Have you ever lost work because of a power failure? This is why.)

ROM, or *read-only memory*, is readable but not writeable (i.e., its value is immutable). It hosts data that never changes during the lifetime of a device (e.g., the computer's serial number). Unlike RAM, the contents of ROM are permanent and survive reboots and power cycles.

Although the details are well beyond the scope of this book, I should note that there are several types of ROM, including EPROM (Erasable ROM) and EEPROM (Electrically Erasable ROM), that, using special techniques, may have their contents modified.

---

[2] We refer to this as *multiprocessing*.
[3] Note that, unlike disk drives, this is not permanent storage.

The Bus

In a computer system, a *bus* facilitates data transport among connected components. It allows all devices to communicate with the CPU and each other (when appropriate). In essence, it serves as the data highway for the system. For example, when the CPU needs to "fetch" the next instruction to execute, it issues a request to the memory component via the bus.

We'll discuss all the preceding hardware components in greater detail in the following sections.

The CPU

Previously, we noted that the CPU serves as the "brain" of a computer because it controls most aspects of system execution. However, although we often speak of it as a single unit, the CPU comprises several subcomponents (Figure 4.6).

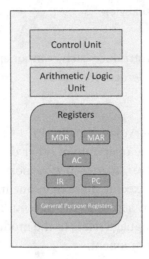

FIGURE 4.6   CPU subcomponents.

We'll begin our discussion of the CPU's subcomponents using some high-level concepts and then explain each subcomponent in detail. Following that, we'll demonstrate how all the modules work in unison to run programs and execute instructions.

The Control Unit

As its name implies, the *Control Unit* (CU) oversees most operations within the system. In addition, it orchestrates all processing within the CPU and schedules the actions of some of the other components that connect to the bus (e.g., main memory). Among its many tasks, the CU ensures that the current instruction executes properly, the "next" instruction is "queued up," and that it has "fetched" all required data from memory.

Registers

Registers (or, more accurately, *hardware registers*) are high-speed memory repositories under the CPU's direct control. There are two classes of registers used in modern hardware design: *General-purpose registers* serve as "scratchpads," and *special-purpose registers* support highly customized tasks. We will present examples of both types later in this chapter.

As it begins each execution cycle (we'll review this in detail below), the CU will copy the instruction and one or more data elements from memory into its registers. After the fetch phase completes, the CU performs the specified operation (as indicated by the instruction) and then copies the results back to memory. Alternatively, the CU may leave data "in place" to be available to subsequent instructions (i.e., the values generated by the current operation may only be intermediate results).

When reviewing Figure 4.6, you may have noticed that some registers have names. That's because system designers have reserved them for specific functions. A typical CPU contains many of these; descriptions of the most common appear below.[4]

Instruction Register (IR)	The IR contains the instruction currently executing. During each instruction cycle, the CPU fetches the next instruction from memory and stores it in the IR.
Program Counter (PC)	Although its name might appear odd, the PC contains the memory address of the *next* instruction that the CU will execute. Typically, this is the instruction immediately following the one in progress. However, as is often the case, the current operation could alter the instruction sequence. When that occurs, the CU copies the new location (address) into the PC before initiating the next instruction cycle.
Accumulator (AC)	The AC is the register into which the CPU stores the results of arithmetic and logic operations. For example, after summing the values contained in two general-purpose registers, the CU stores the answer in the AC. The value is available for additional operations (if it's an intermediate result), or the CU can copy its contents to memory (or both).
Memory Address Register (MAR)	The MAR contains the address (location) of data required by the current instruction. That is, if an operation requires "fetching" data from memory, the CU loads its location into the MAR before initiating the request.
Memory Data Register (MDR)	The MDR contains the data that will be written to or have been previously copied from memory. For example, if the CU needs a piece of data stored at location 011011,[5] it loads that value into the MAR (see above). Then, the Memory Controller (MC; discussed below) fetches the value at that location and copies it into the MAR. The CU now has a copy of the data that it can use to complete the current instruction.

---

[4] Please note that, although most do, hardware manufacturers do not have to adhere to these naming conventions.

[5] Please note that this is a *binary representation* of the data's location (address). Remember, computers only use 0s and 1s.

The Arithmetic/Logic Unit

Most instructions in a computer execute within a component called the Arithmetic/Logic Unit (ALU). There are several classes of operations that ALUs typically support; I've included a sampling below.

Please note, however, that the following are just examples. As such, they may not represent actual operations that you might find included in any computer's instruction set currently in production.

One more point. Many of the operations presented below might look like "software" (i.e., programming) instructions. On the contrary, however, they are simply human-readable representations of instructions that execute in the hardware (i.e., in the circuitry). The distinction will become more apparent in Chapter 5 when we discuss software.

Arithmetic Operations   As you might expect, computers are "whizzes" at math. Here are two examples.

> ADD V1, V2   Add v1 and v2 and place the result in a register.
> SUB V1, V2   Subtract v1 from v2 and place the result in a register.

Logic Operations   Computers are nothing if not logical—sometimes to the point of frustration. Nonetheless, although it may seem counterintuitive, instructions don't usually execute in strict sequence. On the contrary, software developers build "decision processing" into their programs to respond to events.

For example, consider a dialog box that pops up "asking" whether you want to save your work before you exit a program. If you press "YES," then one set of instructions executes; if you select "NO," a different section of code will run.

To implement such processing, programmers use *logical operators*. In contrast to the arithmetic instructions discussed above, logical operators don't compute values as such. Instead, they determine whether a set of one or more conditions are TRUE or FALSE.

We've already seen such processing at work. Please recall that for a keyboard to transmit a capital "A," the user must simultaneously press the "SHIFT" and "A" keys. This is an example of an AND condition. That is, the condition yields TRUE when the user presses *both* keys at once; otherwise, the result is FALSE. In terms of logical operators, when the condition is TRUE, the keyboard transmits an uppercase "A;" otherwise, it sends a lowercase "A."

We can extend this idea to create arbitrarily complex logical expressions. For example, consider a customer at an Automated Teller Machine (ATM) who wants to transfer money from a checking account to a savings account. The bank's software would permit this transaction given that *all* the following conditions are true:

- The customer is the account holder of record on the checking account, AND

- The customer has permission to deposit money into the savings account, AND

- There are sufficient funds available in the checking account to cover the amount of the transfer.

When writing a computer program, a developer would combine these conditions using a logical AND operator to ensure they are all TRUE before allowing the code to complete the transfer.

Alternatively, there are occasions when only one of several conditions must be met for a given section of code to execute. For instance, consider that the bank in our previous example may grant third-party signatories access to accounts. If so, we can reformulate the first condition to read as follows:

The customer is the account holder of record OR is an authorized signatory.

In this case, a developer would use a logical OR operator to evaluate this condition. Specifically, an OR operator yields TRUE when at least *one* of its conditions is TRUE.

Given this rule, the banking software will allow the transaction if the customer is either the account holder OR an authorized signatory. We can now modify the complete set of conditions as follows:

- The customer is the account holder of record OR an authorized signatory on the account, AND
- The customer has permission to deposit money into the savings account, AND
- There are sufficient funds available in the checking account to cover the amount of the transfer

As the previous example demonstrates, programmers may combine logical operators to create arbitrarily complex expressions.

Data Transfer Operations   CPUs spend a significant percentage of their time repositioning data. For example, they move:

- Data from disk into memory
- Data from memory into registers
- Computational results from registers back into memory, and
- Data from memory to disk

As a result, all computers include primitive operations that move data efficiently. Examples include the following:

MOV R1,R2   Move the data in register 2 into register 1.
LOAD R5,M1   Move data at memory location M1 into register 5.
STOR M2,R7   Move the data in register 7 to memory location M2.

Please don't be concerned if the values and terminology of these examples appear strange. We'll explain everything in more detail shortly.

Other Operations   There are several other classes of hardware operations that a typical CPU supports. Some examples appear below.

> **Graphics**   Graphics operations support the sophisticated displays prevalent in modern computer applications such as video streaming, gaming software, and virtual reality.
>
> **Floating Point**   Floating-point computations are mathematical expressions containing real numbers (i.e., values that include a decimal point, e.g., 123.456).[6] As a result, they are among the most complex and time-consuming operations performed by the hardware.
>
> To compensate, system engineers often equip computers with a floating-point accelerator chip (also called a floating-point unit, FPU, or math coprocessor) that contains custom circuitry specifically designed to execute floating-point operations efficiently. When included, the CPU directs all floating-point computations to the FPU. (You may recall that earlier in this chapter, I stated that the ALU executes most instructions—but not all; this is one example.)
>
> **Input/Output**   All computer systems provide instructions that support the reading and writing of data from/to external devices such as disks, printers, and networks.

Main Memory

Main memory is the component that maintains all the information required by the CPU to manage the system. For any program to execute, all its instructions and data must reside in memory.[7]

Conceptually, you can envision memory as rows of uniquely numbered (addressed) lockers in a health club's changing room. The CPU may read (i.e., look inside) or write (replace the current value with a new one) any locker's contents.

Figure 4.7 depicts a conceptual view of memory in a computer. Each box (or cell) is a uniquely addressable memory location (i.e., a "locker") and represents one *byte*[8] of storage. I've arranged the cells in rows and columns for convenience and logical representation.

The numbers appearing to the left of the cells are addresses. Specifically, each value indicates the address of the first cell in each row (up to one *megabyte*[9] in this example). As you scan each row, you add "1" to compute each successive cell's address.

---

[6] In binary arithmetic, a "decimal point" is called a *binary point*.

[7] This statement is not 100% accurate. To reduce memory usage, some systems allow program data to remain on disk until the CPU needs it.

[8] A *byte* contains 8 bits (0s and 1s) of storage. You can think of a byte as a "locker" that can hold one character of data. See the Advanced Section for a more extensive explanation.

[9] 1 *megabyte* equals 1,024,000 bytes; see the Advanced Section for more detail.

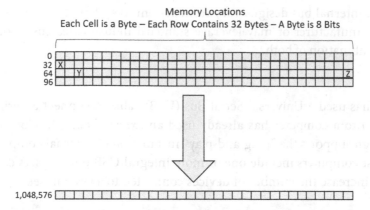

FIGURE 4.7   Main memory.

For example, the address of the cell labeled "x" is 32, the address of the cell labeled "'y" is 66, and the address of the cell labeled "z" is 95. Please take a moment to get comfortable with this addressing notation before reading on.[10]

There are two important points to note about main memory.

First, it's dynamic and volatile. That means that programs can change the contents of memory cells at will,[11] and its contents "disappear" whenever the system loses power or restarts.

Second, applications and system components don't directly access memory locations. Instead, they interact with a *controller* whose job is to store and retrieve data to/from memory (see below).

The Bus

Often called a "data highway," the *bus* facilitates data exchange among components within a computer system. There are many types and classes of busses. For our purposes, we need to discuss only two of them.

Internal Bus

An *internal* bus facilitates data transfer among the computer's internal components.

Figure 4.8 provides an example.

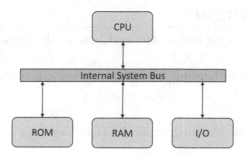

FIGURE 4.8   Internal system bus.

---

[10] I should point out that Figure 4.7 represents addresses in Base-10. As I've stated *ad nauseam*, computers use binary values. See the Advanced Section for more detail.

[11] Security issues aside.

In practice, internal bus designs vary from system to system. In addition, they can be unique to a manufacturer or may leverage standard industry designs. Modern systems often use a combination of both.

External Bus

Anyone who has used a Universal Serial Bus (USB) cable to connect a peripheral device (e.g., a printer) to a computer has already used an *external bus*. Developed in the early 1990s, its design supports the "plug-and-play" installation of external components.

Today, most computers include one or more integral USB ports. Users can also install a USB hub to increase the number of devices connected to a system (see Figure 4.9 for an example.)

FIGURE 4.9   USB hub.

INSTRUCTION EXECUTION

It's time to complete the circle and understand how all the knowledge we've just gained comes together.

A computer is a machine: Nothing more, nothing less. Thus, the *raison d'être* of a CPU is as follows:

1. Fetch the next instruction (instruction FETCH stage)

2. Decode the instruction (instruction DECODE stage)

3. Execute the instruction (instruction EXECUTION stage)

4. Rinse and repeat

The process just described constitutes one *instruction cycle*. Admittedly, it's a simplified description—but only in terms of the details. So long as it has power, that's what a CPU does.

Given the above, let's step through an instruction cycle and understand how it works. While reviewing this example, you might find it helpful to refer to Figure 4.6. Please note that the following discussion omits some of the underlying detail. Nonetheless, it does describe a complete instruction cycle, albeit at a conceptual level.

Instruction Fetch Stage

In our discussion of *registers*, we noted that the PC always contains the address of the *next* instruction to execute. Thus, every instruction cycle begins when the CU copies the PC's contents into the MAR as a prerequisite for the "instruction fetch."

Then, in preparation for the *following* instruction cycle, the CU increments the PC to point to the *next* instruction in sequence. (One caveat: Because programs may alter their instruction sequence, the PC's value might change before the beginning of the next instruction cycle. We can ignore this point for now.)

Next, via the bus, the MC acquires the address contained in the MAR. Again, please remember that the MAR holds the instruction's *address* (memory location), not the instruction itself.

The MC then fetches the instruction from memory and again uses the bus to copy its value into the MDR.

Finally, the CU copies the instruction residing in the MDR into the IR.

The CPU is now ready to move on to the next stage.

Instruction Decode Stage

At the start of this stage, the CPU "decodes" the instruction. That is, it determines what operation it must perform. For this example, let's assume it's an ADD instruction that will sum two numbers as follows:

ADD v1, v2

Next, just like the processing used to fetch the instruction, the MC acquires the required data (i.e., the value of the two operands, v1 and v2) from memory and stores it into registers R1 and R2, respectively.

Okay, let's pause and summarize what has just happened. At this point, the IR holds the instruction (i.e., ADD), and registers R1 and R2 contain the data (i.e., the value of two operands, v1 and v2, respectively).

The CPU is now ready to enter the instruction execution stage.

Instruction Execution Stage

To begin the execution stage, the CU copies the contents of registers R1 and R2 into the ALU.

Next, the ALU performs the addition and stores the result in the AC.

The result of the computation remains in the AC to serve as an operand in subsequent instructions (i.e., the ADD instruction in our example might be part of a more extensive computation) or until a subsequent instruction directs the CPU to copy the contents of the AC to memory.

Rinse and Repeat

Repeat *ad infinitum*. The CPU returns to Step 1 to execute the next instruction whose address already resides in the PC.

Well, that's it—a complete instruction cycle.

You might want to step through this example a few times until you feel comfortable with it. Also, as you reflect on this processing, keep in mind that your smartphone or laptop can execute millions, if not billions, of similar instruction cycles every second.

ADVANCED SECTION

What is a "Bit"?

Thus far, for pedagogical clarity, the examples we've used expressed values using decimal notation or, more precisely, the Base-10 number system that we commonly use every day. For instance, we observed that keyboards represent capital "A" as the value "65."

For reasons that will become clear shortly, computers cannot use Base-10. However, before discussing how electronic circuits process digital data, let's quickly review how number systems work.

When we write a number such as "456," we intuitively interpret it as represented in Table 4.1.

TABLE 4.1   Base-10 Number Representation

Base-10 Digit Value	Operation	Base-10 Column Value		Total
4	Multiplication	100	=	400
5	Multiplication	10	=	50
6	Multiplication	1	=	6
Total (Addition)				456

Progressing from *right* to *left*, each column's value increases by a power of ten (hence the name, Base-10). Thus, the rightmost column (the one containing the digit "6" in the example) is the 1s column. The one to its left (the one with the value "5") is the 10s column. And the leftmost column (the one with the digit "4") is the 100s column.

We "compute" the value of "456" by multiplying each digit by its corresponding column value, then summing the intermediate results. However, because we learned Base-10 at an early age, we are no longer aware that we're performing this calculation; it's become second nature.

The Base-10 number system requires ten digits to display all the possible values in a single column: 0, 1, 2, 3, 4, 5, 6, 7, 8, and 9. Please note, however, that there is no *single* digit representing the value "10." Instead, the value 10 requires two digits: a "1" in the 10s column and a "0" in the 1s column. (This is important; please keep it in mind as you read the following material.)

Although Base-10 is natural to us, it's not well-suited for the digital world, which prefers binary numbers (0s and 1s). Fortunately, there is a name for this scheme: The Base-2 number system.

In Base-2, we form numbers the same way we do in Base-10, but we use fewer digits (just 0 and 1), and the column values increase by powers of two, not powers of ten.

As an example, Table 4.2 shows how to interpret the binary number "101."

Moving from *right* to *left*, column values in Base-2 are 1, 2, 4, 8, 16, 32, 64, etc. The basic computation is identical to the Base-10 example above; the only difference is the column values. Thus, in Base-10, "101" equals the value 101, whereas in Base-2, "101" equals 5.

TABLE 4.2   Base-2/Binary Number Representation

Base-2 Digit Value	Operation	Base-2 Column Value		Base-10 Total
1	Multiplication	4	=	4
0	Multiplication	2	=	0
1	Multiplication	1	=	1
Total Base-10 (Addition)				5

Similar to the way Base-10 has no single digit representing the value "10," Base-2 has no single digit representing its base value "2"; it also requires two digits: A "1" located in the 2s column and a "0" positioned in the 1s column. Thus, the Base-2 (binary) number written as "10" has a Base-10 value of "2."

Please take a moment to convince yourself of that.

Does this seem strange? Well, another example might help clarify things. Let's convert the Base-2 (binary) value "10101" into its Base-10 equivalent. Table 4.3 illustrates the process.

TABLE 4.3   Converting Binary "10101" to Base-10

Base-2 Digit Value	Operation	Column Value		Base-10 Total
1	Multiplication	16	=	16
0	Multiplication	8	=	0
1	Multiplication	4	=	4
0	Multiplication	2	=	0
1	Multiplication	1	=	1
Total Base-10 (Addition)				21

In computer parlance, we refer to each binary (Base-2) digit as a *bit,* which is a portmanteau of the word *binary* and *digit.* Bits serve as the basic unit of information in all digital electronics.[12]

---

[12] IT Professionals commonly use other number bases as well such as octal (Base-8) and hexadecimal (Base-16).

At this point, you may be wondering why computers use the Base-2 (binary) number system and not Base-10. It's because it's very convenient to create transistor circuits that only need to recognize binary values, such as 0 and 1, ON or OFF, YES or NO, TRUE or FALSE.

However, billions of individual bits flying around a computer would confuse the programmers who had to deal with them. Therefore, to simplify matters, engineers combine bits into larger groupings as follows:

- Eight *bits* form a *byte*

- Four *bytes* form a *word*.[13] Thus, there are 32 *bits* in a *word*

- One *kilobyte* (usually shortened to "one-kay") is 1,024 *bytes*

- One *megabyte* (usually shortened to "one-meg") is 1,048,576 *bytes* or 1,024 *kilobytes*

- One *gigabyte* (usually shortened to "one-gig") is 1,073,741,824 *bytes*, 1,048,576 *kilobytes*, or 1,024 *megabytes*

Armed with this knowledge, let's return to our keyboard example from earlier in this chapter. We initially stated that the numerical representation of a capital "A" was the value "65." However, that's its human-compatible, Base-10 representation. Now, given the above discussion, can you compute what its binary equivalent would be?

The answer is "1000001." Thus, when you type SHIFT A, your keyboard transmits a *byte* that contains the bit values "01000001."

Note that although the representation for the letter capital "A" requires only seven bits, the leading zero is needed because, as we learned above, a *byte* comprises eight bits; thus, we "pad" the byte with an extra "0."

SUMMARY

In this chapter, we described how computer hardware works. We began with a discussion of *digitization* which serves as the *lingua franca* of electronic data.

We then discussed the typical components of modern computers: The CPU, registers, main memory, etc. We followed that by describing a CPU's constituent subcomponents: ALU, CU, etc. We then used our newfound knowledge to explain how each hardware component supports program execution by walking through a complete instruction cycle.

In the Advanced Section, we completed our discussions by defining what bits are and why they form the foundation of electronic devices.

---

[13] This can vary by the system and its underlying hardware design.

CHAPTER 5

What Is Software?

Software is the language of automation.

JENSEN HUANG

INTRODUCTION

In the previous chapter, we reviewed the more tangible components of computer systems. The stuff we can see, touch, plug in, and pound with our fists when things aren't working correctly.

However, that's not what jumps to mind for most users when talking about computers. Most people think in terms of *software*—Waze, Grubhub, MS Word, etc.—rather than the Central Processing Unit (CPU), bus, and memory, and rightly so. Like cars, we want computers to take us where we want to go without worrying about such annoying details as engines, transmissions, and fuel injectors.

In the following sections, we'll provide a thorough understanding of what software is and how it works. However, like the material from the previous chapter, our discussions will be conceptual and will not reflect any specific system or application.

What is Software?

As alluded to above, software is the face of computers: We watch news and movies, listen to books and music, chat with friends and doctors virtually, check our mail and calendars, deposit checks and pay bills, purchase and swap concert tickets, etc. Indeed, our reliance (dependence might be a better word) on electronic devices seems to grow by the day. Nonetheless, what might surprise you is that despite the vast range of services available to us, it's (mostly) software that brings them to life.

But how?

DOI: 10.1201/9781003143437-5

Let's begin with a definition.

DEFINITION 1

Software is an organized arrangement of data and instructions that, when executed, direct the operations of the underlying hardware to accomplish a particular purpose.

This definition shouldn't be a revelation to you—especially if you've read the preceding chapter. Nonetheless, we should take a moment to review it.

Let's begin with the first part.

Previously, we learned that computer programs reside in memory when executing and include both instructions and data. Instructions direct the hardware's operations and determine how to manipulate the data.

The second part of the definition, "to accomplish a specific purpose," is why we have thousands upon thousands of apps and not just one. Each program addresses a specific need. For example:

- If you want to file your taxes, you use a program like *TurboTax*, not *Photoshop*

- If you'd like to kick back and watch a movie, you launch *Media Player*, not *Excel*; and

- If you'd like to author the next Great American Novel, you use a word processor, not a calendar program

The critical point is that the hardware remains constant. All the above programs can run on your laptop or smartphone.[1]

Although accurate, the above definition doesn't describe how IT professionals build and organize software. So, let's peel away a few layers of this onion in a way that won't bring tears to your eyes.

Software Layers

Broadly speaking, we can divide software into two major categories: *System* and *application*. For the most part, *system software* runs behind the scenes. Its responsibilities include managing the hardware, protecting the system from unauthorized access, and performing routine maintenance.

The term *application software* refers to programs designed for users which perform clearly defined functions: Browsers, email apps, word processors, social media services, and eReaders (which you might be using right now to read this book).

Although we're off to a good start, these two classes are too broad and require further refinement. Thus, Figure 5.1 depicts the typical *layers* we use when organizing software.

---

[1] Assuming you have them installed on your system.

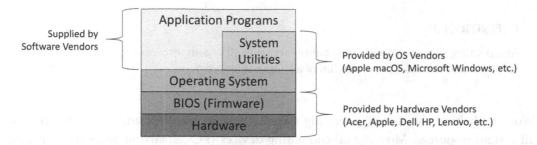

FIGURE 5.1 Software layers.

Let's discuss them from bottom to top.

Firmware and BIOS

Supplied by hardware vendors, *BIOS*, an acronym that stands for Basic Input/Output System, introduces us to a type of system software called *firmware*.

DEFINITION 2

Firmware is software integrated into the hardware that controls the operation of the underlying circuitry.

Conceptually, firmware is like the other types of software we've already discussed. The difference is the level of control. In modern digital devices, engineers design circuitry so that software (i.e., its firmware) controls its operation. Thus, designers can modify and extend firmware to meet changing demands without replacing or upgrading the underlying hardware. In some sense, this means that even hardware has become programmable.

Returning to Figure 5.1, BIOS is preinstalled firmware that controls system initialization (see the discussion on the *boot process* below), identifies connected devices (e.g., mouse, keyboard, and disk drives), and provides run-time support for the *Operating System* (OS; discussed later in this chapter).

As with all firmware, BIOS usually resides in a nonvolatile data store and doesn't change all that frequently. Nonetheless, during system upgrades on your PC, you might occasionally receive a notification that a "BIOS update" occurred.

We won't spend any more time discussing firmware: Its focus is too narrow, and it's so integrated into the underlying circuitry as to become indistinguishable from the hardware (at least for our purposes). Nonetheless, please keep in mind that because it's software, firmware allows for easy extension and upgrade without requiring hardware component replacement.

Operating System and Utilities

The next layer in our software stack is the OS and its associated utility programs. Let's begin with the OS proper.

DEFINITION 3

An *operating system* oversees and controls access to all system resources (both hardware and software) and manages the execution of all application programs.

Working behind the scenes, operating systems host applications and manage access to all system resources. Most digital computing devices (PCs, smartphones, smartwatches, tablets, etc.) rely on the OS for overall command and control. And although you're likely familiar with the names of some of the more popular products—MS Windows, macOS, Linux, Android, iOS—you might not be aware of what they do because you rarely interact with them directly.

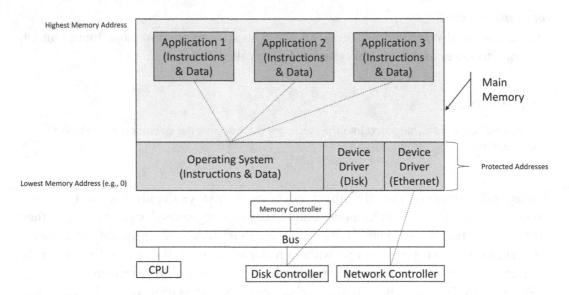

FIGURE 5.2 The OS.

To highlight some of the responsibilities of OSs, please review Figure 5.2, which depicts a representation of the internal state of a running system. Specifically, let's focus on the box representing *main memory*.

As part of system start-up, the initialization process loads the OS into the lower part of memory.[2] Enforced by the hardware, this area is "off-limits" to all other applications; only the OS may access data residing in this section. From this protected memory location, the OS safeguards and manages access to all system resources.

Please note that I added several boxes labeled "Device Driver" in Figure 5.2. Device drivers are custom software components that manage specific hardware devices like disk drives and network controllers. We never interact with them directly. However, whenever

---

[2] We'll describe the system initialization (boot) process in the next section.

an application requires services from a hardware component (e.g., reading a file from a disk), a device driver does the "heavy lifting."[3]

The initialization process loads device drivers into the protected memory segment as well. As a result, they run as extensions of the OS.

As also depicted in Figure 5.2, all user programs (e.g., browsers, word processors, and music players) execute in *application space*, which we define as any memory segment not otherwise reserved for the OS.

Every running program receives its own memory segment. It's the responsibility of the OS to ensure that applications don't expand beyond their allotted boundaries or otherwise interfere with other processes' memory allocations.

Returning to our discussion of layers as presented in Figure 5.1, operating systems also include numerous utility packages. That is, in addition to the system components that load into low-level memory during the boot process, OS vendors provide a suite of programs that help manage the system. These tools usually reside on your hard drive, and you run them like any other application program.

Utility programs offer a wide range of services. For example, you may have used virus scanners, disk repair tools, system monitors that display CPU and memory usage, and diagnostic programs that identify problems. Each OS vendor supplies a suite of tools that they believe serves their customers' needs. In addition, you can also acquire third-party utilities (some for a fee; others are free) that replace, augment, or enhance those included with your system.

Application Software

If the OS is the plate, applications (i.e., the topmost layer depicted in Figure 5.1) are the entrée. They are the reason that we purchase computers. For example, how valuable would an Ultra HD TV be if networks didn't broadcast any shows in that format? The same holds for computers: You could have the most advanced hardware and OS known to humankind, but they wouldn't be much use if they couldn't run any applications.

Formally, we define an application as follows:

DEFINITION 4

An *application* is a collection of one or more programs designed to serve a specific need.

There are more applications than we could cover in a volume of books. They range from:

General purpose	Email utilities, word processors, music players, browsers, spreadsheets, social media apps, etc.
To specific	Banking apps, shopping apps, games, video streaming, billing applications, etc.

---

[3] As we will see later in the chapter, *device drivers* serve as the interface between the Operating System (OS) and the underlying hardware and alleviate the need for the OS to understand how every component functions.

To even more specific	Surgical software, autopilot systems, ground-penetrating radar software that categorizes subsurface structures, facial recognition, robotic Artificial Intelligence (AI), etc.
To custom	Automated trading applications used by brokerage firms, custom order management systems, proprietary market analysis tools, etc.
To personal	I wrote a small program[4] that packages all the files (text, figures, logs, etc.) that comprise this manuscript into a single ZIP file so I could easily email it to my publisher.

I could continue listing applications *ad nauseam*. The point is that if there's a need that software can solve, there's likely (or will be) an application that can fill it. Moreover, despite its obvious triteness, the following assertion is nonetheless true:

The types of software applications are limited only by human imagination.

Now that we understand the software components of a computer system, we can describe each layer in greater detail.

Let's begin with the OS.

WHAT DOES AN OPERATING SYSTEM DO?

As mentioned previously, operating systems manage resources. But that statement is too vague. So, in the following sections, we'll describe some of the specific responsibilities of a modern OS.

Process Lifecycle Management

One essential task of every OS is supervising the execution of running programs. Specifically, whenever we launch (i.e., start) an application, the OS must manage and oversee that process until it terminates.

Before we proceed, we should note the distinction between a *program* and a *process*.

DEFINITION 5

A *program* is an ordered collection of computer instructions contained in a *file*.

DEFINITION 6

A *process* is the running image of a *program* as it executes in memory.

---

[4] Technically, we call that type of program a *script*.

To expand on that definition, consider that when you CLICK on a *program*'s icon (e.g., a browser), the OS copies all the instructions in its disk file into main memory. The image now residing in memory is the *process*; it's only at this point that the program can "run."

With this in mind, let's discuss how operating systems manage the entire execution cycle of a *process*.

Invocation   Initially, when you invoke (run) a program, the OS must locate its file on disk and copy its instructions and data into memory.

Execution   After completing the invocation tasks, your program is ready to begin executing. Indeed, the OS could allow your program to start running immediately. However, in most modern computing environments, there's usually more than one process that's ready to run at any given moment in time. The OS must therefore choose which one executes next. This selection leads us to our next topic: *Scheduling*.

Scheduling   The principal resource in any computer system is its CPU; it's the one resource required by *every* running process. *Scheduling* is the method by which the OS grants CPU access to runnable processes.

Context switching   After determining which process should run next, the OS must suspend the currently running process and begin executing the newly selected one. We refer to this task as *context switching*. (Note that in computer science, we refer to a process's execution state as its *context*, hence the term *context switch*.)

To perform a *context switch*, the OS must save the execution state of the currently running process, restore the previously saved execution state of the process that's about to run, then turn over control of the CPU to the new process.

Process termination   A running process can *terminate* (we also use the terms *stop, halt,* and *exit*) for many reasons. In the best case, programs exit when they complete their assigned tasks successfully. Additionally, users may stop applications at any time.

However, there are occasions when the OS must intervene and terminate an application because it's "misbehaving." For example, a process may only retrieve data from memory locations within its assigned address space. If it tries to access an area that's "out of bounds," the OS will step in and terminate it.

Regardless of the reason, the OS must "clean up" after a process terminates. Some examples of these "housekeeping" tasks include freeing memory so that other programs may use it and aborting any in-progress operations such as previously issued disk read requests that are still in progress.

Resource and Hardware Management

Operating System Architecture

As we noted previously, one of the most important tasks of an operating system is to manage the underlying hardware. To understand how that process works, we need to discuss the structure of a typical OS; we refer to this design as its *architecture*.

Figure 5.3 depicts the logical architecture of a typical OS.[5]

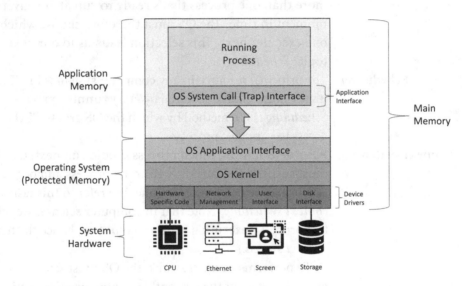

FIGURE 5.3   Logical architecture of an operating system.

As a reminder, the OS usually resides in a protected area of memory reserved explicitly for system software. This design prevents unauthorized access to the hardware.

The following sections discuss the architectural components of an OS in more detail.

Application Interface

When an application program requires a system service, it must call upon the OS to complete the task on its behalf. To initiate such a request, processes use the *system call application interface*, which is a collection of prepackaged functions provided by the OS. Examples include reading data from a disk, displaying text and graphics on the user's screen, and communicating with other systems.

---

[5] As you might expect, the architecture of most modern OS is far more intricate than that depicted.

The Kernel

The *kernel* is the core component of the OS (hence its name). It manages all system-level operations and ensures that applications have permission to access any requested service. It also manages processes, schedules execution, and maintains system integrity.

Device Drivers

Have you ever considered how many types and models of computers (desktops, laptops, tablets, and smart devices) and OSs (e.g., Microsoft Windows, Linux, macOS, and Android) there are? Or the thousands of devices (e.g., disks, printers, and keyboards) that interoperate with them?

The number of combinations is staggering. Nonetheless, when you buy a new component and plug it into your computer, it just *works* (well, usually).

So, how do OS and hardware vendors address this issue through the design and use of *device drivers*?

Device drivers are software components that have two primary responsibilities: "Drive" (i.e., control) the hardware and interact with the OS. By design, when you "plug in" a new device, the OS automatically installs the associated driver (often by downloading it from the Web). At that point, the new component is "visible" on your system and available to all applications.

When a running process needs access to a hardware device (e.g., it wants to read data from a disk file), it issues a request via the *OS application interface* (Figure 5.3). The OS, in turn, forwards the request to the appropriate *device driver,* which supervises the operation on behalf of the requesting application.

When a hardware device completes a request, the device driver delivers the results to the OS, which, in turn, forwards them to the requesting application. This design ensures that neither applications nor operating systems must contend with the intricacies of individual hardware components.

Software Resources

Although hardware serves as the foundation, not all computing services are "hard-wired." Some system features are software-based. Examples include the following:

Security	Authorization to access system resources is a "logical" concept managed through a set of permissions implemented in software. This task includes administering passwords, verifying user biometrics, and enforcing system rules and policies (e.g., preventing a process from accessing a memory location outside its allotted segment).
IPC	IPC, or inter-process communication, is a software service that enables data exchange among executing processes. A common example is *copy and paste*. When using any IPC feature, the OS acts as a "telephone company" routing messages among communicating entities.

Allocation   Many system resources, like the CPU, may require exclusive access. Therefore, the *kernel* arbitrates among requesting applications to ensure that multiple processes do not use such resources concurrently.

Memory Management

Another essential resource in computer systems is its *main memory*. All processes require it, and there is a finite amount of it. Thus, one of the most crucial tasks of operating system is managing it.

However, this task can quickly become problematic. For example, have you ever had to rearrange pots in a dishwasher to make room for a few more items?

OSs deal with similar issues when managing memory. As processes come and go (execute and terminate), they acquire and relinquish memory segments. As a result, memory can become *fragmented*, affecting system performance.[6]

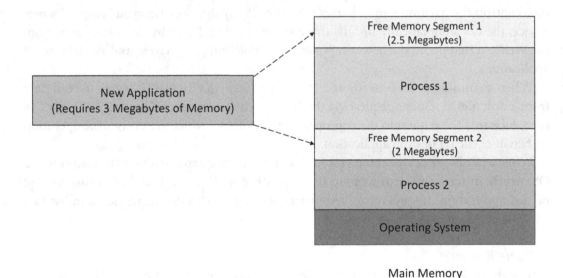

FIGURE 5.4   Memory fragmentation.

For example, as depicted in Figure 5.4, there's sufficient memory available in the system to allow the new application to execute. It requires three megabytes of memory, and Segments 1 and 2 contain 4.5 megabytes collectively. Unfortunately, however, the segments are not *contiguous*, and neither one is large enough individually to meet the need.

One of the most common techniques OSs use to address such fragmentation is through a technique called *compaction*. As illustrated in Figure 5.5, when memory becomes fragmented, the OS can reorganize it such that all the "free" segments coalesce.

---

[6] Does your PC often seem sluggish? Memory fragmentation may be the cause.

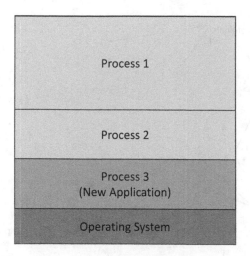

Main Memory

FIGURE 5.5   Memory after compaction.

Several other memory management techniques are available (e.g., *swapping* and *paging*) that are beyond the scope of this text. Nonetheless, regardless of the method, this is one of the most critical and fundamental services provided by every OS.

File System Management

Like managing main memory, organizing disk storage is another essential task for the OS. Otherwise, absent centralized control, using the disk could become a hit-or-miss proposition.

For example, how would we prevent one application from inadvertently (or deliberately!) overwriting another program's data? How would developers know which areas of the disk were available to use? How would programs locate previously stored data? OSs must supervise this resource to ensure privacy and maintain data integrity.

Let's see how.

Most OSs organize disk storage using abstractions[7] familiar to users. One of the most common approaches mimics the way organizations historically managed paper: Files and folders. Data resides in *files*; *files* reside in *folders*.[8] Most modern OSs extend this analogy and allow folders to contain other folders (called *subfolders*), creating a storage hierarchy.

For example, you could create a folder named TAXES to store all your IRS-related files. However, over time, you might find it problematic to locate all the files associated with a specific tax year. However, understanding that folders may contain other folders, you might opt to reorganize your tax records using a structure like the one depicted in Figure 5.6.

---

[7] See the Glossary for a definition.
[8] Some OSs (e.g., Linux) call folders *directories*.

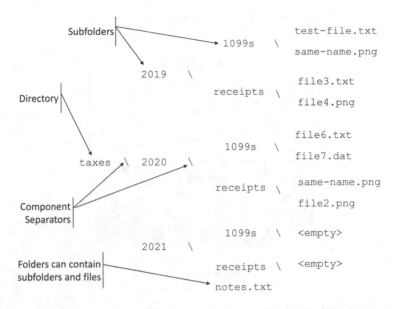

FIGURE 5.6   Example of tax folder hierarchy.

As the diagram demonstrates, you can create a custom *folder hierarchy* to meet your specific needs. In this case, we have a *parent folder* called TAXES that contains *subfolders* named 2019, 2020, and 2021. Note that, as highlighted in the subfolder, 2021, folders may include both files and other subfolders.

One syntactical consideration: The backslash character ("\")[9] does not appear in the file system or on disk. It's for notational convenience and serves to separate components, allowing us to reference a file by its *pathname*.

For example, in Figure 5.6, the *pathname* for the file TEST-FILE.TXT is as follows:

TAXES\2019\1099s\TEST-FILE.TXT

As might be obvious, file names within a folder must be unique. Otherwise, how could we distinguish them?

However, we can name two (or more files) identically if they reside in different folders as follows:

TAXES\2019\1099s\SAME-NAME.PNG

and

TAXES\2020\1099s\same-name.png

Note that the *pathnames* uniquely identify files even though they might share a common file name (i.e., SAME-NAME.PNG).

---

[9] Some file systems (e.g., Linux) use the forward slash ("/") character as the component separator.

The OS implements the file/folder abstraction on your behalf; thus, you typically don't need to concern yourself with the details. For example, regardless of the underlying disk technology, the file system on your 10-year-old laptop will appear to function identically to the one that shipped with your brand-new tablet.

User Interfaces

All computer systems must provide *interfaces* to allow users—or other electronic devices—to interact with them. Otherwise, they would become the metaphorical "closed box:" No data in, no data out.

Typically, the most important (and certainly the most visible) aspect of any program's design is its *user interface*. The IT industry spends untold dollars developing intuitive and straightforward techniques for users to interact with their applications seamlessly. And they're succeeding. Consider how infrequently—if ever—you consult the user manual for newly acquired applications.

Most OSs offer an integrated *Graphical User Interface* (GUI) to support that goal.[10] GUIs employ icons, graphics, and sounds to create an intuitive (and often immersive) experience for users.

As with file systems, GUI designs rely on abstractions. In this case, the metaphor is a desktop. Each running application appears in a *window*, and each window is akin to a piece of paper on a desk. As you are free to move and reshuffle documents on a physical surface, you can rearrange and reorganize application windows on your screen.

As a rule, GUIs divide responsibilities between the OS—as implemented by a service called the *window manager*—and individual applications. The primary task of the *window manager* is to maintain the desktop. Based on mouse clicks or screen touches, it positions windows and determines which parts of any given window are visible.

Applications are responsible for maintaining the *contents* of their windows. Obviously, as data change, programs must update their displays.

System Initialization (Booting)

Now that we understand what an OS does, the next logical question is: How does it start up?

Obviously, nothing is running when you power down your computer, including the operating system. So, when you apply power, how does the OS come to life?

As it turns out, there is an intricate orchestration of events called *system initialization* or the *boot process* that loads and executes the OS.

Every system employs a unique boot process. Some are more elaborate than others based on need and applicability. For example, you might not mind waiting 45 seconds for a desktop computer to boot. However, most people would consider that an eternity for a smartphone. Thus, as with many of our prior discussions, the following material describes the start-up process in conceptual terms.

For most typical computers, the boot process unfolds in *stages*. Initially, when we apply power to a system, a small program—called the *bootstrap loader*—begins running.

---

[10] With some OSs, the *graphical user interface* is an add-on product.

The bootstrap loader ships with the hardware and performs a single task: Executing the OS-specific *stage one loader.* (Please note that many computers allow you to choose which OS you want to run on your machine. Thus, the *bootstrap loader* runs the *stage one loader* specific to your OS.)

Although slightly more elaborate than the *bootstrap loader,* the *stage one loader* has only one task as well: It executes the *stage two loader.*

You may be wondering why the initialization process needs a *stage one loader* at all. After all, why couldn't the bootstrap loader initiate *the stage two loader*?

The reason has to do with a convention. The OS must store the *stage one loader* at a specific location on disk so the *bootstrap loader* can "find" it. In contrast, the *stage two loader* may reside anywhere on the file system and is thus beyond the "grasp" of the *bootstrap loader.* Because the *stage one loader* ships with the OS, it "knows" where the *stage two loader* "lives."

Unlike the programs that preceded it, the *stage two loader* performs several system-specific tasks, including initializing memory, loading the primary OS, and, most importantly, initiating OS execution. (For some systems, the *stage two loader* might be a tiny operating system in its own right.)

Once invoked by the *stage two loader,* the OS verifies the viability of all hardware components, loads device drivers, and initializes the environment. The boot process completes when the OS is ready to execute user applications.

When you start a system by applying power, it's considered a *hard boot.* In contrast, a *soft boot* occurs when you instruct the OS to restart via software. For example, *soft boots* typically take place after a system upgrade when the OS informs you that it must restart the system to complete the installation process. (For many systems, the *soft boot* process may not require as many steps as a *hard boot.*)

Some organizations boot their computers via a network to control software versions and ensure security. In such cases, the loaders and the OS reside on remote servers. Unfortunately, when using this approach, systems are often unable to boot without a functioning network connection.

Security

As noted earlier, in addition to providing a stable, robust execution platform, most operating systems also enforce security policies. This task includes managing users, safeguarding system resources, and protecting running processes from other misbehaving or nefarious programs.

System security is a multifaceted responsibility; let's begin with user management.

User Security

When it comes to security, an OS's highest priority is to ensure that only authorized users may gain access to system resources. In furtherance of that goal, OSs will impose an *authentication process* that users must undergo before granting permission to interact with the environment. This procedure can range from a simple login and password combination to elaborate biometric verification techniques.

Authenticating users has many benefits including the following:

Identification	Typically, systems assign each user a unique ID so that the OS can track resource usage. Thus, administrators "know" what each user does on their systems.
Authorization	Resource entitlement need not be universal. For example, consider systems that support a health-care facility. Clearly, billing personnel should not have access to patient medical histories. To enforce such constraints, system administrators can selectively impose restrictions on data access. We call this process *authorization*.
Auditing	The system can record every command (even every keystroke if required) a user enters. This type of tracking is of particular concern in secure environments like government installations. However, this might also be an important feature used in legal, medical, and laboratory environments.
Monitoring	Systems can track resource consumption by user. Such data collection supports billing processes and alerts administrators when individual users consume resources in excess of their entitlements.

Process Security

On most systems, an executing program assumes the privileges of the user who invoked it. Consequently, the process can only access resources authorized for that user. So, for example, two users could launch MS Word on the same system. However, one user might be able to edit a file that the other user can't. In most cases, it's the OS that usually enforces such restrictions.[11]

The OS also ensures that executing processes don't violate system constraints. For example, in the previous chapter, we noted that addresses are just numerical values. Thus, what's to stop a process from trying to read (or write to) a portion of memory it doesn't control? It's typically the OS that prevents such erroneous or pernicious behavior.

Data Security

When you delete a file, the OS reclaims the now-unused disk storage and makes it available for reuse. Specifically, the file system returns the deleted file's blocks[12] to the "free" list; as a result, other files are free to use them.

However, please take note that the OS **doesn't erase anything**. *Therefore, all the previously written information recorded on the freed blocks remains unchanged.* That's why you can "undo" a file deletion on some systems—no data were lost during the deletion process.

---

[11] This might not hold true for all resources. In some cases, application software—like a database management system—might determine authorization independently of the OS.

[12] Please recall that chunks of memory are called *segments*; chunks of files are called *blocks*.

As a result of this design approach, hackers, computer forensic investigators, and bored teenagers with time on their hands can read "deleted" data if they have access to your system (and the requisite technical competency). Consequently, you risk that financial account information, social security numbers, and your aunt's secret apple pie recipe might fall into the wrong hands.

To thwart this threat, you can use one of the many commercial tools that permanently erase data in deleted files. If protecting personal data is a concern to you, I suggest you invest in one of these products.

Common Services and Utilities

In addition to the services discussed in the prior sections, most OSs provide many other features and utilities. I say "most" because some operating systems that control small devices—like those in smartwatches or electronic thermostats—might not offer as many services as their big siblings.

The sections below examine several of the most common services and utilities provided by full-featured OSs.

File Explorers

Even the most sophisticated file system would be useless if it didn't allow users to review and manage its contents. All PC operating systems provide such tools. I'm sure you're familiar with *File Explorer* for Windows or *Finder* that ships with macOS.[13] Both utilities offer graphical representations of their respective file systems and allow users to open, create, delete, and copy files and folders.

Disk Administration

Over time, files and folders can become fragmented or corrupted. Thus, most OSs provide disk administration tools that repair such anomalies. Many systems also include utilities that optimize file system structures to increase performance.

Backup and Restore

All digital devices fail. And let me be clear on this: It's not a case of *if*, but *when*.

Disk drives are no exception to this rule. As a result, most operating systems include backup utilities that copy files from one disk drive (called the *primary*) to another (called the *secondary* or *backup*).

Because of advances in manufacturing processes, disk technology has become so dependable that many users have become complacent and don't back up their systems regularly. Don't be one of them. If your data is important enough to save to disk, it's valuable enough to back up.

Disk drives have become very inexpensive and are simple to install. Buy one. Better yet, buy two. I know it's easy for me to spend your money—but consider what the cost to you might be if your primary disk drive failed and you couldn't recover your files and data.

---

[13] File system access is slightly different under OSs like Linux.

If you don't like the backup utility provided with your system, there are many reliable third-party offerings. In addition, you can use one of the numerous cloud-based backup services that ensure you can recover corrupted data from anywhere in the world.

Use one of them regularly.

Clipboard

One of the most convenient features of modern computing environments is *copy and paste*. The ability to grab data from one application and insert it into another minimizes human error and saves us from the tedium of retyping information.

Network Administration

Over the past two decades or so, networks have become highly reliable and easy to use. However, that's not to suggest that nothing ever goes awry: Components fail, software has bugs, circuits experience outages, etc.

To help address such anomalies, operating systems provide tools to analyze, diagnose, and repair network problems. In addition, many OSs also supply tools that will display your computer's IP and MAC addresses, evaluate your network's speed, and determine whether a device your system is communicating with is responding.[14]

We'll discuss how computers communicate in Chapter 6.

WHAT IS A COMPUTER APPLICATION?

Previously, we've characterized a computer application as a collection of one or more programs designed to serve a specific need. Let's refine that definition a bit.

DEFINITION 7

An *application* is a finite arrangement of instructions packaged as one or more *programs* that, when executed, use data to accomplish a specific set of tasks within a targeted computing environment.

Let's begin analyzing that revised definition by scrutinizing the phrase: "One or more programs."

Most computer users tend to use the terms "program" and "application" interchangeably. However, in the world of IT, each has a distinct meaning. A *program* is a single set of instructions often contained in a single executable file, whereas an *application* comprises multiple programs, each of which resides in separate files.

Now, let's move on to the phrase "targeted set of tasks."

All applications must limit or focus their functionality. For example, some digital music players support several types of music files (e.g., MP3, WAV, and WMA); others may only support one or two. Word processors don't play music, but besides providing text editing

---

[14] We call this a *ping* test.

features, some might also include advanced tools such as a dictionary, a grammar analyzer, and a spell checker.

The point is that despite any variance in scope, every application addresses a specific, focused set of needs. They are not "all things to all people."

The phrase "use data" in the definition is deliberately vague. Applications may operate on any digital information in any format (e.g., text files, audio streams, numeric data, and biometric input). Moreover, an application's data may reside locally, on a cloud server, or in a database on a remote machine. In addition, some applications might *generate* data. For example, consider a Sudoku game app that uses programmatically generated random numbers to create each puzzle.

Where are Applications Used?

Unless you've lived in solitude for the last 50 years, the answer to the question, "Where are applications used?" is obvious: Everywhere. So, we should bring this section to a quick close.

For completeness, however, I'd like to discuss some uses of software that might not be so obvious.

Business

Most of you use software applications at your workplace: Email programs, word processors, spreadsheets, payroll systems, etc. In terms of direct use, enough said. However, you might be unaware of some indirect interactions you might have with computer software.

For example, some logistics organizations can track their fleets using satellite technology (often without the operator's knowledge). Using this feature, transportation companies can monitor how many hours their drivers are behind the wheel each day and receive real-time alerts when one of their vehicles deviates from an assigned route.

Another example is when you buy a garment in a department store. When the clerk "rings you up," the register might send the purchase information to a system that tracks inventory and automatically initiates replenishment orders with the supplier.

An extreme case of automated ordering is called *just-in-time delivery*. It costs money when inventory sits idle on a shelf. To reduce overhead, companies buy goods only when they need them. For example, a car manufacturer's inventory system can compute how many vehicles the automaker will build tomorrow and automatically order the appropriate number of tires to arrive at the factory's loading dock in the morning. Pretty slick.

Music

Chapter 4 discussed how applications process digital sound via audio files and streaming services. However, you might not know that software *generates* much of the music you listen to today. And I'm not just referring to the "weird" sounds that are "otherworldly" and are clearly artificial.

Familiar instruments such as violins, horns, drums, organs, and pianos are not always performed "live." In many cases, composers use Digital Audio Workstations (DAWs) to create those sounds using software (and sometimes specialized hardware).

As an aside, digitized music is one example of how software has far-reaching and often unintended consequences. DAWs have democratized the world of music and liberated musicians. Anyone with access to a laptop can create, package, market, and distribute music without the need for traditional publishing companies or record labels.

Consequently, we can listen to many artists who, in the past, we might have never known existed. But unfortunately, that also means that we might have to wade through a flood of junk from "artists" who have only a fleeting relationship with talent.

Alas, as with most things in life, we must take the good with the bad.

Education

In recent years, distance learning—where students are physically remote and interact with their instructors via computer—has become commonplace. However, application software is far more integrated into pedagogy than simply connecting pupils and teachers.

Although it might not be obvious, many online courses adjust lessons based on each student's progress and test results. When implemented correctly, this is self-paced, one-on-one education at its best.

Many book publishers can custom-tailor textbooks to align precisely with the syllabus of individual courses offered at various universities. Thus, the contents and sequence of topics for the same book can vary by school.

Educators also use advanced graphics to develop visual images that facilitate the presentation of complex structures and ideas. For example, medical schools create three-dimensional models of complex organs like the heart and lungs that allow students to "travel through" them.

Very cool.

FIGURE 5.7   A model of a human heart generated on a 3D printer.

It may be the case that science will be able to generate customized replacement body parts on advanced 3D printers in our lifetimes (Figure 5.7).

Health Care

In health care, software drives much of the diagnostic testing patients undergo. For example, with the aid of sophisticated computer graphics, MRIs, CAT scans, and sonograms create detailed, three-dimensional images of our internal organs.

But medical software does so much more.

It aids doctors in diagnosing illnesses. As an illustration, recent studies have demonstrated that AI software may be more accurate in identifying disorders of the eyes than ophthalmologists. Moreover, AI technologies may also aid in developing new therapeutic drugs and vaccines[15] and improving the early diagnosis of progressive neurological diseases such as Alzheimer's and Parkinson's.

Military

Much of what the military does with technology is unknown to the public (including me). However, I think we can state without reservation that software drives the modern army. It coordinates battles, repositions personnel, directs smart weapons, and manages encrypted communication.

Moreover, battlefields have become increasingly digital. As a result, armies in the traditional sense are becoming obsolete, replaced by "techies" who, without leaving the comfort of their favorite gaming chair, fight on land (using drones and smart tanks), sea (directing remote-controlled watercraft), and air (controlling pilotless fighter jets).

More alarmingly, however, due to technology's influence, the perception of the battlefield has morphed. Today, "techie" combatants fight for more than traditional military objectives—they grapple for control over private-sector digital resources as well. For example, foreign hackers might attack a country's banking systems to undermine its financial stability or target a region's transportation infrastructure to wreak havoc on roads and debilitate commerce.

HOW DO WE BUILD SOFTWARE?

Thus far, we've discussed the distinction between hardware and software, how instructions execute inside a CPU, and the types of software found in computer systems. In this section, we'll learn how developers build applications.

Software development is part art, part science. Indeed, if you were to assign a hundred professional programmers an identical task, you'd receive a hundred unique solutions in response. Indeed, they might all function correctly, but they would look nothing alike.

At first blush, this might seem surprising—even alarming—but it's no different than any other human undertaking requiring some degree of creativity and interpretation. For example, consider asking every person who attended the same meeting to write a set of minutes. I assure you, no two would read identically.

---

[15] Witness the advances during the COVID-19 pandemic.

WHAT IS COMPUTER PROGRAMMING?

The purpose of computer programming is to develop a specific sequence of instructions that automates a given task. More formally:

> **DEFINITION 8**
>
> *Computer programming* is a set of tasks and procedures conducted by software developers that, when completed, generates a set of executable instructions that achieve a specific result.

However, software development doesn't happen in a vacuum. On the contrary, professional-caliber programming requires that developers have expertise in both computer science and the subject matter they're automating.

For example, consider developing an accounting program. The programmers must understand concepts like *debit*, *credit*, and *depreciation* to write the necessary code. We call this *domain-specific knowledge.*

Professional programmers must also comprehend the fundamental concepts of computer science and the tools and techniques of software development. Serving as a foundation for this knowledge is a thorough understanding of one or more programming languages.

WHAT IS A PROGRAMMING LANGUAGE?

Let's begin our discussion of programming languages by comparing them with natural languages. The objective of both is communication: Expressing ideas, sharing information, and issuing instructions. They also rely on standardized rules of construction consisting of a defined vocabulary, formalized grammar, and permissible operations.

However, that's where the similarities end.

Natural languages are typically large, riddled with ambiguity, and evolve, well, naturally, whereas computer languages are artificial constructs with a finite set of rules that change slowly and deliberately.

To understand the differences, consider the following English sentence:

I didn't start my car because my friend wasn't in it.

Although it's grammatically correct, there are two valid interpretations of that sentence:

1. I didn't start my car because I wanted to wait until my friend got in.

2. I didn't start my car—but for a reason that had nothing to do with my friend's absence.

Another classic example shows us how the use of punctuation can change the meaning of an English sentence:

Let's eat, Grandma.

and

Let's eat Grandma.

In the first version, we're urging Grandma to serve the food; in the second, Grandma is on the menu.

Humans can work through such vagueness—especially when conversing. However, ambiguity of this sort would wreak havoc in the IT world: Each *expression* or *statement* in a computer language—the equivalent of a sentence in a natural language—must have one and only one interpretation. Otherwise, the same statement could yield a different result with every execution. That would be anathema in a world that expects accurate, repeatable results.

Consequently, computer languages are small (comparatively speaking) and impose strict usage and syntactical rules. Thus, we can define a programming language as follows:

DEFINITION 9

A *programming language* is a formalized set of general-purpose instructions that produce a precise result when combined and executed in a specific arrangement.

Computer language design is complicated and worthy of study in its own right. Language creators must consider many attributes: What sorts of problems will it solve? What types of constructs should it provide? On what kinds of hardware will it run?

However, the most important design aspect is consistency. Regardless of how developers use and combine a programming language's constructs, every statement must have one and only one interpretation. As noted above, there can be no ambiguity.

A Brief History of Programming Languages

Despite its relative infancy, the IT industry has developed thousands of computer languages. Some are general purpose; others address specific needs. A brief history of the more significant developments in computer language evolution follows.

1800s	Ada Lovelace developed a program to compute Bernoulli numbers. Historians consider this the first computer program and Ada Lovelace the first computer programmer.
1949	The first assembly language.
1957	J. Backus developed the Fortran (FORmula TRANslation) language. Despite its early origins, it's still in use today.
1958	A committee of American and European computer scientists developed a language called ALGOL (Algorithmic

Language). Although it never achieved independent popularity, ALGOL served as the foundation for many other influential computer languages.

1959   Rear Admiral Dr. Grace Murray Hopper developed a general-purpose computer programming language called COBOL (COmmon Business-Oriented Language). COBOL was significant because it was one of the first languages that could execute on many different brands of computers. COBOL is still in use today.

1959   John McCarthy of MIT developed LISP (LISt Processor), the first language used for AI research. Among many innovative ideas, the language allows programs to modify themselves.

1964   While working at Dartmouth College, John G. Kemeny and Thomas E. Kurtz developed BASIC (Beginner's All-purpose Symbolic Instruction Code). Created as a pedagogical tool, BASIC is often the first language taught to beginning computer science students.

1970   Niklaus Wirth developed a language called Pascal. (He named it in honor of the famous French mathematician Blaise Pascal). Although primarily created as an instructional tool for computer science students, it also served as the primary programming language in early generations of Apple computers.

1972   While working at Bell Labs, Dennis Ritchie created The C Programming Language. (It extended a language called, oddly enough, B.) Ritchie developed C to support the design and implementation of the UNIX Operating System. It also influenced many other computer languages such as Java, Python, Perl, and C#. It's still widely used today.

1972   While working at IBM, Donald Chamberlin and Raymond Boyce developed SQL (pronounced "sequel") a Structured Query Language. Based on Relational Algebra (developed by Dr. Edgar Codd while also working at IBM), SQL supports the querying and manipulating of data stored in a relational database. Variants of SQL are in widespread use today.

1985   While working at Bell Laboratories, Bjarne Stroustrup published the first edition of his book, *The C++ Programming Language*. An extension of C, C++ is an Object-Oriented (OO) language still in use today.

1991   While working as a CERN[16] contractor, Tim Berners-Lee published a document called "HTML Tags" (Hypertext Markup Language), which proposed a language that could format text and images on web pages. As a result of his innovation, historians consider Mr. Berners-Lee the inventor of the World Wide Web.

1991   Guido Van Rossum developed Python (an *homage* to the British comedy group *Monty Python*). Widely used, Python serves the needs of many development organizations.

1995   While working at Sun Microsystems, James Gosling originally developed Java to support small devices such as cable boxes and handheld computers. After subsequent improvements enhanced its power, Java became the *lingua franca* of the Web. To say "Java is everywhere" is an understatement.

1995   Brendan Eich designed JavaScript to enhance browser development. Today, most websites you visit employ JavaScript.

2000   Microsoft developed C#. Based on C++ and Java, it's used primarily in Microsoft components.

This list is but a tiny sample. Existing languages continue to evolve, and the IT industry creates new ones to address emerging needs.

Classes of Computer Languages

There are so many computer languages because they each possess inherent characteristics that address a particular need. Such design diversity is not unique to computer science. For example, in carpentry, there are dozens of distinct types of hammers—each serves a specific task.[17] Similarly, developers will often use multiple languages when writing large-scale computer systems. *The right tool for the right job.*

The sections that follow discuss several classes of programming languages. Please note, however, that some languages fit into multiple categories. For example, C++ is both an OO and a *compiled* language. In contrast, Java is both an OO and an *interpreted* language. (We'll discuss what these terms mean below.)

Machine Languages

The most fundamental class of computer language is the CPU's instruction set. As discussed in Chapter 4, every machine-language *opcode* directs the CPU to execute one primitive instruction.

---

[16] The European Organization for Nuclear Research.

[17] That notwithstanding, I find that a butter knife can accomplish most household repairs. You know what "they" say: When all you have is a butter knife, everything looks like a … well, I'm sure you know what I mean.

Although every executable program ultimately runs as a series of opcodes (we'll describe how this happens later in this chapter), programming in machine language has many shortcomings:

- It's tedious and error prone

- Programs written in machine language are challenging to read; thus, making changes to them is often problematic[18]

- Machine-language instructions are CPU specific: Programs written using one CPU's instruction set cannot run on other processors[19]

Because programming in a machine language is so demanding, the IT community developed computer languages with increasingly greater degrees of abstraction. As we will see, with each increase in the level of abstraction, we reduce degrees of complexity for programmers.

Assembly Languages

The first level of abstraction is *assembly language* (or *assembler language* or just *assembler*). Although still low-level, assembler languages provide human-readable mnemonics for every machine-language instruction. Thus, instead of typing a string of 1s and 0s as given below:

```
01101100 000111001 0110001
```

programmers would code something like the following:

```
MOV B, A
```

As I'm sure you'd agree, assembler mnemonics are more human-friendly. This clarity is especially beneficial when modifying an existing program—the easier code is to read, the easier it is to comprehend (i.e., reverse engineer).

To prepare an assembler program for execution, developers use a tool called an *assembler* to convert human-readable mnemonics into machine opcodes. Returning to the example above, if a program were to contain the statement:

```
MOV B, A
```

the assembler would generate the following:

```
01101100 000111001 0110001
```

---

[18] We refer to this as *readability*.
[19] We refer to this as *portability*.

Though easier than coding using machine instructions, assembler language programming also suffers several deficiencies:

- Writing assembler code is also tedious and still highly error prone
- It also lacks portability because of the one-to-one relationship between assembler mnemonics and machine-language opcodes

As we will see, to address these shortcomings, the IT community developed *high-level languages* that further increase the levels of abstraction.

Structured Programming Languages

Structured programming languages represent the next level of abstraction. Developed in the mid-to-late 1960s, structured languages improve the power, readability, and clarity of computer programs. Some popular examples you might be familiar with include C, ALGOL, and PASCAL.

Although the syntax and semantics of structured languages may vary, they all share the basic *control constructs* described below. Developers may freely arrange them in any combination to achieve a desired result.

Sequence The ordered execution of one statement after another (Refer Listing 5.1).

```
STATEMENT 1
STATEMENT 2
      ...
STATEMENT N
```

LISTING 5.1   A Sequence of Statements.

Selection Choosing which instructions execute based on one or more conditions. For example, most web pages allow users to sign in or create a new account. The code to implement that type of processing might look something like the code presented in Listing 5.2:

```
IF ( THE USER PRESSED THE SIGN-IN BUTTON )
THEN
    EXECUTE THE SIGN-IN CODE
ELSE
    EXECUTE THE NEW ACCOUNT CODE
END
```

LISTING 5.2   Selection Example.

Based on the result of what's called a *conditional expression* (i.e., "IF (THE USER PRESSED THE SIGN-IN BUTTON) "), the program will either execute the sign-in code or the new account code.

Note that I didn't use an actual programming language in this example. Instead, I expressed the logic using a construct called *pseudocode*.

DEFINITION 10

Pseudocode allows developers to describe programming logic using human-readable constructs without becoming mired in a specific language's syntactic details.

Like an artist's sketchbook, pseudocode allows programmers to conveniently capture and convey programmatic ideas in an *ad hoc*, readable format.

Iteration Repeat a sequence of instructions until some *condition* causes the *looping* to terminate. For example, the pseudocode to add the numbers 1–10 (inclusive) might look something like this:

```
SUM = 0                              // INITIALIZE SUM TO 0
COUNTER = 1                          // START COUNTER A 1

// LOOP UNTIL COUNTER REACHES THE VALUE 11
WHILE ( COUNTER IS LESS THAN 11 )
DO
    SUM = SUM + COUNTER       // ACCUMULATE THE SUM
    COUNTER = COUNTER + 1 // INCREMENT THE COUNTER
DONE
```

LISTING 5.3   Iteration Example.

Execution begins with the *initialization* of the variables, SUM and COUNTER, to 0 and 1, respectively. Programmers initialize variables to ensure they have a known value at the beginning of the program rather than acquiring some random bit pattern in their memory locations left behind by a previously running process.

The WHILE loop's body (i.e., the code positioned between the DO and DONE syntactical placeholders) repeatedly executes until the variable, COUNTER, reaches the value 11. During each loop iteration, the code aggregates the sum

(SUM = SUM + COUNTER) and increments the counter (COUNTER = COUNTER + 1).

Note that I've introduced another new statement type in this example. By convention (and language specification), all text following double forward slashes ("//") are *comments* written by programmers for other programmers. *Comments* do not *execute*. When solutions become complex, it's often difficult to understand the meaning of code written by another programmer. Therefore, developers include *comments* to help clarify programming logic.

Blocks   Programming *blocks* allow developers to group multiple statements together and treat them as a single unit. As an example, consider the pseudocode in the iteration section above (Listing 5.3). The statements contained within the body of the WHILE loop (i.e., between the DO and DONE keywords) form a programming block that executes as a unit during each iteration.

Developers may also assign names to programming blocks. Using this construct, coders can reuse a block by referencing its name rather than reinserting the identical code each time they need to use it.[20]

For example, I converted the code from the iteration section above into a named block. (Formally, we refer to this as a *function*). To aid readability, I've added additional comments and highlighted the key changes/additions in gray.

```
SUM_INTERGERS ( MAX_VALUE )          // FUNCTION DECLARATION
BEGIN                                 // BEGIN THE BLOCK
    SUM = 0                           // INITIALIZE SUM TO 0
    COUNTER = 1                       // START COUNTER AT 1

    // LOOP UNTIL COUNTER REACHES MAX_VALUE
    WHILE ( COUNTER IS LESS THAN MAX_VALUE+1 )
    DO                                // BEGIN BODY OF LOOP
        SUM = SUM + COUNTER           // ACCUMULATE THE SUM
        COUNTER = COUNTER + 1         // INCREMENT THE COUNTER
    DONE                              // END BODY OF LOOP
    RETURN ( SUM )                    // RETURN THE RESULT
END                                   // END THE BLOCK
```

LISTING 5.4   Example of a Named Block.

---

[20] Called *code reuse*, this is a *best practice* in software development.

As part of its declaration (the first line), I named the function SUM_INTEGERS. The BEGIN and END keywords delineate its boundaries (i.e., its *body*).

The declaration also specifies that SUM_INTEGERS accepts one *parameter,* which I've named MAX_VALUE. Parameters are placeholders for values that functions may receive when invoked. Thus, instead of stipulating the value 11 as in the iteration example in Listing 5.4 above, MAX_VALUE can contain a different number each time we call the function.

Given this function declaration, we can sum the integers from 1 to 10 as follows:

```
ANSWER = SUM_INTERGERS ( 10 )
```

After this statement executes, ANSWER contains the value 55.

Please note we can pass any valid integer value to this function. For example, to sum the numbers from 1 to 100, we would invoke SUM_INTERGERS as follows:

```
ANSWER = SUM_INTERGERS ( 100 )
```

This expression assigns ANSWER the value 5,050.

Although it requires additional effort to package functionality into reusable named blocks, programmers employ this technique to avoid writing duplicate code.

Object-Oriented Programming Languages

While they incorporate many of the same basic constructs of structured languages (i.e., sequence, selection, iteration, and named blocks), OO languages alter the way developers approach software design. In structured languages, developers tend to think linearly, creating blocks of code that execute sequentially. In contrast, programmers think in terms of *objects* and their *interactions* when using OO languages. This paradigm is much more consistent with the way we view the world.

To highlight the difference between the two approaches, let's consider a typical banking transaction: Transferring money from a savings account into a checking account. When you reflected on that process just now, I bet you didn't think about code blocks like those in our previous example. More likely, what came to mind were *objects* like *bank* and *account*. In addition, you likely envisioned the transfer as an *operation* (or a *behavior*) involving the two account objects.

Similarly, developers design programs that closely align with real-world concepts when coding in OO languages: They identify significant *objects* and ascribe *behaviors* to them.

This is a powerful design paradigm that, when implemented correctly,[21] engenders well-constructed programs that are (relatively speaking) simple to build and comprehend.

Miscellaneous Language Categories

There are many other classes of programming languages that are beyond the scope of this text. Nonetheless, we've included a list below with some examples for those readers who wish to learn more about them.

- Functional programming languages: SML, Scala, Erlang

- Logic-based programming languages: Prolog

- Command-line languages: Windows PowerShell, Bash

- Scripting languages: AWK, Perl

- Web languages: HTML, JavaScript

- Markup languages: HTML, XML

ADVANCED SECTION

How Do Programs Execute?

After we finish writing a computer program, it doesn't just run all by itself. On the contrary, we need to complete a specific set of tasks to prepare the code for execution.

The following sections describe the two most common execution paradigms: *Compilation* and *interpretation*.

Compilation

As noted previously, computers can only execute machine-language instructions. Consequently, to make programs developed in high-level languages *executable*, we need to convert (translate) them into a form that allows them to run.

We refer to this process as *compilation*.

DEFINITION 11

Compilation is the process of translating a computer program written in one language (called the *source*) into another language (called the *target*).

Typically, the *source* is a high-level language, and the *target* is machine code. However, this is not always the case. For example, some compilers convert COBOL into Java.[22]

---

[21] On the other hand, there are few things in life as convoluted and confusing as a poorly designed object-oriented program.
[22] For obvious reasons, we often call such programs *translators*.

Compilation is comparable to translating into English a novel written in French. There is, however, an important distinction. Because they are so complex, quirky interpretations often occur with natural language translations. (I'm sure everyone has heard or used the expression, "Something got lost in translation.")

For example, we cannot translate the English idiom "A chip off the old block" literally. Instead, we must convert such expressions into phrases that are equivalent in meaning in the target language.

In contrast, there is no "wiggle room" with computer language compilation—semantic precision counts. Compiled programs must execute exactly as specified by the statements in the source language.

Let's examine the compilation process more closely.

As depicted in Figure 5.8, the compiler reads code contained in a *source file*. It then stores the machine code in an executable file when it completes.

FIGURE 5.8   Compilations process.

Time for an example. Listing 5.5 contains the source code for one of the simplest programs you can write in the C Programming Language.[23] It's called *Hello World!*[24]

```
#INCLUDE <STDIO.H>                        // IGNORE THIS FOR NOW
MAIN()
{
        PRINTF( "HELLO, WORLD!\N" );      // SAY HELLO TO THE WORLD!
}
```

LISTING 5.5   Hello World Program.

When this program executes, it displays the text HELLO WORLD! on the screen. Not that exciting, I know. But it does serve our needs.

To prepare the program for execution, I created a file called HELLO.C[25] and typed in all the code contained in Listing 5.5. After I saved and closed the file, I executed the following command:

```
G++ HELLO.C
```

The program, G++, is the C compiler on the system I used to create this example.[26] When it finished running, the compiler produced a file called A.EXE, which is the default name used by G++ for every executable file it creates.[27]

---

[23] In any language for that matter.

[24] Dating back to the early 1970s, Brian Kernighan holds the distinction of creating the first version of the *Hello World* program.

[25] To do this, I used an editor called notepad++. It's like Microsoft Word for software developers.

[26] I used Cygwin running atop MS Windows.

[27] You can instruct g++ to change the name of the executable file.

I then executed the command, A.EXE, which displayed the following text on my screen:

HELLO, WORLD!

Despite its simplicity, this example does highlight a few of the tasks undertaken by professional developers to prepare programs for execution.

Interpretation

Another common way that programs execute is through a process called *interpretation*. With this approach, we don't compile a program into machine language. Instead, we translate the source code into an intermediate representation, usually called *bytecode* (or *p-code*[28]), and then another program, called an *interpreter*, executes the intermediate code on our behalf.

DEFINITION 12

An *interpreter* is a software program that executes instructions without requiring compilation.

Though accurate, that definition may seem ambiguous. So, let's see whether we can bring some clarity to this process.

As I've stated previously, one of the most fundamental and powerful design tools in computer science is *abstraction*. Thus far, we've seen several examples of this technique: The file/folder paradigm for disk storage and the desktop metaphor for GUIs.

Extending that idea, what's to stop us from creating an abstraction of a *computer*? Asked another way, why can't we write a software program that emulates the hardware of a computer?

The answer is: Nothing! We call such a program a *Virtual Machine* (VM).

DEFINITION 13

A *virtual machine* is a software representation of a computer system that emulates hardware functionality.

As you may recall from Chapter 4, computers contain many components, ALUs, CPUs, registers, buses, memory, etc. VMs simulate all those components in software.

To see interpretation in action, let's implement our *Hello World* program in one of the most widely used interpreted languages: Java.[29]

---

[28] Shorthand for *portable code*.
[29] For the sake of thoroughness, I should note that compiled versions of Java also exist.

Listing 5.6 contains the source code for a file I created called HELLOWORLD.JAVA.

```
// HELLO WORLD IN JAVA

CLASS HELLOWORLD
{
    PUBLIC STATIC VOID MAIN ( STRING [] ARGS )
    {
        SYSTEM . OUT . PRINTLN ( "HELLO, WORLD!" ) ;
    }
}
```

LISTING 5.6   Hello World in Java.

Again, please don't become mired in language constructs. Like its C counterpart, this program displays the text HELLO WORLD! on the screen when executed.

To generate the *p-code* for this program, I executed the following command:

```
JAVAC HELLOWORLD.JAVA
```

The program, JAVAC, is the name of the Java compiler on my system. However, unlike the C compiler (G++) used in the preceding example, JAVAC doesn't generate an *executable* file. Instead, it creates a file named HELLOWORLD.CLASS, which contains the *p-code* produced by the translation process (see Listing 5.7).

```
CLASS HELLOWORLD {
    HELLOWORLD () ;
        CODE :
            0 : ALOAD_0
            1 : INVOKESPECIAL #1
            4 : RETURN

    PUBLIC STATIC VOID MAIN (JAVA.LANG.STRING[] ) ;
        CODE :
            0 : GETSTATIC      #7
            3 : LDC               #13
            5 : INVOKEVIRTUAL #15
            8 : RETURN
}
```

LISTING 5.7   Bytecode for HELLOWORLD.CLASS.

We will not discuss how to decipher the p-code representation; the key point is that it is not machine code and cannot run on any computer in its current form.

To execute the p-code, we run the following command:

```
JAVA HELLOWORLD
```

The program, JAVA, is the Java Virtual Machine (JVM). When it *interprets* (i.e., runs) our program, it displays the following text on the screen:

HELLO, WORLD!

Please take a moment to note the differences between the C and Java examples. In the Java case, we didn't run the HELLOWORLD program directly as we did when we ran A.EXE. Instead, we invoked an interpreter (JAVA) to execute the instructions (*bytecodes*) contained in the file HELLOWORLD.CLASS on our behalf.

SUMMARY

To understand the nature of software, we described what it is (a set of instructions that drive the hardware), its types (e.g., system and application), how we build it (using programming languages), and how it executes (compilation and interpretation). Nonetheless, despite the intricacies of the material presented in this chapter, I hope you now have an appreciation of what software is and what it can do.

CHAPTER 6

How Do Computers Communicate?

Sometimes when my Internet is down, I forget that the rest of my computer still works.

UNKNOWN

INTRODUCTION

Electronic devices enhance almost every aspect of our lives. However, computers that don't connect to anything are of little practical value.

For example, consider your smartphone. Sure, it's a remarkable example of modern technology. But how much benefit would it provide if it didn't connect to the cell phone network, the Internet, or surrounding devices? It would become a glorified calculator or a portable paperweight. The fact that smartphones connect us to the world makes them the *sine qua non* of modern life.

The above notwithstanding, we also don't want systems to engage in digital anarchy: Allowing any computer to connect to any other device at any time for any reason. That would lead to chaos—not to mention the security concerns. Instead, it would serve us better if components communicated in a controlled, systematic manner such that we would know which systems they are connecting to and understand what data and resources they are sharing.

We call this computer networking.

DEFINITION 1

Networking is the ability to connect two or more electronic devices with the express intent to share data or computing resources.

In the sections that follow, we'll present the technologies, configurations, and organization of the devices involved in "moving bits." Then, once we've poured that foundation, we'll

DOI: 10.1201/9781003143437-6

build upon that understanding and describe how communicating devices use networking technologies to exchange data.

One last point before we jump in: To communicate, electronic devices exchange *messages*. (We'll describe what that means in more detail below.) Messages comprise a series of ordered *bits*. If you haven't already done so, you might find it beneficial to read the *What Is a "Bit"?* subsection (in the Advanced Section) of Chapter 4.

NETWORK TRANSMISSION TECHNOLOGIES

In IT parlance, we refer to any component connected to a network as a *node*.

> **DEFINITION 2**
>
> A *node* is any physical device that can forward or consume data transmitted via a network.

Throughout the remainder of this section, we'll explore the types of devices and their roles in forming and managing computer networks.

Let's begin by discussing how we connect nodes.

Physical Transmission Media

There are two ways by which we can connect network nodes: Wired and wireless. With wired networks, data travels from one node to another via a physical cable. The sections below discuss the most common options.

CAT 5 Cable

One of the most used technologies to interconnect network devices is Category 5 cable (called "CAT 5" or "Ethernet cable" for short). If a cable connects your computer to your router, odds are you're using this type of cable.

CAT 5 installations are simple: Plug one end into a network port on your computer and the other into a port on your router, and *voilà*, you're up and running. Because these connections are "hardwired" (i.e., physical), you typically don't require a password to access the network. (We'll discuss network security later in this chapter.)

Figure 6.1 provides an example of a CAT 5 cable.

Coaxial Cable

Coaxial cable (or "coax" for short—pronounced "co-ax") is an electrical cable that contains an inner conductor (through which the bits move) surrounded by a woven metal shield (to minimize external interference). It's typically used in telephone networks, broadband connections, and television signal transmission. You've likely used coax cables to connect TVs and other video devices to your cable or satellite network at home. See Figure 6.2 for an example.

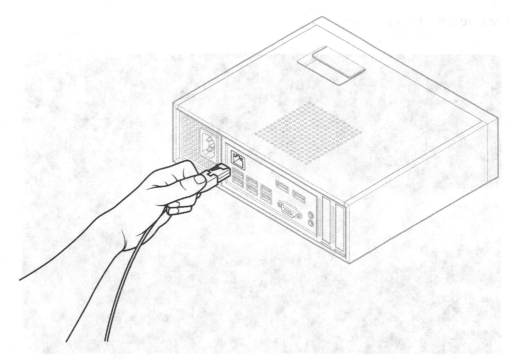

FIGURE 6.1   CAT 5 connection.

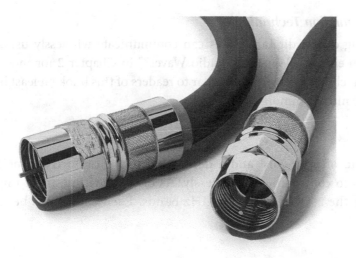

FIGURE 6.2   Coax cable.

Fiber-Optic Cable

When using CAT 5 and coax, information traverses the cable via electrical signals. With a fiber-optic connection, data moves as pulses of light. Some broadband and TV providers deliver service to your home using fiber-optic cable.

See Figure 6.3 for an example.

FIGURE 6.3   Fiber-optic cable.

Wireless Transmission Technologies

Instead of using cables, digital devices can communicate wirelessly using radio waves. (See the section entitled "What Are Radio Waves?" in Chapter 2 for more information.) Many of these technologies will be familiar to readers of this book (at least by name). We'll discuss the two most common below.

Wi-Fi

Wi-Fi is a suite of protocols[1] and a designated set of radio frequencies[2] that allow digital devices to communicate wirelessly. As of this writing, most implementations support either the 2.4 GHz or the 5 GHz bands. Each choice has both benefits and drawbacks.[3]

Bluetooth

Another prevalent wireless technology you've likely used is *Bluetooth*. For example, I'm sure most of you allow your smartphones to connect to your car's audio system so you can make hands-free telephone calls. That connection is Bluetooth-based.

---

[1] Please refer to the section entitled "Network Protocols" in Chapter 2 for more information.
[2] Please refer to the section entitled "Frequencies and Channels" in Chapter 2 for more information.
[3] Of late, price has become less of an issue. Most modern routers support both the 2.4 GHz and 5 GHz frequency bands.

Designed to enable mobile devices to connect to stationary components, Bluetooth technology supports a limited range (approximately 10 meters[4]). Nonetheless, because it doesn't require much power, it's ideal for devices like smartphones and headsets.

The Advanced Section in this chapter discusses Bluetooth technology in greater detail.

NETWORK COMPONENTS

As endpoints, computers are the most critical nodes in any network. They are the devices that send, receive, and process the transmitted data. However, they alone do not form a complete network. As we will see, many other types of devices help transfer messages from senders to receivers.

To clarify this point, we can use a familiar example of a network: The US Postal Service. Consider that any sender can mail a package to any recipient who has a valid address.

In this model, every mailbox (or P.O. box) is an endpoint (i.e., a network node). However, mailboxes don't "move" packages. Instead, the postal service's framework—comprising letter carriers, post offices, substations, and processing plants—collects, sorts, and transports parcels from one mailbox to another. Collectively, these resources form the USPS's *network infrastructure.*

Computer networks function in much the same way. The endpoints (computers) rely on a network's infrastructure to deliver messages reliably from the originator to the designated recipient.

In the following sections, we'll discuss the components that form the foundation of modern networks. However, please keep in mind that although each device described below serves a specific purpose in managing message flow, many are computers in their own right. Nonetheless, we tend to think of them solely as networking components because of their focused functionality.[5]

Interface Controllers

Let's begin our discussions with your computer. PCs require a Network Interface Controller (NIC) to connect to a network. Historically, NICs were available as accessory boards inserted into expansion slots inside the computer. However, the NIC often resides directly on the motherboard in modern PCs.[6]

Regardless of its form factor, an NIC connects to external networks using cables (wired) or via radio waves (wirelessly). Most modern PCs ship with NICs that support both.

To support wired networks, NICs provide a *port*[7] that accepts a cable connection. Typically, this type of connection uses a CAT 5/Ethernet cable (Figure 6.4) to connect your computer to a *router* (we'll describe *routers* in the next section).

NICs also contain circuitry that allows them to connect to radio-based networks such as Wi-Fi or Bluetooth to enable wireless communication.

---

[4] Or, if you must, about 32.8 feet in imperial units.

[5] We often refer to computing devices of this type as *appliances.*

[6] Please refer to the section entitled "Overview of Motherboard Components" in Chapter 4 for more information.

[7] Ports are connection points that allow network devices to interconnect. They are the digital equivalents of electrical outlets.

FIGURE 6.4   NIC port and Ethernet cable.

One of the essential features of an NIC is its Media Access Control address (*MAC address*). Like a telephone number, MAC addresses uniquely identify every NIC, guaranteeing that every network node has a unique ID and that senders can direct messages to specific recipients.[8]

As depicted in Figure 6.5, a MAC address has two distinct parts: The Organizational Unique Identifier (OUI) and a vendor-assigned address. Administered and assigned by an organization called the IEEE,[9] the OUI uniquely identifies every hardware vendor.

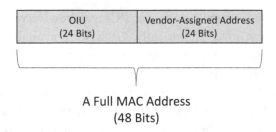

FIGURE 6.5   MAC address components.

Vendors generate the second part of the MAC address and must ensure that the value they assign is unique for every instance of every product they manufacture. Thus, the combination of OUIs and vendor-generated addresses guarantees that every NIC is uniquely addressable.

---

[8] Networks also support the notion of a *broadcast message* that every node receives regardless of its NIC address.
[9] Institute of Electrical and Electronics Engineers.

Routers

The primary function of a *router* is to forward data packets between two or more networks. Most of us are familiar with the routers that we use at home.

Figure 6.6 contains an example.

FIGURE 6.6 Home router.

Typically installed by an Internet Service Provider (ISP), routers support wired connections and establish Wi-Fi networks allowing devices to interconnect with each other and to the Internet.

See Figure 6.7 for an example.

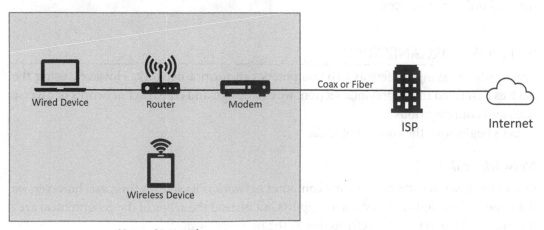

FIGURE 6.7 Home router connectivity.

Hubs

The function of a *hub* is to form a private network, connecting two or more nodes without allowing access to other networks (or the Internet). Upon receiving a packet, a *hub* rebroadcasts the message to all other devices on its network.

Switches

A *switch* functions much like a *hub* in that it forms a private network among its connected components. However, it differs in the way it routes traffic. Instead of broadcasting messages to all connected nodes, a *switch* directs packets to a specific recipient based on the MAC address.

Bridges

Bridges interconnect networks, forming a more extensive, composite network. As a result, nodes on bridged networks can communicate with each other as seamlessly as if they resided on one network.

Modems

A *modem*, or MOdulator-DEModulator, allows network traffic to flow over transmission media not originally intended to support digital traffic (e.g., telephone lines). Although we still use the name (e.g., "cable modem"), modern broadband networks usually don't supply them as separate components because devices such as *routers* and *bridges* usually incorporate modem functionality.

Firewalls

Security is always at the forefront of modern network design. To that end, designers employ *firewalls* to prevent unauthorized network access.

Typically, *firewalls* are the entry ("touchdown") point into a network, and they implement the rules that grant or deny access. In most networks, *firewalls* block access requests from all unknown devices.

NETWORK ORGANIZATION

Practically speaking, as few as two computers can form a network. However, using the devices described in the previous section, we can design and construct networks of diverse sizes and configurations.

Let's begin with the concept of *scale*.

Network Scale

One of the essential attributes of any computer network is its size. In this case, however, we don't mean the number of devices it supports but instead the scope of the geographical area it serves. In IT parlance, we refer to this as the network's *scale*.

The sections below discuss the various categories in order of scope. Please note that there is some overlap in the definitions.

PANs

Personal Area Network (PAN), defines the smallest geographic area. It refers to interconnected personal devices. For example, do you own a smartwatch that connects to your smartphone? Does your fitness tracker transmit data to your laptop?

All devices on a PAN interconnect wirelessly. (It wouldn't be very convenient to have your smartwatch tethered to your laptop by a network cable.) Although not required, PANs may also interconnect with LANs and WANs (see below).

LANs

Local Area Networks (LANs) service a limited geographic range such as a home, an office suite, a single building, or an apartment complex. LANs support wired and wireless connections and vary in size from two interconnected devices to thousands. In addition, most LANs provide a *gateway* node (such as a *router*, see above) that enables access to other networks.

Figure 6.8 depicts a typical home LAN.[10] The *router* drives the network and allows devices to interconnect wirelessly or via cables. All nodes may communicate with each other and share resources. For example, every device can route requests to the printer. In addition, all nodes can access the Internet via the *router*, which also serves as a *gateway*.

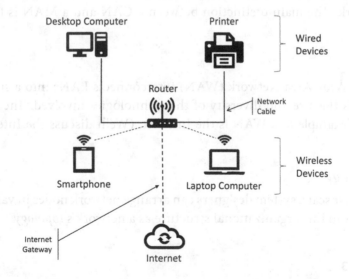

FIGURE 6.8 A typical home LAN.

CANs

Campus Area Network (CAN),[11] comprises two or more LANs connected by a *backbone* that interconnects (joins) multiple network segments. A CAN is typically larger than a LAN but smaller than a Metropolitan Area Network (MAN, see below).

---

[10] You may also see networks of this type referenced as a Home Area Network (HAN).

[11] You might also see this defined as a *corporate area network*.

As depicted in Figure 6.9, the *backbone* allows Computer 1 to communicate with Computer 2 even though they reside on separate LANs. As a security consideration, administrators can configure the network to limit access to the *backbone*.

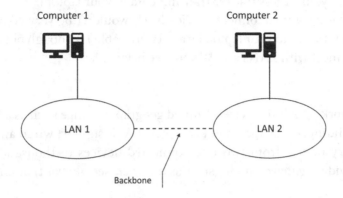

FIGURE 6.9   Campus Area Network.

MANs

The term MAN, Metropolitan Area Network, refers to a network that spans a geographic area as large as an entire city. MANs can interconnect LANs and CANs to form a single cohesive network. The main distinction between a CAN and a MAN is the size of the area it serves.

WANs

Like a MAN, a Wide Area Network (WAN) interconnects LANs into a single network. The difference is the size and diversity of the technologies involved. The most obvious and ubiquitous example of a WAN is the Internet. (We'll discuss the Internet in detail in Chapter 7.)

Network Topology

Regardless of their scale, system designers can arrange network nodes in various configurations. We refer to this organizational structure as a network's *topology*.

> **DEFINITION 3**
>
> *Topology* describes the organization and hierarchy of the nodes residing on a network.

In the sections that follow, we'll discuss several common topologies.

Bus Network

Let's begin with a topology that we've already discussed in Chapter 4: A bus network. Like an internal bus, all nodes connected to an external bus can communicate independently with any other connected node. Figure 6.10 depicts this design.

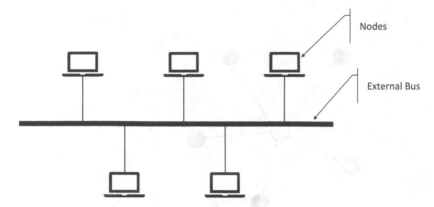

FIGURE 6.10   Bus topology.

This is a commonly used topology. Indeed, anyone who has used a USB device is already familiar with this type of network. (Refer Figure 6.11 for an example.)

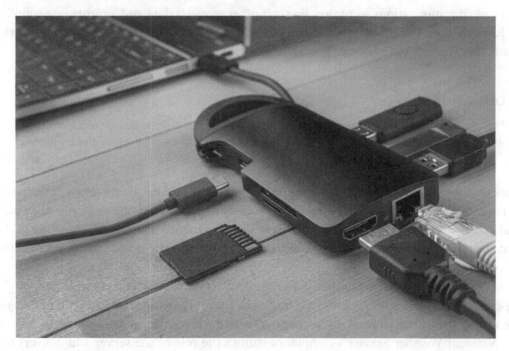

FIGURE 6.11   USB hub.

Star Network

Leveraging a configuration that looks like a bicycle wheel, all star network components connect to a central node called a *hub* (Figure 6.12). All messages traverse through the hub before arriving at their destination.

A star configuration is a common topology you've likely used without knowing it. The Wi-Fi network in your home forms this configuration because your wireless devices connect and exchange messages through a central hub (i.e., your router).

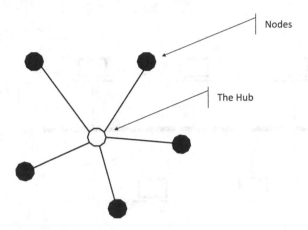

FIGURE 6.12   Star topology.

Client-Server

In most communications scenarios, one computer requests data and another one supplies it. Regardless of the underlying network topology, we call the requesting computer the *client*, and we refer to the device providing the data as the *server*.

DEFINITION 4

The *client-server* model is a communications framework that pairs a service requestor with a service provider via a network connection. The requestor is the *client*; the provider is the *server*.

Note that the relationship among communicating devices is logical and forms at the point of request. For example, when Computer A solicits data from Computer B, A is the client and B is the server. However, computer B might also require data from Computer A. In that scenario, the roles reverse, and Computer B acts as the client and Computer A as the server.

Actually, you're already familiar with the client-server model. For example, you might type HTTPS://WWW.WEATHER.GOV into your browser's address bar when you want an update on the weekend weather forecast. By requesting the report, your browser becomes the client; the National Weather Service's computer assumes the role of the server and delivers the data.

Internetworking

In conjunction with scale and topology considerations, administrators also organize the structure of networks to maintain control over system resources. Specifically, they want to regulate how their networks interconnect with other networks—if at all.

Except in extreme cases (think CIA), this does not mean "locking down" every system resource. On the contrary, many organizations allow external access to trusted partners.

For example, a warehouse company might permit suppliers to update their inventory records after completing a delivery.

The sections below examine the most common examples of such network structures. One note: As you read this material, please keep in mind that some of the designs discussed below are logical and may "overlay" physical networks.

Intranet

An *intranet* is one or more interconnected networks controlled by one organization for the benefit of its users. For example, LANs, CANs, MANs, and WANs individually or collectively can function as an intranet. The key attribute is that the *intranet* remains private, available only to the managing organization's approved user base.

Extranets

Like *intranets*, *extranets* remain under the control of a single organization. However, they do allow limited access to external entities and users. Thus, organizations can selectively grant network privileges to whomever they want. In addition, for security reasons, network engineers usually permit access to the *extranet* only through single entry points called *portals*.

The Internet

Few individuals on this planet are unaware of the Internet. It has revolutionized many aspects of our lives, and its importance cannot be understated. Thus, we will discuss it at length in Chapter 7 to give it its full due.

Darknets

Although available via the Internet, a *darknet* is a private[12] network that restricts accessibility to select groups or individuals. Therefore, you typically require specialized software and a personal invitation to access these networks.

Despite their nefarious reputation, *darknets* support many constructive uses. For example, in countries that impose censorship, *darknets* allow their citizens anonymous access to the Internet.[13]

Sadly, as with any human endeavor, there are always individuals who can find ways to exploit anything. As a result, *darknet* technology does support pernicious activities such as illegal markets, human trafficking, and piracy.

Security

A critical concern of any network designer is security. In general, to gain access to any protected electronic resource, the provider needs to determine who you are and, based on that knowledge, decide what you can "see" and "do."

---

[12] Darknets remain private because they are not indexed by search engines (e.g., Google, DuckDuckGo, Bing) and are thus difficult—if not impossible—to locate.

[13] One such service, the *Tor network*, provides a browser that prevents tracking and masks its user's location.

Authentication is the process of determining your identity. Using preestablished credentials such as login name and password—and other optional safeguards such as biometrics or codes[14] sent to your phone or email—security software verifies the identity of every user attempting to gain access to a network or system.

Authorization is the process of establishing the limits on what system resources individual users may access. For example, we would expect that hospital administrators may review your billing and payment history. However, they shouldn't have access to your medical records.

Network and system administrators don't establish and enforce security policies to annoy you. Instead, they undertake these safeguards to prevent unauthorized use and modification of data (*your* data).

Most folks don't want to think about it, but data and identity theft are rampant. Unlike most people, I am always grateful when the organizations I conduct business with take prudent steps to thwart unauthorized access—despite the annoyance factor.

HOW DO NETWORKS WORK?

Okay, we've just covered a lot of ground, introducing numerous technologies, devices, and definitions. However, we still haven't discussed how network nodes collaborate to transmit messages accurately from senders to receivers.

We call the "glue" that makes that happen the *network layer model*.

Ethernet

In the sections above, we discussed technologies that facilitate the movement of *bits* from one point to another. However, sending devices cannot transmit messages at random and expect receiving devices to understand their meaning. On the contrary, the process of exchanging data requires a significant degree of structure and organization.

That's where *Ethernet* enters the picture. Ethernet is a network protocol that packages, manages, and controls data transmission over LAN connections.

We introduced the concept of network protocols in Chapter 2 using cell phones. Now, let's apply that knowledge to computer networks.

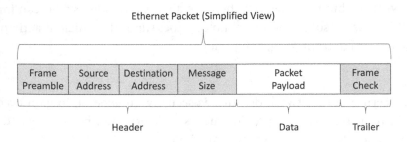

FIGURE 6.13 Ethernet packet—Simplified view.

---

[14] Called one-time passwords (OTPs), the system generates these codes randomly. They are valid for a limited time and only one login attempt.

As depicted in Figure 6.13, the Ethernet protocol groups data into *packets*[15]; packets comprise several subsections: *Header, payload*, and *trailer*.

Like an envelope's mailing address, the *header* contains information that allows senders and receivers to exchange and track messages. It includes the following fields (among others):

Preamble   The preamble is a series of synchronization bits that senders transmit to alert receivers that a message is imminent. It ends with a specific bit pattern indicating that "the rest of the header is about to follow."

Source   This is the source (sender's) MAC address.

Destination   This is the destination (recipient's) MAC address.

Size   The length of the message in bytes. The Ethernet specification defines a minimum and maximum packet size.

Immediately following the header is the *payload*. This field contains the data that the sender wants to transmit to the receiver. For example, the *payload* field holds the message content when you send an email.

The *frame check field*, a component of the message *trailer*, is part of a process that confirms transmission accuracy. Let's see how this works.

During packet preparation, the sender performs a mathematical computation called a Cyclic Redundancy Check (CRC) and stores the result in the *frame check field*.[16] Upon the arrival of a packet, the receiver performs the same calculation and compares the result with the CRC included in the inbound message's *frame check field*. If the two values are not identical, it means an error occurred during transmission. In such cases, the receiver may request the sender to retransmit the packet.[17]

At a conceptual level, Ethernet packets function like traditional snail-mail envelopes. The outside (i.e., the *header*) contains addressing information, and the inside (i.e., the *payload*) holds the letter (i.e., the message). However, Ethernet packets can't "move on their own." Like envelopes, they require an infrastructure to transport them from sender to receiver.

Enter the Transmission Control Protocol/Internet Protocol (TCP/IP) stack.

The TCP/IP Stack

The most common networking model in use today is the "TCP/IP stack." It's a suite of standards used by communicating devices that serve as the foundation of the Internet.

As depicted in Figure 6.14, we refer to the TCP/IP protocol as a "stack" because it comprises four distinct layers, each of which performs a specific set of tasks required to move data from one node to another.

---

[15] Technically, these are called Ethernet *frames*.
[16] A discussion of the actual CRC algorithm is beyond the scope of this text.
[17] There are several other error detection and correction techniques used in data communication.

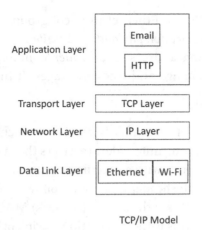

FIGURE 6.14 The TCP/IP "stack".

Conceptually, each TCP/IP layer on the sending side logically interacts with its corresponding layer on the receiving side. However, in practice, the entire message travels via the data link layer, and specific software components on each side of the communication channel process the data for their respective "layers."

In the sections that follow, we'll describe the function and responsibilities of each TCP/IP layer. Please refer to Figure 6.15[18] as you read through this material; it depicts the transmission of an email message.

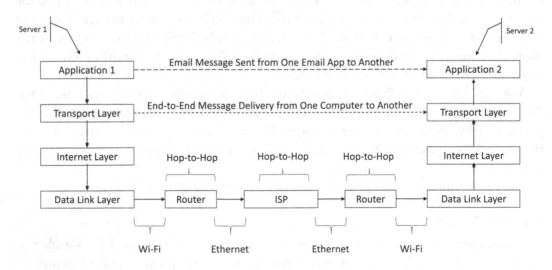

FIGURE 6.15 Example TCP/IP packet movement.

Data Link Layer

As mentioned earlier in this chapter, many individual types of devices comprise a network: Routers, switches, hubs, etc. The data link layer uses protocols such as Ethernet and Wi-Fi

---

[18] Please note that this figure only presents a few examples of the protocols available for use at each layer.

to transmit bits directly from one node to the next. Its primary responsibility is to ensure that messages arrive reliably at each intermediate destination.

The IP Layer

IP is an acronym for Internet protocol. The IP layer moves data packets from one network to another (hence the term "Internet"). In other words, it manages all the *intermediate* hops a message undergoes until arriving at its destination.

As depicted in Figure 6.15, that may include changes in the data link layer protocols (e.g., Ethernet vs. Wi-Fi) as the message moves from node to node through all the intervening networks.

The TCP Layer

The TCP or Transmission Control Protocol layer manages message delivery from a source to a destination. In network terminology, the TCP layer establishes a *channel* between two communicating devices and ensures the accurate delivery of messages between endpoints.

Let's take a moment to summarize the separation of responsibilities of these two critical layers. While transmitting data between nodes, the IP layer must manage issues such as changes in the underlying protocols, packet retransmission requests when failures occur, and payload resequencing when packets arrive in the incorrect order.

The TCP layer ensures that the message arrives at its intended destination regardless of the number of intermediate hops. It also maintains the channel between the communicating entities and manages flow control (e.g., a receiver can tell the sender to "slow down").

Application Layer

The application layer represents the software components that exchange messages via the other layers. For example, in Figure 6.15, Server 1 is sending an email message to Server 2. Because both APPLICATION 1 and APPLICATION 2 understand the content and structure of the payload (an email message in this example), they can logically communicate with each other.

Message Transmission Example

Continuing with the example depicted in Figure 6.15, APPLICATION 1 (the sender) provides its local transport layer a "chunk" of data (i.e., the email message). Next, the TCP and IP layers on Server 1 append routing and addressing information (in the message header) and present it to the data link layer.

The data link layer on Server 1 forwards the message—via multiple intermediate hops using the information provided by the TCP and IP layers—to the data link layer on the recipient's host (Server 2). Upon its arrival, the message is "unwrapped" and delivered to APPLICATION 2 via the TCP and IP layers on the destination host.

The TCP/IP stack makes it appear to both applications that they are communicating directly. Thus, they can remain unaware of the myriad details associated with data transmission.

ADVANCED SECTION

What is Bluetooth?

What do a Danish king and a wireless technology have in common? *Bluetooth*. Let me explain.

In the tenth century, a king named Harald "Bluetooth"[19] Gormsson of Denmark united his people. Then, in the late 1980s, a technology—eventually dubbed Bluetooth in the 1990s—emerged that could "unite" nearby computing devices.

I'm sure most readers of this book have already used Bluetooth. For example, does your cell phone automatically "pair" with your car's entertainment system? Do you listen to music using wireless headphones? Do you use a wireless mouse and keyboard with your desktop computer?

Bluetooth is a radio-wave-based communications technology optimized for a limited range. Typically, this is less than 10 meters, but the technology supports longer distances. (See the section entitled "What Are Radio Waves?" in Chapter 2 for more information.)

When Bluetooth devices connect, they form what's called a *piconet*. (Please refer to the section above entitled Network Scale.) Devices may join and leave a Bluetooth *piconet* at any time. The protocol supports up to eight concurrent connected devices.

As defined by the protocol specification, a Bluetooth network uses 79 channels centered around the 2.45 GHz frequency. (Please refer to Chapter 2's radio frequencies and channels discussion.) When two Bluetooth devices want to communicate, they randomly select a channel. If it is already in use, they randomly switch to another. This process continues until they find one that's unused. Moreover, to enhance security and minimize interference, Bluetooth devices continually change frequencies.

This technique—"hopping" from channel to channel—is called spread-spectrum frequency hopping and was developed during WWII to enable secure communication. Given these historical roots, can we assume Bluetooth is secure?

No wireless network can ever be as secure as one that uses a cable. For example, consider that anyone with a receiver can "listen" to message traffic.

That said, Bluetooth devices do allow you to restrict the class of services (e.g., printers) that may connect to the network and deny access to all devices except those you specifically approve (e.g., only your ear pods).

SUMMARY

In this chapter, we discovered that many "moving parts" are required to enable computers to communicate. And although most of us won't become network engineers, there are several points to keep in mind:

- We classify networks by *scale* (LAN, WAN, etc.)

- Topologies (e.g., bus and star) organize network nodes

---

[19] The true origin of the nickname "Bluetooth" is lost in antiquity.

- Various types of devices may connect to networks in addition to computers (e.g., routers, gateways, and switches)

- Every network node has a NIC that ships with a unique MAC address

- Computer networks comprise several conceptual layers (e.g., data link, Internet, transport, and application)

- TCP/IP is the most used network "stack"

We also discussed how networks send and receive messages using the TCP/IP stack. And in the Advanced Section, we discussed how Bluetooth works.

Given this newfound knowledge, I hope the next time you *google* "movies near me," you'll appreciate how many devices and how much processing might be involved to deliver that information to you.

How Does the Internet Work?

Search engines find the information, not necessarily the truth.

AMIT KALANTRI

INTRODUCTION

Unless you've recently migrated to Earth from a distant galaxy, you're aware that the Internet has affected almost every aspect of life on this planet. Indeed, a sizable percentage of the world's population uses it.[1]

From a practicable standpoint, this means there are a vast number of interconnected devices.[2] Thus, before discussing how the Internet works, we need to understand how we can address every node[3] on this global network.

HOW DOES INTERNET ADDRESSING WORK?

What's an IP Address?

To help explain Internet addressing, let's revisit the cell phone network discussion from Chapter 2. Conceptually, when we want to speak with a friend, we think something like this: *I want to call Joan.* But to establish a connection, the cell phone network uses her telephone number, not her name.

As previously discussed, the cell phone network must coordinate many "moving parts" when connecting a call. For example, your friend can change devices, telephone numbers, and locations. So, how does the network track the information associated with every user to complete every call reliably?

First, let's consider what happens when your friend changes telephone numbers. In the old days, you'd typically dial directory assistance (e.g., 411) and ask the operator for your friend's new number.[4] Today, you'd likely perform a search using the Internet. In either

---

[1] Over 5 billion at the time of this writing.

[2] Some estimates predict that by the year 2025, there will be over 35 *billion* devices connected to the Internet.

[3] See Chapter 6 for a discussion of *nodes* and *networking*.

[4] I know most smartphones capture and save telephone numbers, so we don't dial "411" much anymore; just go with me on this one.

DOI: 10.1201/9781003143437-7

case, the result is that you eventually associate your friend's name with the new telephone number.

Next, what if your friend recently upgraded to the newly released iPhone but retained the same telephone number? In this case, the cellular network must "map" your friend's existing telephone number to the new cell phone. In other words, you'd dial the old number but connect to a new device.

So how do these two examples relate to Internet?

Every device that connects to the Internet requires a unique identifier called an *IP*[5] *address*. They are of the form NNN.NNN.NNN.NNN. [6] So, for example, at the time of this writing, one of the IP addresses for NASA.GOV is 52.0.14.116. Thus, if you wanted to visit NASA's website, you could type either "NASA.GOV" or "HTTP://52.0.14.116/" into your browser's address bar. (Please note that the preamble string "HTTP://" and the trailing forward slash ("/") are required in the second example.)

What's DNS?

Now, returning to our cell phone analogy, a domain name (e.g., "NASA.GOV") is equivalent to your friend's name, and its associated IP address (e.g., "52.0.14.116") is like a telephone number. And as we learned in Chapter 6, the TCP/IP stack requires message packets to specify destinations using IP addresses (i.e., the "telephone number"), not the domain name (i.e., the "user's name"). Thus, when you enter a domain name (e.g., "NASA.GOV") into its address bar, your browser must somehow convert it to its IP address (e.g., "52.0.14.116").

So how is this done? Must every browser store the IP address of every domain on the Internet? That would be highly impractical.

Fortunately, the Internet provides a "411" service called Domain Name System (DNS). When a site "registers" on the Internet, DNS "maps" its name to its public IP address. So, when you type a domain name like NASA.GOV, the browser's first task is to call out to a DNS service to acquire the IP address of NASA's website.

What is DNS-to-MAC Addressing?

Okay, so that covers the mapping of domain names to IP addresses. But what about mapping IP addresses to specific devices?

Please recall from Chapter 6 that computers use NIC cards to connect to networks and that every NIC card has a unique MAC address. For most networks, *routers* manage this mapping by maintaining internal tables that associate external IP addresses with internal MAC addresses. Thus, when processing an inbound message, the router queries the destination IP address (contained in the inbound message header) and routes it to the appropriate computer based on the associated MAC address.

This design also manages server replacement. In this case, the router would direct messages to the new computer by associating the external IP address with the new computer's

---

[5] Yes, this is the same 'IP' as in Internet Protocol discussed in Chapter 6.
[6] The example uses Version 4 ("IPv4") of the IP address format. Due to the explosion of devices connecting to the Internet, IPv4 is quickly running out of addresses. In response, the industry is rolling out Version 6 ("IPv6") which can support 2^{128} addresses.

NIC card's MAC address in its mapping table. (This is the equivalent of your friend purchasing a new iPhone but keeping the old telephone number.)

One last comment on IP addresses. Each time a device connects to a router on a home network, the Internet Service Provider (ISP) assigns it a *temporary* IP address that can vary with each session. As a rule, such transitory addresses do not find their way into the Internet's DNS registries. That's why it's difficult for a third-party server to locate your computer: Your temporary IP address does not appear in the directory.

What's a URL?

As we have just seen, DNS helps us locate computers on the Web. Most of the time, however, we're not interested in *computers*. Instead, we want access to the *resources* they host.

For example, a typical YouTube server manages thousands of media files. But unfortunately, knowing the server's IP address does not help us locate a specific video we want to watch. That's where Uniform Resource Locators[7] (URLs) come into play—they uniquely identify every resource available on a web server.

A URL comprises several elements: A protocol, a hostname, and a resource identifier.[8] As an example, a generic URL might look something like this:

HTTP://WWW.SOMEHOSTNAME.COM/INDEX.HTML

The string, "HTTP" (Hypertext Transfer Protocol), is the protocol,[9] WWW.SOMEHOSTNAME.COM identifies the server,[10] and INDEX.HTML is the resource. (Please note that "://" and "." are required syntactical separators.)

For example, if we wanted to visit NASA's website, we'd type the URL HTTP://NASA.GOV into our browser's search bar. In this case, HTTP is the protocol and NASA.GOV specifies the server. However, in this instance, the resource, a web page, is implied; thus, we need not explicitly provide it.

After we press the ENTER key, our browser would look up NASA.GOV in a DNS server to determine its corresponding IP address, establish a connection with NASA's server, and select the resource (in this case, its home page). In response, NASA's server would send a series of commands instructing your browser on how it should display the requested information on your screen.

As another example, consider this URL:

HTTPS://WWW.YOUTUBE.COM/WATCH?V=CC-z_aBAv6M

When typed into a browser's address bar, this URL will launch a video of a NASA space walk. Note the added component, "/WATCH?V=CC-Z_ABAV6M," appended after the hostname identifies the exact video (resource) we want to play.

---

[7] Considered the inventor of the World Wide Web, Tim Berners-Lee defined URLs in 1994 when he issued Request for Comments (RFC) 1738. The world has never been the same.

[8] More accurately, a URL is one type of Uniform Resource Identifier (URI) which, when fully defined, contains five (5) components.

[9] Formally, this is called the *scheme*.

[10] Formally, this is called the *authority*; it has three (3) subcomponents.

Though less commonly used, URLs can specify many other services and resources beyond web pages and videos. For example, you can download files (FTP), send emails (MAILTO), and log on to remote servers (TELNET), just to name a few. The key point is that because the structure of URLs is flexible, the industry can easily introduce new protocols and resources as the need arises.

HOW DO WEB PAGES WORK?

Okay, it's time for an example. Let's combine the networking knowledge we gained from Chapter 6 and our understanding of Internet addressing from above to understand how web pages function. For your convenience, Figure 7.1 is a copy of the message transmission diagram from Chapter 6.

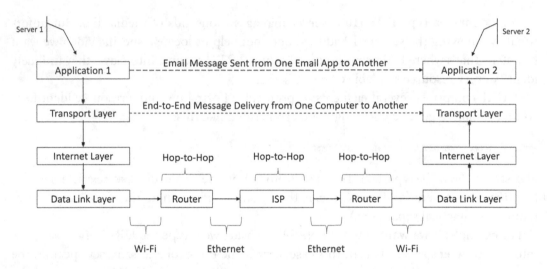

FIGURE 7.1   Message transmission diagram.

We begin the example by launching our favorite browser (e.g., Firefox, Edge, Chrome, Safari, and Opera). Note that the browser represents *Application 1* in Figure 7.1.

After typing a URL in the address bar, let's say, SOME-DOMAIN.COM, you press ENTER. Then, using a DNS server, the browser determines the destination computer's IP address and passes the request to the communication software residing on your local computer (in Figure 7.1, this is the *transport layer*).

Next, the TCP software on your computer establishes a connection (channel) with the destination server. Note that this task includes identifying the intermediate network servers (hops) through which the message packets will traverse. Remember, your PC doesn't have a direct network connection to SOME-DOMAIN.COM. Instead, the TCP layer must find a path from your machine to it.

At this point, the IP and Data Link layers on your computer transmit the message to the first hop (this is the router in Figure 7.1). Then, using the IP information included in the message header, the router forwards the message to the next node in the communication chain.

The hop-to-hop processing continues until the message arrives at the data link layer residing on the destination server. At this point, the network layers on the receiving computer "bubble up" the message to the web server (*Application 2*) that will respond to the URL request by returning content and display instructions back to your browser. When it receives the return message, the browser "paints' your screen, "plays" your song, or "streams" the video you requested.

HOW DOES EMAIL WORK?

Despite the explosion and adoption of other messaging platforms, email remains a vital form of electronic correspondence—especially in business and commerce. Indeed, most folks I know complain about the volume of emails they receive every day—both expected and *spam*.

> **DEFINITION 1**
>
> *Spam* refers to unwanted electronic junk mail. It derives its name from a 1970s *Monty Python's Flying Circus* comedy skit set in a restaurant wherein the characters repeatedly recite the word "spam."

Email came into existence on a network called ARPANET,[11] a precursor to the Internet. Initially, only users on the same server could exchange messages. However, in 1971, Raymond Samuel Tomlinson designed the first system that could send/receive emails to/from users on separate computers.

Since then, sending and receiving emails have become as easy as it is commonplace. Nonetheless, a significant amount of processing occurs after you press the SEND button. In this section, we will clarify how this works.

However, before we discuss how emails fly across the Internet, let's review how the US Post Office handles mail. When we send a letter to a friend, we have two considerations: The content of the message we insert inside the envelope and our friend's address that we write on its exterior.[12] Once we deposit our correspondence into a postbox, the postal infrastructure takes responsibility for delivering the letter to our friend's mailbox.

Figure 7.2 presents a simplified diagram of this process.

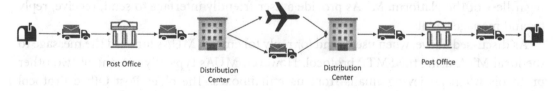

Post Office   Distribution Center   Distribution Center   Post Office

FIGURE 7.2 Simplified post office delivery process.

---

[11] Developed by the Advanced Research Projects Agency (ARPA) of the United States Department of Defense, ARPANET was the first wide area network and an early adopter of the TCP/IP protocol suite.

[12] And, of course, we need to include the correct postage.

As Figure 7.3 depicts, email processing functions similarly, except that the infrastructure components are electronic rather than physical.

When the sender presses the SEND button, the email app, called a Mail User Agent (MUA), forwards the message to a component called the Mail Transfer Agent (MTA). Then, using address information (e.g., JANESMITH@SOMESERVER.COM) and DNS (see above), the sender's MTA routes the message to the recipient's MTA.

Upon receipt, the recipient's MTA forwards the messages to a Mail Delivery Agent (MDA), which stores inbound emails in the user's mailbox until they are retrieved using another MUA. (MUAs periodically poll the MDA to determine whether new mail messages have arrived; we discuss this below in more detail.)

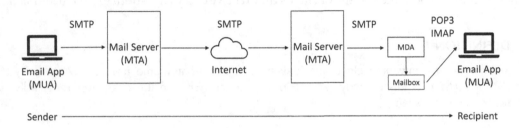

FIGURE 7.3 Simplified email delivery.

MTAs are the backbone of the email infrastructure. They use the Simple Mail Transfer Protocol[13] (SMTP)[14] to send email messages via the Internet. Note that MTAs only store emails until they forward them to the next MTA.

To determine the IP address[15] of the destination server, MTAs use the domain portion of the email address (i.e., the part after the "@" sign). So, for example, given the email address SOME-USER@SOME-SERVER.COM, an MTA will perform a DNS lookup using SOME-SERVER.COM and forward the message to the corresponding MTA running on that server. Upon receipt, the receiving MTA will deliver the message to the SOME-USER's mailbox (see below).

MDAs receive emails from MTAs and store them in the appropriate user's mailboxes. Messages remain there until the user deletes them.

MUAs come in many forms: Desktop, web-based, and smartphone apps. Nonetheless, regardless of the platform, MUAs provide a user-friendly interface to send, receive, reply to, and manage emails.

As discussed above, when users send (or reply to) emails, MUAs forward the message to the local MTA using the SMTP protocol. However, MUAs typically use one of two other protocols when retrieving emails from user mailboxes. The older Post Office Protocol (POP3) provides limited functionality and supports only one-way synchronization. That is, it allows users only to download email.

---

[13] See Chapter 6 for a discussion of Network Protocols.
[14] Because they use the SMTP protocol, MTAs are often called STMP servers.
[15] See above.

A more modern protocol, Internet Messaging Access Protocol (IMAP), allows for two-way synchronization and multiple, concurrent MUA connections. Thus, your desktop, smartphone, and tablet-based MUAs can remain synchronized.

One final comment: Email messages are routed like any other communication packet using the TCP/IP stack. (See the discussion in Chapter 6.)

WHAT IS CLOUD COMPUTING?

Cloud computing is one of the most overused and overhyped terms in the IT world. Moreover, because of its diverse services and emerging technologies, it can mean different things to different people. However, at its core, cloud computing is a remarkably simple concept.

Let's begin with a definition.

DEFINITION 2

Cloud computing is the use of remote (off-site) hardware and software computing services, such as servers, storage, applications, and databases.

In this context, the term "Cloud" is synonymous with "the Internet."[16] Thus, instead of hosting your own servers and software, you can lease these computing resources from third-party "cloud providers." That is, instead of setting up a data center[17]—with scads of computers, networking equipment, cables, software, and all the requisite maintenance issues, you can "rent" a computing environment from an organization that will do it for you.

Figure 7.4 provides an example of a cloud computing environment.

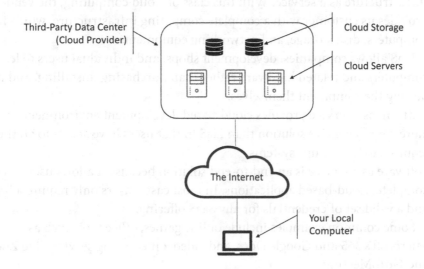

Third-Party Data Center
(Cloud Provider)

Cloud Storage

Cloud Servers

The Internet

Your Local
Computer

FIGURE 7.4   Example of cloud computing environment.

---

[16] Strictly speaking, you could establish a private cloud using a private network.

[17] We use the term *data center* to refer to any facility (e.g., a room, a floor, a building) that hosts computing equipment and software.

When referring to cloud computing, we often speak of "virtual servers," which might lead some folks to think that the hardware (e.g., computers and networking equipment) doesn't exist. On the contrary, cloud environments need real, tangible components to run. We use the term "virtual" to mean that computing environments are shared among many users and that your environment can migrate from one server to another without your knowledge and without affecting your service.

Some of you might think this is a strange way to design systems: *My* computers, *my* programs, and *my* data need to reside in *my* data center. But I assure you, this concept is not new, and every reader of this book has already engaged in cloud computing.

For example, have you installed an MTA[18] on your home computers? The answer is likely no.

Instead, you probably use an email service sponsored by a third party (e.g., Gmail, Outlook, and Yahoo). That means that your email provider hosts the requisite MTAs, MDAs, and mailboxes to support this service on *their* computers located in *their* data centers. In other words, when your local MUA calls out to the appropriate provider (i.e., "in the cloud"), you do not know where or how your messages are stored and maintained; a third-party provider does all the work for you.

Another type of cloud computing you might be familiar with is remote storage. For example, have you ever used Dropbox, Microsoft OneDrive, or Google Drive? These services allow users to store files remotely in the cloud, so they're sharable and accessible anywhere in the world via the Internet.

Cloud vendors provide many other services; the industry groups their offerings into the following categories:

IaaS   Infrastructure as a service. With this class of cloud computing, the vendor provides its customer with a complete computing infrastructure, which includes computers, disk storage, and networking equipment.

IaaS allows companies, development shops, and individual users to lease computers and related hardware rather than purchasing, installing, and maintaining the equipment themselves.

PaaS   Platform as a service provides cloud-based development environments. It is a more comprehensive solution than IaaS in that users have access to all the tools required to "stand-up" systems.

SaaS   Software as a service is an end-to-end solution because it allows users access to complete, cloud-based applications. In most cases, users only require a browser and a valid set of credentials for any SaaS offering.

Some common examples include online games, office tools such as Microsoft's 365 and Google Docs, and videoconferencing services like Zoom and GoToMeeting.

---

[18] Please refer to the discussion in the section above.

ADVANCED SECTION

Security and Privacy

I'd be willing to wager hard cash (or Bitcoin?) that most readers of this book rarely pay for software. For example, most of you get your email from one of the major providers, listen to music from one of the leading streaming services, and check your credit score with one of the primary reporting agencies. So, what's the common attribute? They're free. It can't get any better than that, right?

Have you ever wondered what the business model for these organizations might be? Consider that we've just spent the last several chapters of this book explaining how difficult and costly it is to design, develop, and deploy software systems. Do you think the organizations sponsoring these "free apps" spend all that money because of some misplaced altruistic largess? Or do you think they've found another way to "monetize" their investment?

Before we continue, I'd like to make one point: I'm not about to start bashing "big business" or the right to pursue profits. Free enterprise is the economic engine of liberty. Based on supply and demand, the market (producers and consumers collectively) determines the cost of goods and services, not some anonymous, unnamed bureaucratic governmental agency.

Overall, a free-market economy works well—but it's not without its challenges and abuses. As is always the case, *caveat emptor*.

Returning to the main point, how do organizations whose primary purpose is to pursue profits generate revenue when they practically give away their products and services? Facebook is a perfect example. Most users don't pay a fee to use this service. Nonetheless, at the time of this writing, the company's market capitalization is over 600 billion dollars. How is that possible?

One way software service providers generate income is by selling advertising. But that's only part of the story. So, what is it that we're missing?

The answer is as follows: *You. Moi,* did you say? Yes, *vous.*

These companies are selling *you*—or, more accurately, your *Personally Identifiable Information* (PII). How? They collect, store, and repackage your PII and market it to other organizations, such as other corporations, advertising firms, or even governments.

In the following sections, we'll present some obvious and devious ways organizations acquire and resell your PII—with or without your knowledge and consent. After reading this, if you become as angry as I am, all I can say is: Welcome to the club.

What Do People Know about You?

As noted above, your PII is a valuable commodity. But what exactly is it?

DEFINITION 3

Personally Identifiable Information (PII) is data that identify a specific individual.

The following list is a sample of the data elements collected about *you*. I don't want to sound like an alarmist, but it's likely that much of this information is already available for purchase from legitimate vendors or is otherwise accessible from more nefarious suppliers operating in the dark shadows of the Internet (more on this later).

Please note that this is not an exhaustive list.

Name	Current full name, former name (e.g., maiden), nicknames, your mother's birth name
Demographic data	Date of birth, race, religion, marital status
Contact information	Telephone numbers, including mobile, home, and business
Personal attributes	Education levels, degrees, security clearances, pet ownership
Location data	Home street address, email address, PO box numbers, city of birth
Relationships	Family members, friends, business associates
Associations	Employers, employment history, clubs, organizations, volunteer groups
ID numbers	Social security number (scary!), driver's license number (also scary!), license plate tag, passport number, credit card numbers, financial account numbers, electronic toll collection account IDs
Digital data	The IP address and MAC addresses of the computing devices you commonly use (e.g., your phones and laptops)
Physical characteristics	Photographs (digital images), biometric data (fingerprints, retinal scans, etc.)
Financial assets	Banking data, property ownership, owned or leased vehicles (VINs), credit cards, loans, debts, bankruptcies

Speaking for myself, I find the scope and extent of this list disturbing at best and terrifying at worst.

Why Should You Care?

So, why should you care? After all, you're getting free stuff, right?

At a high level, that seems like a straightforward question with a straightforward answer: Because you're the one who pays the price when something goes awry. The burden falls on you to reconcile accounts, repair your credit, get refunds for products you didn't purchase, etc.

But the actual answer to that question is a bit more subtle. Why? Because your PII data are often used without your knowledge and consent and in ways that are not so obvious.

The sections that follow describe how this happens.

General Concerns

Does it bother you that:

- When you walk into many casinos, the staff knows who you are before you place your first bet

- Search engines know more about your life than your family does

- When you drive, traffic cameras and electronic toll devices trace your trip

- Your phone continually tracks your location

- Social media outlets can accurately determine sexual orientation, race, relationship status, political leanings, etc.

Have you experienced any of the events described below?

- Did you suddenly receive email ads for cheap airfares after discussing vacation options with your significant other within "earshot" of your smart device (e.g., Alexa or Google Home)?

- When you window-shop in front of a store in a mall, do discount coupons arrive as alerts on your phone?

Have you considered these issues?

- How can you determine whether every cell tower your mobile phone connects to is part of your provider's network? Could a government (the US or otherwise) or a third-party data collector own and manage fraudulent cell towers?

- Wi-Fi and cellular networks are becoming so accurate in determining your phone's location that they'll be able to identify which products you're browsing in a store.

- Do you allow your cell phone to connect to public Wi-Fi networks? If so, do you know whether unknown third parties are monitoring your data traffic?

- Are you concerned that identity thieves can file false tax returns in your name? These scammers enter false deductions to ensure a refund and then have the Internal Revenue Service (IRS) wire the payment into one of their bogus bank accounts. Try getting that money back.

I could continue, but I'm sure you get the point.

You may think I'm paranoid, but I assure you that every one of the above examples is real. And they happen every day. Sadly, I'm sure some readers of this book have been victims of one or more of these attacks—including me.

But it doesn't end here. In addition to the general concerns noted above, you can find specific issues outlined in the following sections.

Monetization of Data

The title of this section sounds very professional and businesslike. But what it really means is that companies you do business with every day—cellular providers, electricity suppliers, banks, to name a few—sell your data often without your knowledge and consent. But what galls me is that it's *my* data, and I don't get to authorize who gets it, nor do I receive any remuneration.

Data Breaches

Organizations lust after your PII—as much of it as they can get their digital digits around. And sometimes you have no choice but to give it to them. For example, it's impossible to apply for a credit card, register a car, or receive medical care without providing a wealth of personal information.

Unfortunately, once you provide your PII to some third party, you're no longer in control of it—it's in someone else's hands. Thus, you must rely on them to protect your data as vigorously as you would.

But do they?

Regardless of their diligence and competence, security professionals must design systems to protect your data 24×7×365. Remember that a hacker needs to get lucky only once; the safety measures defending your PII must be 100% accurate 100% of the time. The odds are in the hacker's favor.

Right now, unbeknownst to you, your data might be for sale to anyone willing to pay for it. Moreover, there's no way to anticipate how criminals might use it—they're *highly creative.*

If you think I'm exaggerating, just launch your favorite search engine[19] and query "data breaches." The length of the list returned is staggering. Moreover, whether you're aware of it or not, it's likely you've been involved by one or more of them.

Identity Theft

Identity theft is rampant, but many folks believe it's limited to credit card fraud. But, unfortunately, it's much more pervasive and pernicious than that.

Given enough of your PII—much of which might already be available on the Web—cybercriminals can create a "shadow identity" that looks and acts like you to the rest of the world. They can apply for credit cards, passports, driver's licenses—anything they want in your name.

When the dust settles, and the payments come due, who do you think will be left holding the bag?

---

[19] We'll discuss the security shortcomings of search engines later in this chapter.

Malware

The term *malware* refers to any software written for malicious purposes. Some common examples appear below.

Adware	Adware is an aggressive form of advertising that typically presents as annoying pop-ups; they are more irritating than malicious. However, if you see them, it's likely that your computer has been compromised and that other, more malevolent forms of malware may have already "piggybacked" their way into your system.
Viruses	A computer virus inserts itself into "clean" files and then attempts to infect other documents. They are so named because their behavior imitates their biological counterparts. Unfortunately, they do more than just replicate. They also delete files, corrupt folders, and damage systems.
Spyware	As its name might suggest, the intent of spyware is to snoop—on you. It lurks in the background and surreptitiously collects data such as logins, passwords, and account numbers. It then packages and sends this data to its "creator," who will gladly make it available for purchase.
Ransomware	This might be the most heinous form of malware. Ransomware assumes complete control of your computer. It then issues you an ultimatum: Pay a ransom, or it will delete all your files and render your system unusable.

How Do Organizations Acquire Data?

Humans are incredibly innovative. You see evidence of this in museums and theaters, hear it in music and poetry, and smell it in the kitchens of Michelin four-star restaurants.

Sadly, however, ingenuity is not the sole province of kindly, well-intentioned individuals. Some of the most inventive minds you've never heard of focus their faculties on finding imaginative ways to acquire and use *your* PII. To that end, there are many means—both obvious and devious—by which organizations can track you online. Let's unveil some of them.

Free Services

It may surprise you that organizations have developed a very ingenious way to acquire data from you: They ask you for it.

As we discussed above, there are no free lunches. So, be very wary of any complimentary service you see marketed on the Internet.

Of course, the provider will ask you many innocent and helpful-sounding questions when you sign up. But I assure you, it's not because they care about you; on the contrary, they need something to sell to maintain their revenue streams.

Tracking Your Surfing

Most users would find it annoying having to enter a password every time they press a button on a web page. Thus, websites save session data in files, called *cookies,* and your browser automatically includes this information with every message it sends to the web server.

In addition to retaining authentication data, developers use *cookies* to streamline your interaction with their sites. For example, they maintain lists of items recently viewed, track products placed in shopping carts, and store previously entered data (such as credit card numbers) for later use. Very convenient, to be sure.

Unfortunately, everything that can be exploited will be exploited.[20] *Cookies* are no exception to that rule because advertisers and search engines can create *tracking IDs* that uniquely identify you (or your device) and save them. Advertisers (and other nefarious organizations) can use this ID to monitor browsing history and target advertising.

How targeted advertising works is as simple as it is ingenious. When you direct your browser to a website, say SOME-WEBSITE.COM, you might see an ad positioned somewhere on the web page. That random, innocuous-looking advertisement is associated with its own website, let's say, SILENT-TRACKER.COM which, in *its* cookie, will record the fact that you visited SOME-WEBSITE.COM. (To be clear, the website associated with the ad—SILENT-TRACKER.COM—tracks that you visited SOME-WEBSITE.COM.) Later, when you visit other websites, that same ad may appear, and the same action occurs: SILENT-TRACKER.COM saves each site you visit in its cookie.

As this process continues and data accumulate, advertisers can paint a surprisingly good picture of your life and lifestyle: You're now subject to targeted advertising. For example, let's say you're shopping for a new car and visiting dealership websites. You may start getting ads for other vehicle models, automobile insurance, and bank loans.

At the time of this writing, there has been some legislative progress in this area. For example, in Europe and the US, websites must request permission to use *cookies.* The request is typically in the form of a "pop-up" that appears when you visit each website. Though not a "cure," users are at least made aware of the possibility of "infection."

Device Fingerprinting

Because techniques to impede tracking *cookies* are becoming prevalent (see below), advertisers need to develop more subtle methods to monitor your surfing activity. One approach gaining popularity combines such data elements as your device's IP address, location information, system configuration, and sophisticated algorithms to create a *device fingerprint* that uniquely identifies your system. Thus, advertisers can track all activity originating from your computer.

Did you ever agree to this? I know I didn't.

Device fingerprints are just as effective as tracking IDs but are far more difficult to thwart because the data used to create them are unavoidably visible.

Social Media

Social media giants—Facebook, Twitter, WhatsApp, YouTube, Instagram, etc.—likely know more about you than your lover. Secrets you wouldn't hint at to close friends or family are easily inferred based solely on your "click" history: Postings, likes/dislikes, video

---

[20] A wise person once said that. Well, to be honest, it was me and I'm not so wise—I'm simply tired of feeling exploited.

selections, etc. Furthermore, these service providers aggregate such data and combine it with information garnered from other sources, such as credit reports, web searches, and shopping tendencies, to build a complete and all-too-accurate picture of you.

Armed with this knowledge, these organizations can precisely predict personal attributes such as sexual orientation, political leanings, legal and illicit drug use—the list is endless. In addition, they can accurately anticipate that you're going to buy a particular make and model of an automobile before you even walk into the showroom, know that you're expecting a child before you announce the good news to the world, and correctly forecast how you'll vote in the next election.

What's worse—at least in my opinion—is that these companies sell these prognostications about *you* without your knowledge or consent.

I find this type of electronic stalking both alarming and creepy. So much so that I don't have any social media accounts. None. The benefits these sites offer do not outweigh what I believe is an outrageous and morally reprehensible violation of my privacy.

But to each their own.

How Can You Protect Yourself?

To protect yourself, start by accepting that you're a target and may have already fallen victim to many of the attacks discussed above. Once you've adopted that mindset, you can use the techniques described below to make it difficult for organizations to invade your privacy.

Think before You Share

The title of this section speaks volumes: Don't give away personal data thoughtlessly. Just because a website asks you for information doesn't mean you *must* provide it. Before sharing your PII, ask yourself whether the organization seeking it truly needs it to provide the service in question. If not, say "no."

If it's a "free" site and the provider won't take "no" for an answer (i.e., they won't grant access to their site without acquiring some questionable PII), pull your hands away from the keyboard and ask yourself, is it worth it? Do I really need this service?

If the answer is "yes," you still have two options: Search for another "free" provider or find a fee-based alternative that purports to protect your privacy. Consider spending a little money now to avoid significant issues in the future.

If you opt to use a free service, keep in mind that, even if the provider appears socially responsible, they still glean knowledge about you based on your interactions with their site. Every one of your "clicks" says something about you. Thus, as painful as it is, read the provider's Terms of Service (ToS). That's the only way to understand the level of risk you're assuming.

Once you've completed the registration process with any new site, immediately locate the privacy settings and opt out of every data collection option you can find. For example:

- Many sites ask whether they can track and share usage data: Select "no."

- Other sites ask whether they can monitor activity to improve their product or service: Select "no."

- If a product—typically browsers—provides an option to delete cookies after a session terminates, select "yes."

Scrutinizing such detail is distressingly dull and tedious—but I assure you that identity theft is far more agonizing and painful.

As an aside, this advice holds true in the legacy world of paper as well. When you enter data on forms, questionnaires, and documents, view every field as a *request* for your information. Feel free to say "no."

Whenever and however you provide personal data, you're relying on a third party to protect it. If they experience a security breach, it's a bad *day* for them—but it could be a bad *decade* for you.

Protect Passwords

We live in an extraordinary age of digital convenience. We shop, bank, and communicate with the press of a button—or by verbal command. But there are risks.

For example, would you ever (deliberately) leave your house keys where they could be stolen or copied? Of course not. But most folks don't recognize that passwords are just as important.

Hackers and cybercriminals are continually trying to gain access to your accounts. They are intelligent, motivated, and use powerful computer systems customized to "crack" passwords. Moreover, they have all the time in the world and only need to get lucky once.

Don't be a victim. Below are some guidelines for protecting passwords. Please note that by no means should you consider this an exhaustive list.

- Passwords should be at least 12 characters long, contain upper and lowercase letters, and include numbers and symbols (e.g., "$" and "+").

- Don't jot down passwords on post-it notes and stick them to your monitor.

- Don't choose passwords that relate to you in any way. For example, don't use your dog's name, birth date, or favorite song title. (As per our earlier discussion, cybercriminals can acquire such information from social media sites and use it to compromise passwords.)

- Never reuse a password. Ever.

- Never use the identical password for more than one site. Remember that, through tracking IDs, hackers may know all the websites you visit. Therefore, a password for a closed account should never allow access to an active one.

- Don't use "formulas" to create passwords. For example, if you have an account at SOMESITE.COM, don't create passwords of the form: SOMESITE123 or ABCSOMESITE. Though easy to remember, passwords generated in this manner are a hacker's dream.

- Change passwords frequently and routinely. Yes, this is painful, but it's worth it.

- Unless there's a compelling reason, never disclose passwords to anyone—including work or school colleagues. On those rare occasions when you must reveal a password, change it as soon as possible afterward.

- If your device supports biometrics, use them. Fingerprints are unique, require no memorization, and travel with you.

- Many sites allow you to use third-party authenticators (e.g., Facebook and Google). Consider taking advantage of this service.

Log Off

Take the extra moment to log out.

When you initiate a session with a website, servers often store (or *cache*) some of your data in memory—rather than on a secure disk—so that it can respond to subsequent requests quickly and efficiently. These data are often stored *en clair*. That is, it's not encrypted and thus subject to hacking. The server clears its cache and removes your data from memory when you log out.

Browsers and Search Engines

There are several popular browsers and search engines available today. Like any product, each offers various levels of service. I suggest you use a browser and search engine combination that vigorously safeguards your privacy and doesn't facilitate the use of tracking IDs (see the discussion above).

Once you select a browser, there are several options you should configure. Of course, each product is unique, but here are some general tips to protect your privacy.

- Clear the *cache* and *cookies* on exit.

- Prevent the creation of *tracking IDs* and device *fingerprinting*.

- Inhibit social media tracking.

- Install third-party add-ons from trusted providers that block ad trackers.

- Use *private browsing*. This option prevents recording your browsing history on the device you're using. However, this is not a panacea; the rest of the Internet can still follow your every move. For greater privacy, use a Virtual Private Network (VPN, see below).

Wi-Fi Networks

Do not use public Wi-Fi networks. Ever. Anyone could be eavesdropping on the connection. Instead, pay the data charges for a private service. Trust me: It's cheaper in the long run.

Update Software

For most software products, every update contains security improvements. It's a constant cat-and-mouse game: Hackers identify new flaws; vendors mitigate them. Your best defense is to keep products current.

Anti-Malware Software

Purchase and install *anti-malware* software. The purpose of these products is to deter, detect, and delete all types of malware. Moreover, reputable vendors continually update their products whenever new risks emerge. I, therefore, fervently encourage you to invest in one.

I know it's easy for me to spend your money, but consider the cost if you don't.

Use a VPN

As discussed in Chapter 6, most computers connect to an ISP to access the Web or communicate with devices outside a home or office network. Consequently, your ISP can scrutinize, filter, or even censor Internet traffic.[21] Unfortunately, it also means that third parties—such as advertisers and governments—can also monitor your activity.

One way to increase privacy is by using a personal VPN.

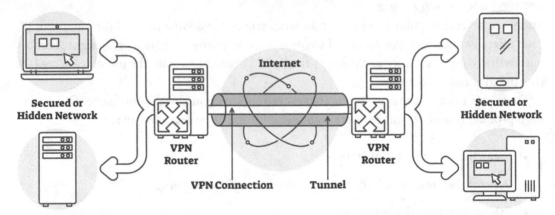

VPN
Virtual Private Network

FIGURE 7.5 VPN topology.

As depicted in Figure 7.5, VPNs create an encrypted connection—called a *tunnel*—between your device and a VPN router. To do that, VPN software installed on your computer encrypts all message traffic before transmitting it.

Upon receipt, the VPN router decrypts the message and forwards it *en clair* to the intended destination. However, the IP address visible on the Internet is that of the VPN's server, not yours. In this manner, *VPN Tunneling* masks your identity and location and makes it difficult to track your activity.[22]

Verify Invoices and Bills

This suggestion may seem obvious but carefully peruse invoices, receipts, credit card bills, and bank records. Unexpected entries on statements may be your first indication that cybercriminals have compromised an account or stolen your identity.

---

[21] There seems to be *big brothers* everywhere you look these days.
[22] Nota bene: If your VPN service provider maintains activity logs, your browsing history might be available *post facto*.

If there's any doubt whatsoever, apply some tourniquets and stop the bleeding as quickly as possible: Change passwords, lock accounts, and call financial institutions immediately.

Clean Up

Delete (close) unused accounts. Though dormant, they still contain your PII and remain targets for a data breach. Moreover, it might take a while to realize that hackers are wreaking havoc with your information because—like most people—you pay little heed to inactive accounts.

Remain Wary

Hackers and cybercriminals are after your data. That's a fact—not paranoia. But unfortunately, despite the constant threat, we receive precious little help from governments and police departments.

In the end, it's up to you to protect yourself. Below are some guidelines I suggest you follow:

- If you see an email that looks *hinky*, delete it without opening it. If you think it might be from someone you know, ask the sender if the message is legitimate.

- Never "click" on a URL included in an email from unknown senders. Doing so is just asking for trouble.

- Similarly, don't "press" any buttons on any questionable websites.

- Never open an email attachment sent by somebody that you don't know. If you're unsure, delete the message and ask the sender to resend the attachment.

- Type important URLs directly into your browser—don't rely on links sent to you. Cybercriminals can mask URLs. Thus, you might think you're interacting with your bank's website when, in reality, you just typed your username and password into a hacker's database.

- Don't download anything from a dubious website. Ever.

- Install anti-malware and antivirus software and never turn it off.

The Dark Side

As discussed earlier, the Internet is an interconnected set of independent networks that adhere to the TCP/IP protocols. That said, anyone can connect any computer to any Internet-based network at any time. However, not every connected device is part of the World Wide Web.

For example, consider that laptops and smartphones gain access to the Internet by connecting to an ISP's network. However, does that mean every Web-based system can locate these devices? It's not likely because ISPs assign them *temporary* IP addresses[23] that

---

[23] ISP-assigned IP addresses may change with every session.

are valid only for the current session and are not known beyond the boundaries of their local network.

In general, for a server to be visible on the Web, search engines such as Google, Bing, and DuckDuckGo must know of its existence.[24] That begs the question: What's a search engine?

DEFINITION 4

A *search engine* is a software application comprising two main parts: A *cataloging component* that scans the Web,[25] indexing every data element found on every website, and a *searching component* that, based on user queries, displays the URLs of previously indexed websites.

Search engines organize and catalog vast amounts of information and provide powerful query tools that allow users to locate data, sites, and services with minimal effort. It's not hyperbole to state that they've become the *sine qua non* of the Internet. Indeed, consider that they've also changed the cultural landscape: We no longer "search for stuff"—we "*google*" it.

Nonetheless, remaining "off the grid" is often beneficial.

For example, consider vendors that offer paid subscription services for news, games, movies, proprietary research, etc. Such sites will often deploy public-facing web pages indexed by search engines but keep their content servers private. Thus, users would only acquire the URLs for the content servers after rendering payment.[26]

This collection of unindexed servers forms what's called the *deep web*.

DEFINITION 5

The *Deep Web* comprises all unindexed servers connected to the Internet.

Most of the deep web is benign and supports constructive uses such as online access to financial accounts, medical data, and business-to-business transactions. But as I stated previously, everything that can be exploited will be exploited.

To that end, sites on the deep web host more nefarious activities such as drug trafficking, illegal weapon sales, marketplaces for stolen PII—and much worse. This subset of servers forms the *dark web* or *darknet*.

DEFINITION 6

The *Dark Web* (or *Darknet*) is a subset of the deep web that requires specialized software, custom configurations, and explicit authorization to access any of its servers.

---

[24] Getting your web page indexed by search engines "puts it on the map." This is important for any site that wants traffic directed to it.

[25] IT professionals refer to this process as *crawling the Web*.

[26] We say that such servers reside behind *paywalls*.

Using specialized software,[27] users can remain anonymous on the dark web. As a result, cybercriminals can conduct their nefarious transactions in the dim recesses of cyberspace. When hackers acquire your PII, this is where they go to sell it to the individuals who will exploit it.

The dark web is not a place to visit for the casual user. So, despite any curiosity you might have, I'd urge you to avoid it.

SUMMARY

This chapter discussed Internet addressing and how servers use DNS to acquire IP addresses. Based on that knowledge, we learned how web pages, email, and cloud computing work.

In the Advanced Section, we discussed some of the darker aspects of the Internet. Specifically, we learned that cybercriminals target anyone and everyone and that every individual must take adequate precautions to protect themselves while surfing the net. To that end, this chapter outlines many ways users can protect themselves.

Finally, we also described the Wild West of the Internet: The deep web and its more nefarious subset, the dark web. The dark web facilitates some of the most heinous activities that occur on the Internet.

---

[27] This discussion is *well* beyond the scope of this text.

CHAPTER 8

How Do Cryptocurrencies Work?

I trust bitcoin more than I trust my bank.

ADAM DRAPER

Well, bitcoin is a currency. Bitcoin has no underlying rate of return. You know, bonds have an interest coupon. Stocks have earnings and dividends. Gold has nothing, and bitcoin has nothing. There is nothing to support the bitcoin except the hope that you will sell it to somebody for more than you paid for it.

JOHN C. BOGLE

INTRODUCTION

An old saying declares that money makes the world go round. This adage holds as true today as it did when first uttered. The only difference is that we now have another option for a medium of financial exchange: Cryptocurrencies.

For many folks, cryptocurrencies are a radical departure from the familiar forms of money because they don't require a central authority (i.e., a government), typically only exist electronically (i.e., there are no physical coins or banknotes), and, most alarmingly, are not considered legal tender.

Not to worry. In the following sections, we'll learn what money is, what cryptocurrencies are, and how digital exchanges function.

However, before we move on, please note that I've included two quotes at the beginning of this chapter. I did this because cryptocurrencies are controversial and provoke polarizing viewpoints. By the end of our discussion, you'll understand why.

WHAT IS MONEY?

Before money existed, people exchanged goods and services via bartering. For example, a farmer and a rancher might trade corn for beef.

DOI: 10.1201/9781003143437-8

Bartering, however, is often inefficient. Consider the following:

- If your commodity has a limited shelf life (e.g., fish), you have little time to trade it.

- Parties had to establish an exchange rate with every deal (e.g., how many bushels of wheat for how many pounds of beef).

- Traders had to find exact matches. For example, a farmer who had an abundance of wheat and wanted beef had to locate a rancher who had excess beef and needed grain.

In response to these issues, societies established money as an alternate medium of exchange. Below, we'll discuss the development and evolution of the three most significant forms of money.[1]

What is Commodity Money?

The oldest type of money has its roots in the bartering system. As its name implies, Commodity Money relied on specific goods to serve as mediums for exchange. That is, the commodity itself served as "currency." Examples include dried corn, pelts, and spices.

When using a commodity as a form of money, barterers no longer had to search for the right deal or worry whether their product would become worthless. Thus, a farmer could now "sell" wheat for pelts and then, at some later point, exchange the pelts for beef.

Regardless of their type, all forms of Commodity Money share the following attributes:

Intrinsic Value	The underlying commodities were valuable in their own right. For example, you could make clothing from pelts; you can cook with spices.
Durability	The value of the commodities would not degrade over time.
Portability	Commodities were easily transported and stored.

What is Commodity-Backed Money?

The next step in money's evolution was creating currency *backed* by a commodity—typically a precious metal such as gold or silver. For example, in Anglo-Saxon England (circa 775 AD), each one pound "note" was a proxy for one pound of actual silver. Thus, because the notes represented tangible units of the underlying commodity, when buyers used silver-backed paper currency, they were, in fact, using silver to purchase bread or meat.

Note the subtle differences between Commodity Money and Commodity-Backed Money.

When using Commodity Money, the commodity itself served as the medium of exchange. (i.e., *I'll trade you seven pelts for a bushel of corn.*)

However, when using a Commodity-*Backed* currency, buyers used "cash" (i.e., paper notes) that *represented* a specific quantity of the underlying commodity to purchase goods and services. (e.g., I'll *give you "two pounds" for seven bushels of wheat.*)

---

[1] There are several others, but they are beyond the scope of this book.

Indeed, in some cases, the holder could even "redeem" the notes for an equivalent amount of the underlying commodity. (We'll return to this point later in this chapter.)

It is often the case that the underlying commodity in a Commodity-Backed currency has no intrinsic value. Consider gold, for example. You can't wear it (as jewelry, yes, but not as a garment that can protect you from the elements like a pelt), you can't eat it (yes, chefs and bakers use gold foil to decorate food, but it has no nutritional value), and you can't use it to build a shelter. Instead, its value is purely perceptual: It's shiny and relatively rare. Nonetheless, we humans still ascribe it "monetary worth"—despite its lack of intrinsic value.

Please keep this point in mind as you read the rest of this material.

What is Fiat Money?

We refer to the next step in currency evolution as Fiat[2] Money because it doesn't require a physical commodity to back it. Instead, this type of currency derives its value because a government *declares it* as legal tender.

Thus, like a Commodity-Backed currency, Fiat Money (in paper form) has no intrinsic value. (In fairness, a minted metal coin might hold some independent worth. For example, one could imagine transforming smelted copper coins into electrical wiring.)

However, unlike Commodity-Backed currency, Fiat Money has nothing "backing" it. Instead, it derives its value from market forces—such as supply and demand—and agreement among members of a society that it serves as a legal form of currency.

Fiat Money serves as the foundation for most modern economies. For example, in 1971, the US Government moved away from the gold standard (i.e., a Commodity-Backed Currency), and thus, the US dollar became a fiat currency.

This decision had several significant implications as noted below:

- First, the price of gold could fluctuate because it's no longer tied to the US Dollar.

- Second, the exchange rate of individual currencies could vary because they no longer share the same underlying commodity.

- And finally, the US Government now has the license to print more paper money than it had gold to back it. (This is the definition of *inflation*.)

To hone the previous point, I've copied the following text directly from the US Treasury's website.[3]

> Federal Reserve notes are not redeemable in gold, silver, or any other commodity and receive no backing by anything. This has been the case since 1933. The letters have no value for themselves but for what they will buy. In another sense, because they are legal tender, Federal Reserve notes are "backed" by all the goods and services in the economy.

---

[2] A *fiat* is an authoritative command or order.
[3] https://www.treasury.gov/resource-center/faqs/Currency/Pages/legal-tender.aspx

So, in plain terms, nothing backs your hard-earned dollars except the good faith and credit of the US Government.

How is Money Created?

Because this is not a book on macroeconomics or monetary policy, we cannot dive too deeply into this subject. However, to appreciate how cryptocurrencies emerged and evolved, we need to understand how to create traditional money.

Broadly speaking, money enters into circulation in one of several ways.

- A country's central bank[4] can print it

- A country's central bank can purchase fixed-income securities such as treasury bonds, thus increasing the money supply

- And, by far, the largest source of funds for any economy: Banks create money as electronic deposits whenever they issue loans

We need to discuss the last example in more detail.

Let's say you borrow $1,000.00 from your bank. After approving the loan, the institution gives you a check for the amount in question.

But how did that money come into being?

The bank created it by borrowing it from another depositor's account. We call this Fractional Reserve Banking because financial institutions may lend a portion of the deposits they manage, retaining only a fraction in reserve.

However, even though the money supply increased, your wealth didn't change: You received $1,000.00 from the bank, but you have also assumed a debt for the same amount; wealth-wise, it's a wash.

But here's where it gets interesting.

Let's say you're an entrepreneur with dreams of expansion, so you deposit that $1,000.00 into your business account you hold at another bank. The second bank can now loan out a portion of your deposit to someone else. Thus, we've almost tripled the money supply based solely on the original depositor's $1,000.00.

To complete the circle, your bank "destroys" the previously created money when you pay back the loan. And again, although this represents a change in the money supply (i.e., the previously borrowed money is no longer in circulation), there is no change in your wealth.

Why Do Currencies Have Value?

As we noted above, one advantage of using Commodity Money over bartering is that the mediums of exchange are durable and portable. For example, pelts, spices, and gold last longer than bushels of corn or bales of wheat and are easier to transport.

---

4 In the US, the central bank is called the Federal Reserve (i.e., "The Fed").

As we moved to fiat currencies, the intrinsic value of money became a little murkier. Yes, they are durable and portable—but that's not enough. Fiat currencies must also possess the following attributes because they lack the backing of an underlying commodity.

Supply	Issuing agencies must control the amount of money in circulation. Too little could negatively affect the economy, increasing the supply causes inflation.
Divisibility	From gumball machines to corporate mergers, currencies need to be divisible to support all types of transactions. (Once you cut up a pelt, it loses some of its intrinsic value.)
Reliability	Consumers and trading partners must have confidence that they can exchange a currency for all goods and services in a given market.
Security	Fiat currencies must be difficult to counterfeit. Otherwise, phony bills and coins could undermine confidence in the money supply.

We will return to these attributes when we discuss cryptocurrencies.

What is a Digital Currency?

Now that we understand how traditional money works, we can turn our attention to the world of cybercash. One caveat: The realm of virtual money is evolving. As a result, the lexicon is in flux, and experts often disagree on terminology and definitions.

That said, let's begin by defining digital currency.

DEFINITION 1

Digital currency[5] is money that is available only in an electronic form.

Digital currency never assumes tangible, physical forms, such as coins or banknotes. Instead, it exists only as a balance in a database. Financial transactions (i.e., payments and deposits) occur electronically using technology hosted on digital devices like computers and smartphones.

Nonetheless, we can use "electronic cash" to pay for products and services like traditional money. However, some digital currencies may have limited use, such as those used to pay for services offered by online streaming, gaming, and gambling sites. (When used in this capacity, they are the electronic equivalent of casino chips.)

---

[5] Other terms for digital currency include virtual money, digital money, virtual currency, and cybercash.

Some advantages of digital currency include the following:

- Exchanges can occur directly between participants without an intermediary (such as a bank or government)

- Trading can cross international boundaries

- Transactions complete almost immediately

Examples of digital currencies include cryptocurrency (discussed below), PayPal, and eCash. In addition, some experts assert that electronic payment services like Zelle, Venmo, or even wire transfers also fit into that category. However, many of these examples are not "money" in and of themselves. Instead, they use an underlying currency (e.g., the US Dollar) to effect financial exchanges.

WHAT IS CRYPTOCURRENCY?

I'm sure most of you have traveled someplace that required you to swap your money for the local currency. For example, you may have had to convert US Dollars into Yen when traveling in Japan. After the exchange, the rules and regulations of the local country's central authority govern your financial transactions. (The Bank of Japan in this example.)

Nonetheless, despite any confusion dealing with a foreign currency, most travelers take this in stride. For example, instead of paying about $2.65 for a fast-food hamburger in the US, you would fork over around ¥291 for such a delicacy in Japan.

However, consider that both the US Dollar and the Yen are fiat currencies (see above). So, when you convert US Dollars into Yen, what are you really exchanging? Yes, you traded two countries' legal tender. But, more specifically, because both currencies have no intrinsic value, you've based your exchange on the good faith and credit of the two central authorities.

Let's compare this with cryptocurrency.

> **DEFINITION 2**
>
> A *cryptocurrency* is a digital monetary system with no central authority or issuing agency but instead uses a distributed, decentralized design to track transactions and create new monetary units.

From a monetary perspective, both crypto- and fiat currencies are similar in that neither has any intrinsic value. The only difference is that cryptocurrencies lack a central authority.

Let's see how that works.

What are the Attributes of Cryptocurrency?

Before describing how cryptocurrencies operate, let's discuss their most important attributes.

Irreversibility	Once completed and confirmed, all cryptocurrency transactions are irreversible. You can't place a stop notice (as with a check), reverse a funds transfer, or cancel an electronic payment. If you sent someone digital money, it's theirs.
Anonymity	Although all trades are public, user identities are rarely (if ever) recorded as part of a cryptocurrency transaction. As we'll see, this approach has both advantages and disadvantages.
Immediacy	Most cryptocurrencies complete and confirm transactions in seconds to minutes.
Security	Because they rely on *cryptology* (hence their name), cryptocurrencies are almost impossible to counterfeit.

Why Do Cryptocurrencies Have Value?

As noted previously, cryptocurrencies have no intrinsic value. Thus, to understand why they can serve as a medium of exchange, we should compare their attributes with their fiat currency counterparts.

Durability	Because they are digital, there is no issue with durability. However, you *must* safeguard your "wallets." (More on this later.)
Portability	You can conduct a cryptocurrency transaction from anywhere globally, assuming you have access to a digital device (e.g., laptop, smartphone, and tablet) and an Internet connection.
Controlled Float	As we will see, all cryptocurrencies cap their supply.
Divisibility	Most cryptocurrencies are far more divisible than their fiat counterparts.
Reliability	Based on their underlying technology (e.g., *blockchain*—see below), cryptocurrencies are highly reliable. Moreover, as we will demonstrate, all transactions are subject to verification and public scrutiny.
Anonymity	Cryptocurrencies provide anonymity and are thus appealing to users who value privacy.
Security	Because they rely on cryptology, cryptocurrencies are highly secure and are not subject to fraudulent activities.

Because of these attributes, cryptocurrencies can serve as an alternative to traditional fiat currencies.

How Do You Use Cryptocurrencies?

With most electronic forms of payment, you don't need detailed knowledge of the underlying technologies or behind-the-scenes processing to use them. So, for example, when paying with a credit card, customers can remain blissfully unaware of the intricacies of the international banking system. Likewise, Zelle and Venmo users don't need to concern themselves with cross-institutional networking challenges when sending or receiving money. Instead, there are user-friendly applications that make these services easy to use.

The same holds for cryptocurrencies. To get started, all you need to do is the following:

Select a cryptocurrency	Choose a cryptocurrency from among the thousands (yes, thousands!) available today.[6]
Select a Wallet	Cryptocurrency wallets are devices or software apps that manage digital currency. They are freely available for most platforms (e.g., laptops, tablets, and smartphones) and serve as the digital equivalent of billfolds, purses, and wallets—except they hold virtual money, not physical bills or coins. Please note that some digital wallets may only support one type of cryptocurrency; others can manage multiple.
Acquire Virtual Money	Several methods are available to "seed" your digital wallet with some cryptocurrency. But, of course, the most direct way is to buy some.
Use	Locate a store, merchant, or service provider that accepts your cryptocurrency and then render payment using your newly acquired digital wallet.

As just described, this cryptocurrency start-up process is straightforward and equivalent to selecting and using a credit card or electronic payment service.

There are caveats, however.

As with any emerging product or service, you might encounter issues using cryptocurrency in the general marketplace. Moreover, because investors trade cryptocurrencies like other commodities, their relative value (compared to other crypto- or fiat currencies) may fluctuate dramatically. Therefore, before committing to one, you should undertake some due diligence to understand the risks and benefits.

The scenario we just described is from the perspective of a user. Now, let's peek behind the curtain and explain how cryptocurrencies work.

---

[6] The term, *altcoin*, has evolved to mean any cryptocurrency other than Bitcoin.

HOW DO CRYPTOCURRENCIES WORK?

All cryptocurrencies must provide all the functions and services described below. However, the implementation may vary widely among the offerings. Thus, we will discuss all the features generically first. Then, in the following section, we will explain how the first cryptocurrency, *Bitcoin*, implements them.

What is a Public Ledger?

Regardless of the currency, when you purchase any product or service, the transaction flow is as follows:

Your Wallet (or account) -> Money -> Someone Else's Wallet (or account)

This process is similar whether you're using cash, credit cards, PayPal, Zelle, etc. The differences are the monetary units and the methods by which the transaction completes. In most cases (other than a direct cash payment), a central authority (e.g., a bank or a credit card company) ensures the accuracy and timely completion of the financial exchange.

However, unlike traditional fiat currencies, cryptocurrencies are *decentralized*. Thus, lacking a central authority to record and validate transactions, how do cryptocurrencies track who has paid what to whom? The short answer is that they use a *ledger*.

The use of ledgers dates to ancient times when merchants recorded transactions on papyrus, clay tablets, and ultimately, paper. Indeed, this early method of record-keeping eventually served as the foundation for the formal double-entry accounting systems still in use today.

However, to ensure accuracy and prevent fraud, cryptocurrencies maintain their ledgers publicly. Thus, all participants may review and verify all transactions. (We'll understand how cryptocurrencies achieve this goal while maintaining anonymity below.)

The concept of a public ledger is not new. Let's start with a non-digital example.

Amaya, Joey, Nora, Matt, and CJ are all "foodies" and formed a Diners Club[7] group. One day, the members agreed that instead of constantly chipping in for every meal, one person would pay for each dinner, and the others would collectively record and track how much they owed. Then, at the end of every month, the participants would reconcile with each other.

Thus, after the agreement is in place, Amaya pays for the first meal, and the "public ledger" might look something like this:

Joey owes Amaya $23
Nora owes Amaya $41
Matt owes Amaya $32
CJ owes Amaya $37

---

[7] Founded in 1950, the original Diners Club charge card was the first independent payment card.

After Joey pays for the next meal, the ledger might look as follows:

JOEY OWES AMAYA $23
NORA OWES AMAYA $41
MATT OWES AMAYA $32
CJ OWES AMAYA $37
AMAYA OWES JOEY $57
NORA OWES JOEY $47
MATT OWES JOEY $63
CJ OWES JOEY $51

At the end of every month, it's simple to "settle up." Members whose meals cost more than they paid would compute the difference and *deposit* that sum into a "communal pot." Alternatively, diners who spent more than the total sum of their meals would *withdraw* the appropriate amount from the "communal pot."[8]

This simple approach works great when dealing with trustworthy individuals. However, because it's public, anyone can add an entry to the ledger at any time. So, what's to prevent a new, less-than-honest member from adding phony entries?

At this point, nothing.

So, to address this concern, your club might adopt the approach that each record must include the signature of the member who owes the money.

For example, consider the following ledger entry.

CHRIS OWES MICHAEL $123

To minimize "mistakes," the club should require that Chris reviews, approves, and then signs this entry to confirm its validity.

Again, this simple approach works well for a small, controlled environment. But how would we implement an equivalent process to support a global currency?

Let's start with *digital signatures*.

What is a Digital Signature?

The signature approach described above works fine for a while. However, it becomes increasingly challenging to track transactions manually as your club grows. Consequently, the group collectively decides to "go digital" and convert the ledger into a "Google doc."[9]

Although this approach makes the ledger more accessible and easier to maintain, it reintroduces the verification and trust issues. That is, using modern graphics tools, it's effortless to copy and paste signatures.

So, does this mean we are right back where we started?

No, not quite.

---

[8] Yes, I'm well aware that there are other, electronic, ways to address this type of cost sharing these days. Please just go with me on this one.

[9] Google Docs is a suite of free, web-based document processing applications.

Because we are now in the electronic world, Diners Club members can sign the ledger *digitally*. One of the most common ways to accomplish that is by using *public-key encryption*.

Public-key encryption is a cryptographic technique that requires two keys, each of which comprises a string of bits (i.e., binary digits—see Chapter 4). The first, called the *Public Key* (PK), is for public distribution and consumption. The second, called the *private key* or *Secret Key* (SK), must always remain confidential.

The mathematics required to generate these keys is beyond this book's scope. However, when used correctly, you can create highly secure, non-repudiable digital signatures.

As mentioned above, your physical signature is easy to forge—relatively speaking. However, with public-key encryption, we can create unique digital signatures for every ledger entry. (Moving forward, we will use the term "message" to represent the data we want to encrypt or sign digitally.)

Figure 8.1 depicts how this process works.

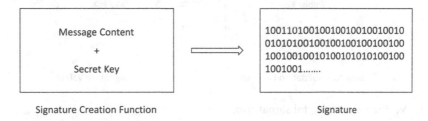

FIGURE 8.1   Digital signature creation.

The signature creation function uses a mathematical formula, the value of the secret key, and the contents of individual messages to create unique digital signatures.

Again, leaving the implementation details to the computer scientists, I will only note that the formulas and algorithms involved in this process ensure that it's tantamount to impossible to calculate the private key, given the public key and digital signature. In colloquial terms, this means the encryption process is a "one-way street." That is, we can use the message and the secret key to generate the digital signature, but we can't use the digital signature to "reverse engineer" the content of the message or the value of the secret key.

For our purposes, the crucial points to consider are as follows:

- Because the signature function uses a secret key, digital signatures are unique to individuals (or their accounts)[10] (assuming, of course, that users maintain the secrecy of their private key).

- The digital signature would change if you were to modify even a single bit of the original message's content. In other words, the process can only recreate the original digital signature from the unaltered original message. Thus, any change to the content would generate a different digital signature, and we'd know someone has altered the original message.

---

[10] And to *digital wallets*, as we will see in the next section.

In short, this means that a digital signature is unique to every combination of user/account and message (e.g., an individual ledger entry). Thus, it would differ if some other user (using a different private key) sent the same message or if the same user sent a different or altered message.

As an example of how this processing works, let's discuss how email users might use digital signatures.

When posting an email, correspondents can include their public key and a digital signature along with the message content. Upon arrival, recipients can verify the authenticity of a message based on the digital signature generated by the sender's private key.

Figure 8.2 depicts this processing.

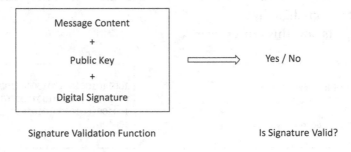

FIGURE 8.2   Verification of digital signatures.

Before opening an email, recipients execute a validation function that determines whether the private key used to create the digital signature is the one associated with the public key included in the message. If it yields TRUE, the message is valid: It's from the purported sender, and its content is unaltered. Otherwise, it's counterfeit, spam—or worse—malware (see Chapter 7).

Let's return to our foodie example. As depicted below, we can use public-key encryption to ensure that the digital signatures associated with every ledger entry are valid.

```
JOEY OWES AMAYA $23 <DIGITAL SIG>
NORA OWES AMAYA $41 <DIGITAL SIG>
MATT OWES AMAYA $32 <DIGITAL SIG>
CJ OWES AMAYA $37 <DIGITAL SIG>
```

Okay, this solves our problem. Or does it?

What prevents unscrupulous individuals from simply copying a message and repeatedly pasting it into the ledger? Clearly, each inserted copy will appear legitimate because it would include a valid digital signature.

```
JOEY OWES AMAYA $23 <DIGITAL SIG>
NORA OWES AMAYA $41 <DIGITAL SIG>
MATT OWES AMAYA $32 <DIGITAL SIG>
CJ OWES AMAYA $37 <DIGITAL SIG>
```

CJ owes Amaya $37 <DIGITAL SIG> ⎫
CJ owes Amaya $37 <DIGITAL SIG> ⎬ Copied Messages
CJ owes Amaya $37 <DIGITAL SIG> ⎭

One way to address this issue is to include a unique transaction identifier with each entry. For example, we could incorporate the ledger's sequence number when creating the digital signature.

<SEQ#1> Joey owes Amaya $23 <DIGITAL SIG>
<SEQ#2> Nora owes Amaya $41 <DIGITAL SIG>
<SEQ#3> Matt owes Amaya $32 <DIGITAL SIG>
<SEQ#4> CJ owes Amaya $32 <DIGITAL SIG>

It now becomes impossible to duplicate previously approved ledger entries because new records would contain either a duplicate sequence number or an invalid digital signature.

What is a Digital Wallet?

Now that we've secured the ledger, there's another issue we need to address: What if one of the members spends more money on dinners than they can afford to pay? For example, let's say one club member orders the most expensive entrees and buys the costliest wines with every meal and, at the end of the month, doesn't have enough cash to put into the pot?

Obviously, this scenario is unacceptable because one or more club members will not receive adequate reimbursement. Thus, we must ensure that diners cannot spend more money than they can afford to pay.

To ensure fair and accurate settlement, the club can enact two new policies:

- Like a poker game, members must "ante" into the communal pot at the beginning of each month

- Member spending may not exceed the amount they have on deposit

That's all well and good, but how does the club monitor and enforce these new rules?

One way is to create a system of debits and credits that we track in a *digital wallet*. Using this approach, every time a member adds money to the pot, we credit the member's wallet by that amount. And after every dinner, we subtract the appropriate number of credits from the member's digital wallet based on the cost of the meal.

Moreover, to ensure that members can't misrepresent the number of credits in their wallets, we can use the public ledger to track every ante. Thus, we can include entries like the following:

<SEQ#> Amaya adds $200 to wallet <DIGITAL SIG>
<SEQ#> Joey adds $150 to wallet <DIGITAL SIG>
<SEQ#> Nora adds $250 to wallet <DIGITAL SIG>
<SEQ#> Matt adds $175 to wallet <DIGITAL SIG>
<SEQ#> CJ adds $220 to wallet <DIGITAL SIG>

Given this approach, the public ledger now ensures that every member has sufficient credits in their digital wallets to cover the cost of the meals that they've ordered. In addition, during reconciliation, we can subtract the appropriate number of credits from each member's digital wallets.

At this point, because wallet entries also appear in the public ledger, all Diners Club transactions are public, validated, and are no longer subject to "spoofing."

Given these "lessons learned," let's revisit cryptocurrencies.

What is Digital Currency—Redux?

In the prior section, we introduced a system of credits to track antes and disbursements. Specifically, when club members contribute to the communal pot, we credits their wallets. Likewise, we subtract from their balances when they "pay" for meals. Moreover, when members reconcile each month, they swap US Dollars for credits. Thus, credits serve as a medium of exchange among club members.

Does this seem familiar? Aren't Diners Club *credits* serving as *currency*?

Let's take this one step further and rename the club's credits Member Currency, or "MC," for short. Now, when members ante, we can say that they are converting US Dollars into MCs. Similarly, we can say that members "pay" each other using MCs. And, during reconciliation, members exchange MCs for US Dollars.

Congratulations, you've just created a new currency.

Jokes aside, I believe every reader would feel comfortable if we were to replace "MC" with "Yen" or "Euro" in the preceding example. It would then resemble a typical travel scenario: When you arrive in a new country, you exchange US Dollars for the local currency. Then, throughout your stay, you conduct all financial transactions using the local currency. Finally, before you return home, you convert any remaining local currency you might have back to US Dollars.

To hone the point further, let's compare MCs with some of the cryptocurrency attributes we discussed earlier. As our scenario demonstrated, MCs are durable, portable, dependable, divisible, and secure. Moreover, because club members "support it," the MC monetary unit "has value" and functions as a fiat currency.

Now, let's stretch this scenario to its limits.

What if the club expanded to include everyone in the country? And let's get really crazy and allow MCs to serve as a medium of exchange for all financial transactions—groceries, tolls, taxes, etc.—not just meals. Would folks who use MCs need US Dollars anymore?

In the following sections, we'll see that this scenario serves as the foundation for all cryptocurrencies.

HOW DOES BITCOIN WORK?

As the oldest and still one of the most widely traded cryptocurrencies, Bitcoin embodies all the features and functionality discussed previously. Below, we'll describe how its designer implemented them.

Before we begin, however, I'd like to share two caveats.

First, the implementation approach discussed below is specific to Bitcoin. The design and implementation of other cryptocurrencies may vary widely.

Second, the underlying Bitcoin software seamlessly executes all the processing we'll describe without any user intervention—we're just peeking "under the hood." Thus, like using a credit card, Bitcoin users need only concern themselves with the debits and credits applied to their respective wallets (accounts).

What is Bitcoin's Public Ledger?

In our Diners Club example, we decided to host the member's public ledger on a website using Google Docs. This solution is more than adequate for a small, trusted group of friends.

However, this approach would raise many questions and concerns for a publicly traded cryptocurrency like Bitcoin: Who maintains this website? Who has permission to add entries to the ledger? Even though each entry is "signed," how secure is the overall environment?

Most importantly, using a single consolidated website has the appearance of a central authority, which is anathema to Bitcoin's stated goal of decentralization.

Regardless of its design, users of any cryptocurrency must feel confident that their money and transactions are not subject to fraud or hacking. Thus, the question becomes: How do we decentralize control and still meet these objectives?

The first step is to distribute the public ledger. That is, Bitcoin requires that every participant maintain copies of the ledger. This approach is both simple and direct and eliminates any notion of central control.

However, it does introduce a new concern: How and where do participants record new transactions? For example, how would Bitcoin memorialize the fact that CJ paid Nora 5Ƀ?[11]

Because it relies on a distributed design, Bitcoin software broadcasts every transaction to every active participant who, upon receipt, must record it into their copy of the public ledger.

Problem solved, right?

Well, not really. Once again, we've alleviated one issue only to introduce another. In this case, several.

First, what if one or more participants don't receive some transactions due to software, hardware, or network error? In such cases, ledgers will be inconsistent.

Second, how does a given recipient know whether every transaction is valid? For example, what stops a hacker from creating and distributing bogus ledger entries?

We can summarize these concerns as ones of trust and consensus: Every transaction must be legitimate, and all ledgers should always correlate.[12] Otherwise, potential participants would not likely adopt a cryptocurrency if they couldn't rely on the integrity of its public ledger.

So, let's review the measures Bitcoin software incorporates to address these issues.

---

[11] Both the symbol Ƀ and the acronym "BTC" serve as Bitcoin currency designations.

[12] This statement is not entirely true. When dealing with the physical implementation of large networks (i.e., the Internet), message transmission is subject to the laws of physics. For example, transit times will vary as a function of the recipient's distance from the sender (among other factors). That said, the key point is that every participant's ledger will at some point receive and process every message and thus become consistent over time. Computer scientists refer to this type of design as *eventually correct*.

What is a Hash Function?

Before discussing how Bitcoin ensures the integrity of its public ledger, let's look at how a typical homeowner secures a dwelling.

Most folks understand that the typical array of locks, dead bolts, and alarms do not render a home impregnable—a determined intruder can always find a way to gain entry. Thus, the object of home security is to make a house so arduous to burglarize that it becomes infeasible.

Bitcoin takes the same approach to secure its distributed ledger. However, it uses *cryptography*—rather than locks and alarms—to accomplish this objective. Specifically, the Bitcoin design ensures that to "break its security," a potential hacker would require more computational power than is practically available. As we will see, this makes it tantamount to impossible to alter ledgers or insert fraudulent entries.

At the heart of Bitcoin's security measures is a calculation called a *Cryptographic Hash Function (CHF)*. This computation is like the public-key encryption methodologies discussed earlier in this chapter.

DEFINITION 3

Cryptographic Hash Function (CHF) is a mathematical computation applied to a series of *bytes*[13] (often called the "message") that generate a unique value called the *hash*.[14]

Figure 8.3 depicts how a CHF works.[15] For each message it receives, a CHF performs its calculation and generates the hash.

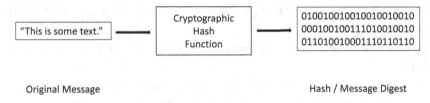

FIGURE 8.3   Cryptographic Hash Function (CHF).

There are several important points to note regarding CHFs:

Deterministic   A CHF computation creates a unique hash value for any sequence of bytes (or *message*). If you apply a CHF to a message multiple times, it will generate the identical hash.

Unique   Hash functions are message specific. If you change, add, delete, swap, or otherwise alter the bits in any way, the

---

[13] See Chapter 5 for a definition of *bytes*.

[14] Hashes go by other names as well: *Hash value, message digest,* or *digest.*

[15] Designed by the United States National Security Agency (NSA), the current industry standard, called SHA-2 (which stands for Secure Hash Algorithm Version 2), includes several cryptographic hash functions, the most common of which (at the time of this writing) is SHA-256.

resulting hash value will change. We'll understand the importance of this feature shortly.

Generic CHFs are not the sole province of cryptocurrencies. We can create a hash on any type of message (i.e., any sequence of bytes). This includes, for example, text documents (e.g., MS Word files), music files (e.g., .MP3 files), and images (e.g., .GIF files). We will see other uses of CHFs later in this chapter.

Unidirectional CHF functions are "one way." Specifically, you apply a CHF to a message to generate a hash. However, there is no practical method by which you can reverse the process. This fact is important to note: You CANNOT use the hash to recreate the original message.

Efficient Most CHFs execute quickly and efficiently.

Fixed Sized Typically, CHFs are fixed sized. Thus, a 100-byte email message will create the same-sized hash as a 1000-page text document when using the same CHF function.

Uniqueness A CHF must have the property that it's tantamount to impossible for two different messages to yield the identical hash. Moreover, there's no way to predict how the hash value will change when you alter the original message. Specifically, changing just one bit in the original message or swapping the order of two random bytes will alter the resulting hash in an unpredictable way.

Okay, at this point, we have a lock and a key, but we still need to understand how Bitcoin uses hashing algorithms to secure its public ledger.

What is a Proof of Work?

As discussed above, an essential task of any cryptocurrency is to ensure the integrity of its public ledger. Bitcoin uses a CHF and what's called a *Proof of Work* (PoW) to achieve this goal.

Consider the ledger appearing in Figure 8.4.

```
JACK PAYS JILL 10 BTC

CAROL PAYS BOB 5 BTC

TED PAYS ALICE 9 BTC
```

FIGURE 8.4   Sample Bitcoin ledger.

As noted above, regardless of its size and content, when we apply a CHF to a message, the result is a fixed-length unique digest (hash). For this discussion, let's assume that the length of that digest is 256 bytes (i.e., SHA-256).

Let's further suppose that when we run SHA-256 on the ledger in Figure 8.4, the resulting hash might look like the output depicted in Figure 8.5. (As will become clear shortly, for this discussion, we don't need to know the exact value of all the bits in this hash.)

```
010010010010010010010100100100100100001

111010010010010010010011100100100100111

...

100110010010010010010011100100100100011
```

FIGURE 8.5   Sample hash output.

So far, so good. Now, let's imagine the following challenge: Find a unique value that we can insert into the ledger such that the resulting hash value begins with 30 zeros. In other words, as depicted in Figure 8.6, we need to add an entry to the ledger such that the CHF will generate a hash that begins with 30 leading zeros.

```
JACK PAYS JILL 10 BTC

CAROL PAYS BOB 5 BTC

TED PAYS ALICE 9 BTC

<SOME ENTRY>
```

FIGURE 8.6   Ledger with new value.

Figure 8.7 depicts the resulting hash value after computing and adding the last entry to the ledger.

```
000000000000000000000000000000XXXXXXX

XXXXXXXXXXXXXXXXXXXXXXXXXXXXXXXXXXXXXX

...

XXXXXXXXXXXXXXXXXXXXXXXXXXXXXXXXXXXXXX
```

FIGURE 8.7   Hash with 30 leading zeros.

Note that I've replaced all the other 1s and 0s with the character "X" because, as noted above, we needn't concern ourselves with the other bits' values.

Returning to our challenge, the objective is to insert a value into the ledger such that when we apply the SHA-256 algorithm, the resulting hash digest begins with 30 leading zeros.[16] However, please recall that we're using a unidirectional CHF. Thus, we can't com-

---

[16] As the processing power of computers increase, the number of leading zeros required in Bitcoin's hash also increases.

pute or "reverse engineer" the unique value we'd need to add to the ledger to accomplish this task. So, instead, our only option is to undertake a brute-force approach—much like the one outlined using the pseudo-code appearing in Listing 8.1.

```
STEP 1:  SET A COUNTER TO THE VALUE 0
STEP 2:  INSERT THE COUNTER INTO THE LEDGER
STEP 3:  EXECUTE THE SHA-256 ALGORITHM
STEP 4:  DOES THE RESULTING HASH BEGIN WITH THIRTY 0S?
    4A:  IF "YES" – STOP PROCESSING
    4B:  IF "NO" – ADD ONE TO THE COUNTER AND RETURN TO STEP 2
```

LISTING 8.1   Brute Force PoW.

The point to note is that there is no computational "shortcut": It's simply a matter of trial and error.

Thus, as you might expect, this type of processing requires a great deal of computing power. On average, it requires multiple millions of "guesses" to determine an appropriate value for the counter. (In the parlance of Bitcoin and cryptography, we refer to the counter as a "nonce" or a "number used once.")

Please note, however, that once we've computed the nonce's value, confirming its correctness is simple: Simply rerun the SHA-256 algorithm and verify that the first 30 bits are zeros.

We call the above processing a "Proof of Work," and Bitcoin uses this approach to confirm the integrity of ledger entries. For example, the resulting hash will no longer begin with 30 zeros if the ledger changes after inserting the nonce. Consequently, to "forge" a transaction, a hacker must modify the registry and compute a new value for the counter.

As we will see shortly, Bitcoin incorporates several techniques to prevent these types of attacks on its ledger.

What is a Blockchain?

Given the PoW processing described in the prior section, we can now ensure that every transaction remains immutable. This approach works particularly well for cryptocurrencies like Bitcoin that use distributed ledgers: Every participant can verify the integrity of their individual copies by simply rerunning the SHA-256 algorithm and confirming that the hash begins with the correct number of zeros.[17]

However, as described thus far, the Bitcoin ledger appears as one massive register. So, this begs the question: If transactions continue to accrue over time, at what point can we use the PoW processing to "lock" the ledger?

In other words, while the ledger remains unlocked, participants may alter its contents. However, Bitcoin's ledger becomes locked once we compute and insert a PoW. Thus, we could no longer record new transactions, and Bitcoin would no longer remain a viable currency.

In other words, How can we periodically "lock" transactions but still leave Bitcoin's ledger "open for business?"

---

[17] The number of required zeros changes over time.

The first step is to divide Bitcoin's ledger into smaller chunks called *blocks*, each of which comprises a group of transactions and a PoW (i.e., the counter or "nonce"). Thus, as depicted in Figure 8.8, each block serves as a mini, self-contained ledger. Moreover, as in our previous examples, signatures validate entries, and the PoW ensures the block's integrity.

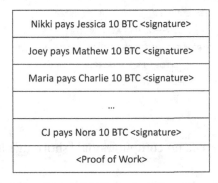

| Nikki pays Jessica 10 BTC \<signature\> |
| Joey pays Mathew 10 BTC \<signature\> |
| Maria pays Charlie 10 BTC \<signature\> |
| ... |
| CJ pays Nora 10 BTC \<signature\> |
| \<Proof of Work\> |

FIGURE 8.8   Bitcoin block structure.

Using this innovative design, we can distribute blocks of transactions to every participant who, upon receipt, can validate them using the SHA-256 algorithm. However, as is often the case, solutions to one problem often introduce new ones. In this case, the issue is one of sequencing.

For example, consider the following scenario:

1. Ahmet currently has 1Ƀ in his wallet.

2. Siobhan sends Ahmet 4Ƀ. This transaction appears in Block 1.

3. Next, Alicia sends Ahmet 5Ƀ. This transaction appears in Block 2.

4. Finally, Ahmet sends Jorge 10Ƀ. This transaction appears in Block 3.

Based on the above sequence, Ahmet accrues 10Ƀ in his wallet before he pays Jorge. That's fine. However, recall that earlier in this chapter, we noted that networks are imperfect and, as such, are subject to error.

Thus, what would happen if a segment of the Internet experienced an outage that delayed Block 2's transmission? That is, Block 3 arrives before Block 2. Consequently, it would appear to some Bitcoin participants that Ahmet was spending 10Ƀ when he was only in possession of 5Ƀ at the apparent time of the transaction.

To address this issue, we need some way to sequence the blocks.

As depicted in Figure 8.9, each block points to its predecessor. This "chaining" arrangement—formally called a *data structure*[18] in computer science—forms a series of blocks that collectively constitute Bitcoin's public ledger and is the reason we refer to it as a *blockchain*.

---

[18] See Chapter 3.

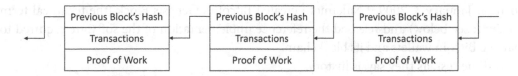

FIGURE 8.9   Simplified example of a blockchain.

As an added security measure, each block includes the previous block's hash as part of its PoW.[19] This feature impedes hackers from changing the contents of previously inserted blocks.

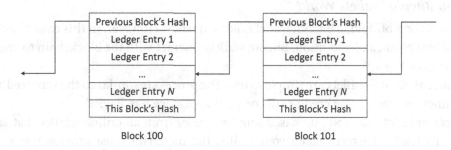

FIGURE 8.10   Example of a blockchain state.

For example, consider the blockchain depicted in Figure 8.10. If a hacker were to change any ledger entries in Block 100,[20] it would also require a concomitant change to its PoW. Thus, the hacker would have to compute and insert a new hash value for that block.

However, the hacker still can't rest because Block 101 still contains Block 100's original hash value. Therefore, the hacker now must modify Block 101—and every subsequent block in the blockchain—in an equivalent manner. And keep in mind that Bitcoin replicates its ledger. Thus, in addition to all the work just described, the hacker must also modify every participant's copy of the blockchain.

Given the design of these safeguards, it's tantamount to impossible to hack Bitcoin's blockchain.

What is the Genesis Block?

In the examples above, we noted that every block on Bitcoin's blockchain points to its predecessor. Obviously, that backward chaining can't go on forever; there must be a "first" block. In the world of blockchains, we call this the *Genesis Block* or *Block 0*.[21]

As a historical note, Bitcoin's ostensible creator, Satoshi Nakamoto,[22] published the original whitepaper entitled *Bitcoin: A Peer-to-Peer Electronic Cash System*[23] on October 31, 2007.

---

[19] Please note that Bitcoin blocks contain several additional fields such as version and timestamp.

[20] This assumes that the hacker can generate valid signatures for the forged entries.

[21] In the world of computers, we usually start counting at 0.

[22] Satoshi Nakamoto is a pseudonym for the person or persons behind Bitcoin's development. Despite several bogus claims by various individuals, the identity of Satoshi Nakamoto is unknown at the time of this writing.

[23] Visit HTTPS://BITCOIN.ORG/EN/BITCOIN-PAPER to download and read a copy of Satoshi Nakamoto's original whitepaper.

Then on January 3, 2009,[24] Nakamoto created Bitcoin's Genesis Block (the technical term is *mined*; see below) and released the reference implementation of the software required to manage Bitcoin wallets and its blockchain.

And the rest, as they say, is history.

One final note. Interested readers can examine Bitcoin's blockchain using a tool called the *Blockchain Explorer*. Enter the search term "bitcoin explorer" into your favorite search engine to get a list of sites.

At this point, we're comfortable with tracking and validating Bitcoin transactions. The next question is: How do we use Bitcoin to buy stuff?

How Do Bitcoin Wallets Work?

Like a purse or a billfold, a Bitcoin wallet holds currency. However, in this case, the money is digital, not physical. In addition, Bitcoin wallets interact with the blockchain to send and receive transactions.[25]

In concept, digital wallets are simple to use. The process is similar to the way credits and debits function when using credit cards or an ePay service like PayPal.

For example, let's say you purchased some groceries from an online retailer that accepts Bitcoin. To render payment using your wallet, the merchant must provide you with an *address*. You can think of an address as an account number, except that its value may change with every transaction. (We'll discuss the reasoning for this approach later in this chapter.) To complete the transaction, you direct your wallet to send the appropriate amount of Bitcoin to the merchant's address. Conversely, when you are the recipient, you instruct your Bitcoin wallet to generate an address that you provide to whoever is sending you a payment.

Before continuing, let's review some security measures discussed earlier in this chapter. Then, we will describe how Bitcoin wallets integrate these features to ensure transaction integrity. (Feel free to skip over this summary if you feel comfortable with hash functions and keys.)

Hash Function	A *hash function* returns a fixed-length value for a given input. Thus, if you applied the identical "hash" algorithm to the message "Hello, World!" and a pdf file containing the full text of this book, the length of the output would be the same (e.g., 256 bits). However, the resulting bit values for each result would be unique.
	Hash values are repeatable: Every time you run a hashing algorithm on the same input, it generates the identical output. Thus, you can ascertain whether someone "tampered" (i.e., added, deleted, or rearranged) a message's contents simply by rerunning the hashing algorithm and determining whether it produces the same output.

---

[24] At 1:15 p.m. EST.
[25] Some Bitcoin wallets can hold and manage cryptocurrencies other than Bitcoin.

Hashing algorithms are one-way. So, for example, if given the hash value for a pdf file, you could not recreate its original content.

Public/Private Keys We use public/private key pairs to encrypt and decrypt messages. We begin this process by generating a *public key* from a *private key*. The private key must always remain secret. However, we can share the public key with the world. Once we do so, anyone can use our public key to encrypt a message that may only be decrypted using our private key.

Another feature of public/private key pairs is that we can create digital signatures. For example, senders can "sign" an email using a private key. Then, recipients can use the corresponding public key to validate that the associated private key created the digital signature.

Note that public key generation is also one-way: We can't derive the private key from the public key.

Okay, let's see how Bitcoin wallets leverage these security measures.

Regardless of their type (see below), all Bitcoin wallets require a private key when created. For some wallets, the cryptocurrency software generates the private key automatically during account initialization; for others, the user can select it.

The wallet uses its private key to sign all transactions. As a result, you must keep the value of your private key secret. If hackers discover it, they can quickly transfer the contents of your wallet to theirs. As noted previously, all Bitcoin transactions are anonymous and irreversible. Therefore, it's doubtful that you'd ever get your money back. Thus, I highly recommend choosing a wallet that allows you to create your own private key and keep it safe.

Once configured, Bitcoin wallets process transactions as depicted in Figure 8.11.

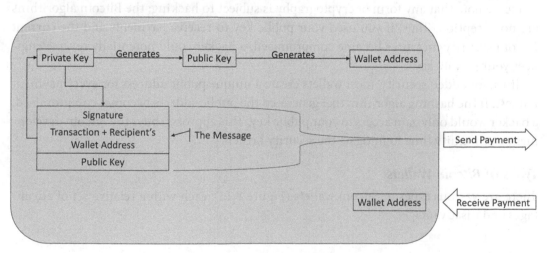

FIGURE 8.11   Inside a Bitcoin wallet.

When preparing to make a payment, the wallet confirms that it has sufficient "funds" to complete the specified transaction. Next, it creates a public key based on its private key and the hash function. It then combines transaction information with the recipient's wallet address to generate the payment "message," which it then "signs" using the private key. Thus, a complete "payment packet" includes the message (i.e., the transaction information), the wallet's signature, and the transaction's public key (Figure 8.12).

After "publishing" the transaction, the wallet deducts the payment amount from its available funds.

To accept a payment, recipients direct their wallets to generate a public address based on a "hash" of the user's public key. Once created, the recipient forwards that address to the person sending them money. After receiving the remittance, the wallet adds the amount collected to its spendable balance.

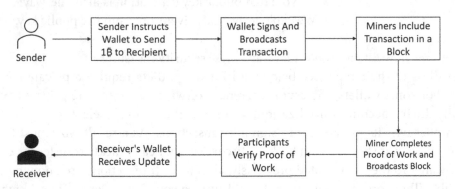

FIGURE 8.12   High-level Bitcoin transaction flow.

Please note that any form of cryptography is subject to hacking; the Bitcoin algorithms are no exception. Thus, if you used your public key to receive payments and the current Bitcoin security measures became compromised, a hacker could potentially reverse engineer your private key.

Thus, for added security, most wallets create a unique public address for every payment request. If the hashing algorithm that generated the public address becomes compromised, a hacker would only gain access to your public key. This approach buys the Bitcoin development community time to mitigate the security breach.

Types of Bitcoin Wallets

There are various types of Bitcoin wallets (Figure 8.13), each with a relative set of advantages and disadvantages.

FIGURE 8.13   Physical Bitcoins.

Paper   A paper Bitcoin "wallet" is not a wallet *per se*. Instead, it's simply a piece of paper with the wallet's private key printed as a QR code.[26] Although they are intuitive to use, paper wallets are subject to many of the issues associated with traditional cash: They are easily misplaced, vulnerable to theft, and are subject to damage (e.g., spilling coffee on them) and physical deterioration (i.e., the ink could fade over time). Moreover, because they have only one address printed on them, they foster address reuse for every transaction. (As noted above, this is a security issue.)

Nonetheless, paper wallets do have some advantages. Because they are not "online," they are not subject to hacking. A thief must gain access to the physical piece of paper, not its digital footprint. Moreover, you can store them for extended periods at home, in a safe, or in a bank's safe deposit box.

However, if you acquired (i.e., printed) a paper wallet from a third-party service, hackers could access the provider's systems and obtain the paper wallet's private key. Later, when you try to use it, you might discover that your wallet is empty.

---

[26] QR codes are a "rectangular" type of barcode.

Coin   There have been some attempts to create tangible forms of cryptocurrencies that look like coins. Typically, each coin (or *token*) would contain a key that remained hidden under a holographic label. To use them, owners would peel back the sticker to reveal the private key.

Alas, the US Government quickly quashed this option, declaring that such a process was equivalent to minting coins and, therefore, violated federal law. However, as of this writing, previously "minted" Bitcoin tokens still retain their value.

Exchange Wallets   Exchange Wallets are like online bank accounts. A third party (usually called an *Exchange*)[27] creates and manages the Bitcoin wallet on the owner's behalf—for a fee.

Although many experts consider them relatively safe, there have been numerous instances of hackers gaining access to an exchange's database and appropriating all the Bitcoin contained in every managed wallet. Thus, because you're relying on the integrity and diligence of an intermediary, you should consider Exchange Wallets the least safe option for storing your Bitcoin.

Hot Wallets   The most common and convenient form of Bitcoin depository is a *Hot Wallet*. A Hot Wallet is an app that runs on computers and other intelligent devices (e.g., a smartphone).[28] As used in this context, the term "hot" indicates that smart devices immediately connect to the Internet when powered on. Therefore, any Bitcoin wallets they host are always available for use.

Hot Wallets are the safest way to store and manage Bitcoin because the wallet's owner manages the keys. Nonetheless, though the instances are exceedingly rare, Hot Wallets are subject to hacking attacks while the underlying devices remain connected to public networks.

Cold Wallets   As depicted in Figure 8.14, a Cold Wallet is a hardware device designed to manage cryptocurrency. Often USB-based,[29] Cold Wallets remain offline until the owner plugs them into a computer or smart device. As a result, they are convenient, highly secure, and require an owner present when sending or receiving Bitcoin.

---

[27] Exchanges are private enterprises that, as of this writing, are not federally regulated, so *caveat emptor*.
[28] Some Hot Wallets are accessible via browsers as well.
[29] Please see Chapter 6 for a discussion of USB devices.

FIGURE 8.14   A Bitcoin Cold Wallet.

What is Mining?

Previously, we discussed how Bitcoin manages its ledger: Pending transactions accumulate into "blocks" that become part of a "chain." We also noted that each block requires a "PoW" and that, when adding new blocks to the chain, participants must include the previous block's "hash." In addition, the "PoW" secures Bitcoin transactions by ensuring that potential hackers must commit significantly more time and resources to an attack than any benefits they could expect to gain. That is, the intricacy of the process itself discourages hackers from even trying.

However, we still need to discuss how participants confirm the accuracy of Bitcoin's distributed blockchain, receive compensation for their work, and how new Bitcoin comes into existence. Because all these issues are related, we will discuss them together.

Let's begin with *mining*.

Because it's the digital equivalent of "digging for gold," we call the creation of new Bitcoin *mining*. Continuing the metaphor, we refer to the participants who engage in this process as *miners*.

The Bitcoin mining process achieves several important objectives including the following:

- It serves as a financial incentive for participants (e.g., miners). Otherwise, why would anyone commit the computing resources to the task?

- It ensures the integrity of Bitcoin's public ledger (i.e., its blockchain). As we will see, part of a miner's responsibility is to authenticate every transaction included in a block. (As discussed above, for added security, every participant also certifies the integrity of every block added to the blockchain.)

Before we describe Bitcoin's mining process in detail, let's take a moment to review the sequence of events involved when adding a new block to the blockchain.

1. Every Bitcoin exchange begins as a *pending transaction* that the originator's wallet broadcasts to all nodes in the network.

2. Upon receipt, miners aggregate pending transactions into *candidate blocks*. As part of this process, miners validate signatures and ensure that each transaction it adds to its candidate block does not appear in any prior blocks. (We can't allow wallets to spend the same Bitcoin twice.)

3. When blocks become "filled," miners "race" to compute[30] the candidate block's PoW. As soon as they complete their work, miners share the block with all participants.

4. Upon receipt, all participants validate the contents of every block added to the block-chain. Post validation, the miner receives an award of newly minted Bitcoin—in addition to any transaction fees they may have collected.

5. Miners begin processing the next block as soon as participants declare the current candidate block "accepted."

Now, let's discuss how the Bitcoin software completes these tasks.

As noted in Steps 1 and 2, miners aggregate pending transactions into the next candidate block. However, this is not necessarily on a first-come, first-served basis. On the contrary, miners may select transactions based on fees: The higher the compensation a pending transaction offers, the more likely a miner would include it into its next candidate block.

Note that this is nothing more or less than free enterprise in digital form. However, this does imply that because they can "cherry-pick," each minor can create blocks with a unique set of transactions that appear in any sequence.

That said, transaction ordering *within* a block is significant. For example, consider a Bitcoin wallet containing 5Ƀ and the following two pending transactions:

A. The wallet receives 10Ƀ

B. The wallet spends 12Ƀ

Miners must ensure that transaction A occurs before transaction B. Otherwise, they would reject transaction B.

In addition to ensuring proper sequence, miners must validate each transaction and ensure that wallets do not double spend.

As indicated in Step 3, after completing a candidate block, miners race to compute the PoW. When finished, miners broadcast the new candidate block to all Bitcoin participants. We will return to this point shortly.

---

[30] As we will see, this is a competition and computing power counts.

In Step 4, all participants certify that the candidate block meets all Bitcoin requirements. Specifically, they must:

- Validate all transactions contained within the block,

- Ensure that "sending" wallets have sufficient Bitcoin to complete the transaction (i.e., wallets can't spend Bitcoin they don't have), and

- Verify that all transactions are unique (i.e., wallets can't spend the same Bitcoin more than once).

A candidate block becomes "accepted" and officially joins the blockchain when participants complete their validation. At this point, the miner receives a "reward" of newly "mined" Bitcoin.

Although the processing we just described is conceptually straightforward, we must consider a few practical considerations.

- Multiple miners can complete and broadcast candidate blocks simultaneously.

- Because they are free-to-choose transactions based on self-interest, each miner's block may vary in content.

- Bitcoin depends on a network: The Internet. In turn, networks rely upon physical devices that can fail and are subject to propagation delays.[31] Thus, candidate blocks can arrive at different destinations at different times and in different sequences—or not at all.

Given that miners can distribute differing candidate blocks and the network is subject to anomalies, how do individual Bitcoin participants determine which block to add to the chain? Or, more to the point, two (or more) divergent blockchains could arise, resulting in multiple versions of the "truth."

Obviously, few investors would support a currency market where such situations could remain unresolved. Not to worry, however, because Bitcoin participants will eventually converge on *one* version of the truth.

The best way to understand how this process unfolds is by way of an example.

Suppose two miners,[32] A and B, generate two different candidate blocks and publish them simultaneously. Let's further assume that 80% of the other miners (we'll call them Group 1) received the candidate block from Miner A, and the remaining 20% (let's call them Group 2) received the candidate block from Miner B. Thus, after each group validates its respective blocks, the result is that the Bitcoin community has two divergent— seemingly valid—blockchains. (Let's call them Chain A and Chain B, respectively.)

Fortunately, this situation is temporary and self-resolving. Let's see how that happens.

The miners in Group 1 will construct their next candidate block using Block A. Likewise, the miners in Group B will base their next candidate on Block B. However, because Group

---

[31] As discussed in Chapter 6.

[32] It can be more, but we will limit our example to two to simplify the discussion. Nonetheless, regardless of the number of miners involved the reconciliation process functions the same way.

A has four times as many miners, it's statistically unlikely that the next candidate block will come from a miner in Group B. Thus, Chain A will grow faster than Chain B. In addition, because miners always choose the longest chain, Chain B will quickly become "ancient history." (We call this an *orphan chain*).

Note that any unconfirmed transactions in Block B (now on the orphan chain) are not lost because they will eventually become part of a future block on Chain A. That is, at some point, the Group A miners will include any remaining unconfirmed transactions in one of their subsequent candidate blocks.

How is a Bitcoin Transaction Confirmed?

As noted above, Bitcoin transactions may become part of an orphan block and are not confirmed until they appear on a block that eventually resides on the main blockchain. Given that this might take some time to resolve, how do recipients know when they can spend the Bitcoin someone else sent them? In other words, when is a Bitcoin transaction *confirmed*?

Let's take this by the numbers.

- First, a miner must select a given transaction to include in a candidate block. Until that happens, the transaction remains unconfirmed.

- On average, miners create a new Bitcoin block every 10 minutes. Thus, once selected, it could take up to 10 minutes for a transaction to receive its first confirmation (i.e., when participants validate the block on which it resides).

- As the blockchain grows, existing blocks and transactions receive an additional confirmation with every newly added block.

So, given this sequence of events, how many confirmations are sufficient?

Because of the possibility of divergent chains, the recommendation is that a Bitcoin transaction must receive six confirmations before it's considered "complete."[33] Thus, it takes about 1 hour (six confirmations at 10-minute intervals) to confirm a Bitcoin transaction.

ADVANCED SECTION

What are Other Uses of Blockchain Technology?

As we have discovered, blockchain is a revolutionary technology that affords many benefits. To summarize, blockchain implementations are as follows:

- *Decentralized:* No single person or agency maintains control or asserts influence

- *Trustless:* They minimize—and often eliminate—the need to rely on the integrity of any single person or entity

---

[33] The math to demonstrate this is beyond the scope of this text.

- *Transparent:* Every participant has access to the public ledger and can review and validate every transaction

- *Economical:* Their designs make them relatively inexpensive to implement and maintain

- *Anonymous:* If used appropriately, participant identities may remain undisclosed

- *Verifiability:* Signed entries (i.e., the hashing function) ensure and maintain the provenance of all messages added to the ledger

Given these advantages, blockchains can serve as the underpinning for many other solutions beyond digital currencies.[34] Below are descriptions of some noteworthy applications of this powerful technology.

Intellectual property	As noted earlier, blockchain "messages" can comprise any string of characters.[35] Thus, we could "hash" a file containing a manuscript, screenplay, or recorded piece of music. Then, when we insert its signature on a blockchain, we've registered an immutable timestamp for its creation. Please recall that because the hash is "one way," no one could recreate the original content. Many organizations offer blockchain-based timestamp registration services. Such applications could eventually alter or obviate the need for copyright registration in the future.
Medical records	Today, health records are often scattered and are subject to unwarranted prying eyes. Blockchains could provide a secure, centralized, and convenient place to maintain medical data. Then, when required, patients could provide their health-care providers a one-time key to access their personal information.
Supply chain logistics	Blockchains would allow a secure, permanent record tracking the provenance of goods and services. For example, some companies support the real-time tracking of food products from farm to store. In addition to the transparency-afforded consumers, public health authorities will benefit from the detailed traceability if issues arise (e.g., a salmonella outbreak).
Government accountability	All levels of government—from federal to municipal—could open their accounting systems to their constituents by recording all transactions—payments, receipts, contract awards, etc.—via a public ledger.

---

[34] When used in more general applications, we often refer to blockchain technology as Distributed Ledger Technology (DLT).

[35] In this context, we would use the term *bytes* rather than *characters.*

Authenticated voting Although it would require some changes to the voter registration process, a blockchain-based public ledger could record all votes and ensure accurate counting.

Property management Blockchains can record property ownership and title transfers simply and inexpensively.

SUMMARY

From early forms of bartering to modern-day cryptocurrencies, this chapter presented the history, development, and management of currency.

We began our discussions by understanding the nature of money. We then reviewed the emergence of financial exchange from bartering to commodity-backed transactions to cryptocurrency and learned that all forms of monetary systems rely on trust.

Our discussion moved on to the design and implementation of Bitcoin, the oldest form of cryptocurrency. We reviewed how Bitcoin uses various technologies—from hashing to blockchains—to ensure a transparent, secure, and reliable implementation.

In the Advanced Section, we also discovered that Bitcoin's underpinning—blockchain technology—can serve as the basis for many future applications.

CHAPTER 9

What Is Artificial Intelligence?

The development of full artificial intelligence could spell the end of the human race.... It would take off on its own and re-design itself at an ever-increasing rate. Humans, who are limited by slow biological evolution, couldn't compete, and would be superseded.

STEPHEN HAWKING

Artificial intelligence would be the ultimate version of Google. The ultimate search engine that would understand everything on the web. It would understand exactly what you wanted, and it would give you the right thing. We're nowhere near doing that now. However, we can get incrementally closer to that, and that is basically what we work on.

LARRY PAGE

Forget artificial intelligence – in the brave new world of big data, it's artificial idiocy we should be looking out for.

TOM CHATFIELD

Before we work on artificial intelligence why don't we do something about natural stupidity?

STEVE POLYAK

INTRODUCTION

Let me begin by apologizing for the number and variety of quotes introducing this chapter. The fact is, however, most folks I know express polarizing views on this subject: They believe that Artificial Intelligence (AI) is either the best or the worst technology ever developed by humankind.

Nonetheless, as with most issues of this nature, I'm sure the truth lies somewhere in the middle. Because, like all technologies, AI's power to benefit or undermine the human condition resides in the hands of the individuals wielding it.

DOI: 10.1201/9781003143437-9

As an example, consider social media. It indeed allows folks to share information and knowledge—this is fantastic. However, as an unintended consequence, it also allows a small group of individuals to control the dissemination of information—this is scary.

Although you might not appreciate it, AI is pervasive. Indeed, you're already interacting with it: You can find it used in email spam detectors, response suggestions when texting, asking Alexa for a weather report, etc. Nonetheless, by the time you conclude reading this chapter, you'll be able to develop your own informed opinion on the relative merits of this powerful technology.

WHAT IS HUMAN INTELLIGENCE?

The definition of human intelligence is a complex question and is the subject of many books and ongoing scientific research. Thus, we will not do justice to the topic in just one section of one chapter in a technology book. Nonetheless, I believe it's essential to understand human intelligence before presenting the artificial version.

Researchers[1] have developed many theories and models that describe human intelligence, each defining a unique set of attributes and characteristics. For our purposes, we will distill these ideas as follows.

At a minimum, human intelligence comprises the following capabilities:

- *Learning:* Gaining knowledge from experience

- *Adapting:* Reacting to new experiences

- *Manipulating:* Changing one's environment

As you read this list, I'm sure many more capabilities came to mind. However, these three form the foundation of human intelligence. We will use these attributes as a baseline when discussing AI later in this chapter.

How Does the Human Brain Work?

As previously mentioned,[2] we can liken the human brain to a computer's CPU. However, instead of an array of integrated circuits, it comprises an amalgamation of 80–100 billion[3] interconnected nerve cells called *neurons*.

See Figure 9.1 for an example.

There are several types of neurons, each of which differs in structure. However, as depicted in Figure 9.2, they all contain a *cell body*, a *nucleus*, an *axon*, a *synapse*, and as many as 100,000 *dendrites*.

Dendrites serve as inputs: They receive impulses from other neurons and pass the signal onto the *cell body*. *Axons* serve as the output channel: They forward information to other neurons or cells. The point of connection is a *neuronal junction* called a *synapse*. When sending messages, neurons release a *chemical messenger* called a *neurotransmitter*.

---

[1] Lewis Terman, Edward L. Thorndike, Raymond B. Cattell, John L. Horn, and John B. Carroll, just to name a few.
[2] Please refer to Chapters 4 and 5.
[3] Estimates vary.

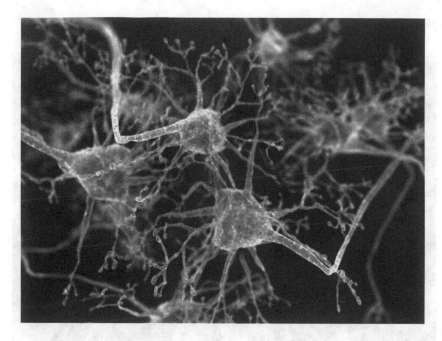

FIGURE 9.1   Interconnected neurons.

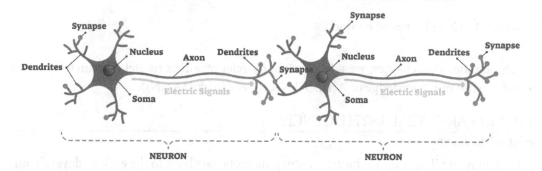

FIGURE 9.2   Neuron anatomy.

What are the Types of Neurons?

We classify neurons as follows:

Sensory	As their name implies, *sensory neurons* receive input from the senses. For example, when you hear a bird singing on a beautiful spring day, sensory neurons carry the sound information to the brain.
Motor	Located in the spinal cord, *motor neurons* send impulses to your muscles and thus trigger and control movement.
Interneurons	The function of *interneurons* is to interconnect motor and sensory neurons. They may also interact with other interneurons.

As depicted in Figure 9.3, neural networks can grow arbitrarily complex.

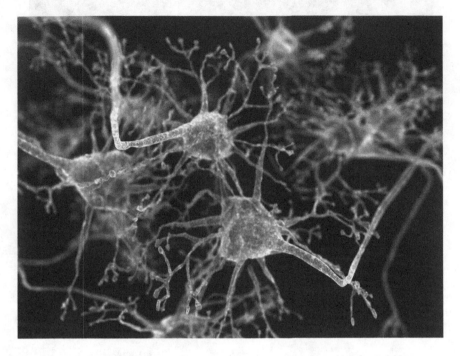

FIGURE 9.3   Complex neural network.

Throughout this chapter, we will continually reference this model of human neurons as we expand our knowledge of Artificial Neural Networks (ANNs).

WHAT IS ARTIFICIAL INTELLIGENCE?

Historical Roots

Although AI is all the rage in the 21st century, its roots date back to the earliest days of computer science. In 1950, in his publication entitled *Computing Machinery and Intelligence*, Alan Turing[4] posed the question: Can machines think?

To address this problem, Mr. Turing proposed a test he called "The Imitation Game" (Figure 9.4)[5] The rules are as follows:

1. There is a human interrogator and two participants (Figure 9.4)

2. One of the participants is human; the other is a machine that can provide anthropomorphic (human-like) responses

3. The interrogator and the two participants must remain isolated throughout the test

---

[4] Among his many achievements, Mr. Turing was instrumental in breaking the German Enigma code during WWII. Historians estimate that his work shortened the war by at least 2 years and saved more than 14 million lives. Nonetheless, despite his status as a war hero, he was prosecuted in 1952 for engaging in "homosexual acts." Sadly, in 1954, less than a month before his 42nd birthday, Mr. Turing died of an apparent suicide.

[5] This is now commonly referred to as the Turing test.

4. The interrogator is aware that one of the participants is a machine

5. The interrogator may question each participant using natural language

6. Participants must respond using natural language

7. Interactions take place using a keyboard and screen

8. Participants don't have to answer questions correctly, but all interactions must appear human

9. If the interrogator cannot accurately determine which participant is human after completing the questioning, the machine "passes the test."

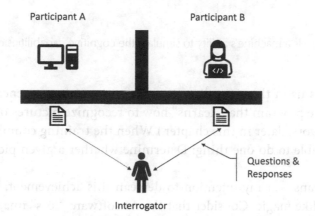

FIGURE 9.4 The Imitation Game.

Though both lauded and criticized, the Turing test set the foundation for future research into AI.

A few years later, in 1956, John McCarthy coined the phrase "artificial intelligence" at the first-ever AI conference (held at Dartmouth College). (Mr. McCarthy would go on to invent the Lisp language in 1958.) Later that year, Allen Newell, J. C. Shaw, and Herbert Simon created the Logic Theorist, the first AI software program.

In the 1980s, neural networks that use *backpropagation*[6] algorithms for training became widely used in AI applications. Then, slightly more than a decade later, in 1995, another significant development occurred. In their coauthored book entitled *Artificial Intelligence: A Modern Approach*, Stuart Russell and Peter Norvig further refined the definition of AI as follows:

- Systems that think like humans

- Systems that act like humans

- Systems that think rationally

- Systems that act rationally

---

[6] Discussed later in this chapter.

Today, AI has exploded onto the computing scene. We have chess games that can beat grand masters, medical diagnostics systems that are more accurate than doctors, self-driving cars, automated image recognition, smart speakers—and the list is growing.

However, before we can delve more deeply into these applications, we need an intuitive understanding of AI.

What is the Definition of AI?

Unfortunately, there isn't a single industry-accepted definition for AI. However, there are several ways by which we can arrive at a common understanding of its nature.

Let's start with the following definition.

DEFINITION 1

Artificial intelligence is a machine's ability to simulate the cognitive capabilities of human beings.

Although it moves us in the right direction, Definition 1 is too general. For example, consider a software program that "learns" how to recognize pictures of cats.[7] (We'll see how this process works later in this chapter.) When the training completes, the application will only be able to do one thing: Determine whether a given picture contains an image of a cat.

Now, by no means is it my intention to demean this achievement. On the contrary, it almost appears like magic. Consider that the AI software "sees" images as an array of pixels[8] (picture elements). It has no context, only a series of "dots." Yet, such programs are astoundingly accurate.

Nevertheless, the question remains: How do we equate such processing to human intelligence?

Image recognition programs such as the one discussed above must often undergo extensive training to recognize various objects. Let's compare that to the human experience: Show a 5-year-old one picture of a cat; subsequently, that child will be highly successful in identifying other photos containing felines. Thus, by comparison, humans usually *learn* much faster that an AI application.

But how quickly and efficiently can humans process images compared to an automated approach? Let's consider a more significant use of image recognition software to address that question.

Military strategists require information about their adversaries to develop successful plans. Thus, they often sortie aircraft to fly over and photograph enemy installations. When each flight returns, which would serve them better: Asking humans to review the thousands of pictures taken? Or process them using a program specifically "trained" to recognize images of military weaponry?

---

[7] The Internet's enduring fascination with felines never ceases to amaze me.
[8] See Chapter 5.

Obviously, the automated approach would classify images faster and more accurately. However, after performing the analysis, human strategists would be far better at formulating a plan of attack—another form of intelligence.

The previous example highlights the chasm in the current state of AI applications. They are highly efficient at many complex tasks. However, they cannot "think" and "react" like humans.

That said, consider the complexity involved in developing self-driving automobiles. The vehicle's AI software must:

- Acquire images from onboard cameras

- Classify the objects appearing in the images (poles, cars, people, cats, etc.)

- Determine which objects might serve as directives (e.g., stop signs, traffic lights)

- By processing successive images (along with input from other sensors such as radar),[9] determine which objects are moving and compute their trajectories (i.e., is the car going to collide with a bike that might be traveling across the street)

- While doing the above, maintain control of the vehicle (i.e., keep it on course toward its destination)

Please note that all the processing described above must be accurate and occur in real time (i.e., as fast as possible). Nonetheless, despite the level of complexity, AI holds the promise of safer roads and more relaxing commutes.

What are AI Levels?

As alluded to previously, there are levels of complexity within AI software. Broadly speaking, we can group AI solutions into three distinct categories.

Weak[10]	We define a weak AI solution as one that can perform a single task better than a human being—this represents the current state of AI technology. Examples include chess games, smart assistants (e.g., Google Home, Alexa, Siri), language translators, and self-driving cars.
	Despite their almost fantastic ability to perform human-like tasks, we classify these AI solutions as "weak" because they don't possess human-like intelligence. Specifically, they are not *self-aware* and don't *think* in any human sense of the term.
Strong[11]	We define a strong AI solution as one that can perform any intellectual task associated with human capabilities.

---

[9] Self-driving cars integrate many technologies such as GPS (Chapter 3), radar, and lasers.
[10] This category is also referred to as Narrow AI.
[11] This category is also referred to as General AI.

Such machines are sentient and self-aware and can reason, think, and emote like their human counterparts. At the time of this writing, this is the stuff of science fiction.

Super If ever achieved, super AI will surpass human intelligence. This potential future capability fuels the fears of individuals who believe machines will one day lead to the demise of the human species. We'll return to this concern later in this chapter.

AI Cognitive Skills

Analogous to the way humans process information, AI solutions require some "intellectual" abilities. Referred to as "cognitive skills," the following list describes some essential capabilities of all AI applications.

Learning AI applications "learn" by uncovering relationships among data elements to produce rules that inform future processing. Ignoring the details for a moment, a "cat recognition" program is an excellent example of AI learning. After it's developed, the program undergoes a training phase.[12] Once completed, it can successfully identify images that include cats.

Reasoning In the world of AI, reasoning is the ability to select the appropriate *algorithm* to achieve a specific result. An algorithm is like a recipe: If you start with the proper ingredients (i.e., the data) and accurately follow all the steps (i.e., the instructions), you'll eventually enjoy a delicious treat.

More formally, we can define an algorithm as follows:

> **DEFINITION 2**
>
> An *algorithm* is a solution methodology suitable for implementation on a computer.

Thus, to "reason," AI programs must select the appropriate algorithm and apply it to the data at hand.

Self-Correction Self-correction is the process by which AI programs adjust their algorithms based on feedback. For example, an image recognition program will "guess" whether a given photo includes a feline image during its training phase. Then, based on each result (i.e., "correct" or "incorrect"), the program will adjust its algorithm accordingly.

---

[12] We'll discuss this in more detail later in the text.

Human Intelligence vs. AI

Before we move too far ahead, let's pause for a moment to compare humans and AI.

- Humans naturally use innate cognitive processes when adapting to new environments or solving problems. AI solutions only mimic human behavior for some very narrow tasks.

- The human brain contains somewhere between 80 and 100 billion neurons; AI neural networks have on the order of hundreds to thousands.

- The human mind is the seat of consciousness; AI has no equivalent.

- The human mind is analog; computers are digital.

- Humans can reason, recall, and think; AI relies on programmed instructions.

Please keep these differences in mind as we explore this topic further.

WHAT ARE THE BASIC TYPES OF AI?

Thus far, we've considered AI-based solutions that can drive cars, play games, respond to spoken commands, and classify images. However, you also may have noticed that, thus far, we haven't spoken about AI-based machines that are sentient, self-aware, and possess human-level intelligence.

That's because science is not there yet.

That begs the next obvious question: How advanced is AI technology? In other words, how long until we can no longer distinguish humans from *replicants*?[13]

The discussions below describe the different classes of AI:

TYPE I   Often called *reactive machines*, Type I AI solutions lack "memory" and the ability to leverage past experiences to improve future choices. A typical example is a chess-playing game. Such software can:

- o Identify each chess piece and its relative location on the game board

- o "Understand" how each chess piece moves (i.e., the rules of the game)

- o Examine a board position

- o Determine the best move for itself and its opponent

- o Select an optimal move from a set of legal choices

---

[13] *Replicant* is the term used to describe bioengineered beings appearing in the 1982 film *Blade Runner*.

Chess computers have become quite "expert" and regularly beat human grandmasters. Nonetheless, they cannot learn from the past. That is, they can't leverage the results of previous choices to improve future ones. Nor can they derive any advantage from understanding how a given opponent plays (i.e., their tendencies). Instead, they repeatedly "start over" and reexamine the game's current state during each round to compute their next move.

TYPE II A Type II, or limited-memory AI solution, "remembers" past events and uses that information to inform future decisions. For example, to compute trajectories, self-driving cars must track and record the motion of moving objects.

Nonetheless, the "memories" are not permanent. That is, self-driving cars can't learn to be better drivers. Currently, such improvements still require human intervention.

Type III Human beings have thoughts, ideas, memories, emotions, etc., that affect behaviors. Psychologists refer to this phenomenon as the *theory of mind*. Future AI research focuses on machines that can simulate the human mental state by developing representations of their environment, thus allowing them to alter behavior based on human interactions and perceived intentions.

Type IV Type IV machines are self-aware. Thus, they can form representations about themselves. However, researchers must fully understand human consciousness before simulating it in an inanimate object.

Types I and II exist today. Types III and IV are not even on the horizon. We'll discuss the ramifications of future AI research later in this chapter.

What are AI Subclasses?

Now that we understand its types and levels, let's head to the deep end of the AI pool and discuss its *subclasses*.

General AI We can say that any program has some level of *cognition* if it can perceive its environment and adjust its behaviors accordingly.

Machine learning Machine Learning (ML) is the ability of AI programs to infer correlations among data elements and adjust behaviors based on experience. Specifically, ML allows programs to recognize patterns and "decide" on the best course of action with little (or no) human intervention.

Deep Learning Like ML, Deep Learning (DL) trains AI algorithms to categorize, infer, and predict outcomes. The difference is that DL implementations use many more *layers*. This distinction will become more apparent when we discuss neural networks later in this chapter.

What are the Types of Learning Algorithms?

As we have already mentioned, most AI programs must undergo "training" before becoming functional. There are several types of learning algorithms: Unsupervised, supervised, and reinforcement.

Unsupervised	With *unsupervised learning*, AI algorithms uncover patterns in unstructured data sets without human intervention. Examples include categorizing news articles, recommending purchase suggestions to customers, and identifying anomalies in system logs such as security breaches and component failures.
Supervised	All *supervised learning* requires structured data sets to ensure the algorithm's accuracy. Examples of this approach include classifying images, identifying objects within images, and sentiment analysis.[14]
Reinforcement	Quite possibly the most complex form of ML, Reinforcement Learning (RL) requires that the algorithm learns how to make decisions by trial and error. It determines success by maximizing a reward. For example, consider an industrial robot that tries many different packing approaches to identify the one that maximizes the number of orders it can fulfill.

Some Thoughts about Machine Learning

Like any technology in its infancy, AI is subject to urban legend, hyperbole, marketing hype, and, in many cases, a thorough lack of understanding. Thus, let's take a moment to separate fact from fallacy.

Existing AI solutions don't *reason* or *think* in any human sense of these terms. Thus, based on the current state of AI technology, one can view ML and DL as just other ways to program computers. Indeed, they can "learn" to perform some incredible tasks. But it's still software, and it's still a form of programming.

Moreover, training is not "free," nor does it occur "in a vacuum." As mentioned earlier, it typically requires enormous data sets, statistical analyses, and significant human intervention. Additionally, this process is not a "one-and-done" proposition. Training of ML- and DL-based systems must persist as long as the underlying data sets evolve. Thus, ML and DL programs don't improve without continuous training and feedback.

Unlike their portrayal in science fiction books and movies, ML and DL solutions are not 100% accurate. They are only as good as the underlying training data sets. For example, image recognition applications are subject to both false positives and false negatives. Thus, depending on the significance of the application (think military intelligence), training-based solutions will still require some level of human verification and oversight.

---

[14] Sentiment analysis derives subjective information from text, voice, and biometric data.

The above notwithstanding, I'm not advocating AI avoidance. On the contrary, given that it's here to stay, I think we should embrace and leverage the power of this remarkable technology. Nonetheless, I also believe you should retain a healthy dose of human skepticism when dealing with AI hype.

USES OF AI

Natural Language Processing

Natural Language Processing (NLP) is the ability of AI solutions to "understand" spoken words (speech recognition) and convert them into text for further processing (speech to text). In addition, NLP solutions can also transform text-based results into verbal responses.

NLP should be familiar to anyone who uses Siri, Alexa, or Google Assistant.

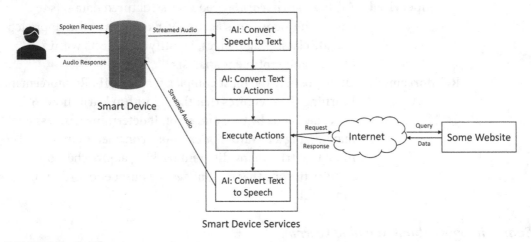

FIGURE 9.5   Inside a smart assistant.

As depicted in Figure 9.5, most smart devices rely on AI-based algorithms to implement many of their features. However, note that they also rely on traditional processing techniques (e.g., accessing data via the Internet) to satisfy user requests.

Computer Vision

In its simplest form, computer vision is the ability of AI programs to classify images. In more advanced applications, computer vision solutions extract information from the content of pictures, videos, and streaming data, allowing systems to analyze and respond to their environments.

Most folks are familiar with self-driving cars. However, computer vision applications are far more prevalent. Examples include automated inspection of products on assembly lines, medical diagnostics, and animal monitoring on farms.

Putting It All Together

As depicted in Figure 9.6, AI solutions can accept input of various forms, convert it to a digital representation, store it in a suitable format, process it, then execute commands, and generate human-compatible output (spoken or visual) as appropriate.

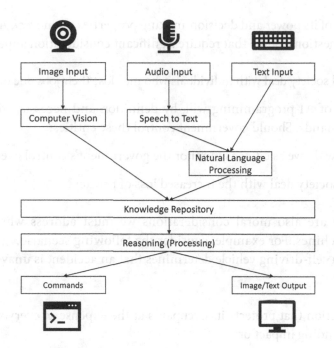

FIGURE 9.6 A complete AI solution (conceptual).

AI: ADVANTAGES AND DISADVANTAGES

Like any technology, AI has advantages and disadvantages. In addition, because of its autonomous nature, AI poses some ethical concerns as well.

The following are some benefits provided by AI-based solutions.

- Algorithms don't need vacations, sick days, breaks, etc. They are available 24×7×365.

- Machines don't get tired or bored. Thus, they are well-suited for all types of monotonous tasks that would quickly fatigue a human being.

- Unlike humans, machines provide predictable and repeatable results regardless of the time of day, day of the week, or season of the year.

- Many AI solutions perform better than their human counterparts.

- Machines are not subject to emotions.

- AI-based customer service solutions never grow exasperated with callers.

Despite its prevalence and power, we can't ignore AI's disadvantages.

First, AI will likely eliminate many jobs: Truck drivers, factory workers, medical professionals, etc. But to be fair, this is not a new phenomenon: All forms of automation are guilty of that charge. Historically, however, employment gains in existing or new professions often offset the losses.

Next, because of its power and decision-making properties, even *weak* AI solutions raise several ethical questions. Some that require significant consideration appear below.

- How should society deal with individuals who may lose their jobs due to AI automation?

- The power of AI programming will, by definition and necessity, reside in a small number of hands. Should government control these entities?

- In turn, how do we as citizens monitor the government's control over AI solutions?

- How does society deal with the increased loss of privacy?

Ironically, there are also moral considerations we must address when dealing with autonomous machines. For example, consider the following scenario.

Assume that a self-driving vehicle determines that an accident is unavoidable. Given a choice, should it:

- Select an action that protects its occupants at the expense of everyone else involved in the impending impact or

- Take measures to minimize overall damage but at the risk of injuring its riders.

Stated another way, should a self-driving car protect its passengers at all costs? Or should it opt for the "greater good?" Moreover, if this is a configurable option, who gets to choose: The vehicle owner or the government (society)?

One final thought: If AI ever attains the level of *super* (see above) by definition, it will have exceeded every aspect of human intelligence. Many people believe this scenario will inevitably lead to the "rise of the machines." To protect the public, should government enact laws requiring AI designers to integrate "hooks" (i.e., controls) into all AI-based devices to ensure society can control them?

HOW DO NEURAL NETWORKS FUNCTION?

Now that we're familiar with the AI paradigm, let's consider a specific implementation: *Neural networks*. We'll begin our discussions by describing how humans learn. We'll then review how AI developers use that understanding to create systems that model that behavior. Finally, for more adventurous readers, we'll include Java code that implements a rudimentary neural network in the Advanced Section.

Let's get started.

How Do Humans Learn?

Earlier in this chapter, we discussed *neurons*, a fundamental component of human brain anatomy (see Figure 9.7). As this is not a textbook intended for medical students, we need only note that neurons contain a *cell body* (including the *nucleus*), an *axon* that transmits messages to other neurons, and *synapses* that serve as the "contact points" to connect with other neurons.

NEURON

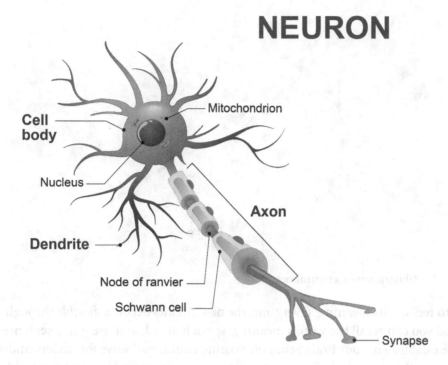

FIGURE 9.7 Anatomy of a neuron.

However, neurons do not exist in isolation. That is, the brain consists of an intricate web of interconnected neurons. For example, Figure 9.8 depicts how two neurons connect, and Figure 9.9 illustrates how many neurons connect to form a network.

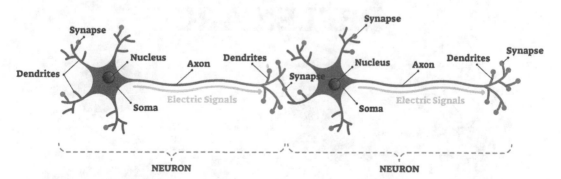

FIGURE 9.8 Two connected neurons.

When we learn, the brain alters neural circuits; this facilitates the transmission of signals along new or modified paths. For instance, while reading this book, you may have encountered a new idea or phrase. A good example might be the word "interneuron," which, as we learned earlier in this chapter, is a type of neuron that interconnects other neurons.

When you read that definition for the first time, your brain created several new neural paths: One to recognize the word's spelling, one to understand its pronunciation, and

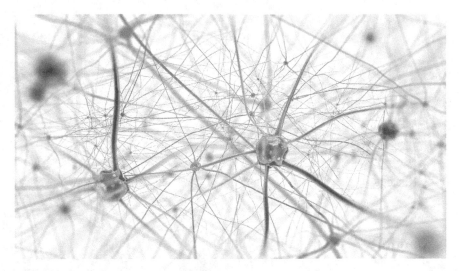

FIGURE 9.9   Illustration of a neural network.

others to register its meaning. Over time, the new circuits become *durable* through repetition, and you can recall the word's meaning, speak it aloud, and use it in a sentence.

Once established, your brain relies on existing neural pathways for understanding and recognition. For example, let's say you've never seen a cactus before, and you touch one of its thorns. Your hand reflexively pulls away at the moment of contact to prevent further discomfort. This type of response to pain is a previously learned behavior.

A simplified demonstration of the processing required to implement this scenario appears in Figure 9.10.

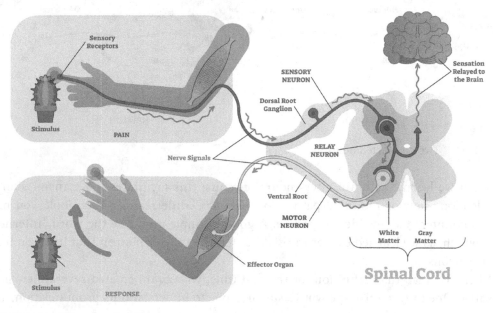

FIGURE 9.10   The arc of a reflex.

Again, as this is not a medical textbook, we need not describe the biological activity in excruciating anatomical detail; the main points for our discussion are as follows:

- There are preexisting (i.e., previously learned) neural pathways that allow the transmission of sensory input to the brain.

- Other preexisting pathways allow the brain to control (i.e., contract) the body's muscles.

- There is a learned response to touching something painful: Based on the input from sensory neurons, interneurons transmit signals to the brain, and output (motor) neurons generate (trigger) the response.

AI designers leverage this model of the brain to design and construct ANNs that mimic this behavior.

However, before we describe that process, we need to review the concept of *abstraction*.

What is an Abstraction?

When we build representations of real-world entities, we don't replicate every detail. If we did, we wouldn't have a model; we'd have the actual object. So, for example, if you were to purchase a model airplane, you wouldn't assume the kit included every nut, bolt, and rivet used to build the original. On the contrary, we'd expect only a set of representative parts that, when assembled, *resemble* the aircraft in question.

This approach holds true in the field of computer science as well.

When software engineers model real-world objects, they identify the essential attributes and ignore the rest. A typical example is a shopping cart. I'm sure every reader of this book has used one while purchasing goods and services from an online merchant. It behaves as we would intuitively expect it to: We can add, remove, and change the quantities of products in the cart. However, we don't have to deal with the squeaky wheel that thwarts our best efforts to steer straight and avoid colliding with displays of breakable products.

More formally, in computer science, we define an abstraction as follows:

> **DEFINITION 3**
>
> An *abstraction* is the distillation of a problem domain's essential and relevant attributes to simplify its representation.

Thus, when developing software abstractions, we must identify and implement the *relevant* features of real-world objects that mimic their behaviors to the extent *necessary* for our purposes.

In the sections that follow, we'll see how we can create abstractions of neural networks that mimic human learning.

How Do We Model Neurons?

Obviously, we can't implement a "real" neuron in software. Thus, as noted in the previous section, we need to create an abstraction that includes all the relevant features of the component we're modeling.

In the case of a human neuron, this consists of the following:

Nucleus	The *nucleus* controls and regulates all actions within a neuron.
Axon	The *axon* serves as the output channel of the neuron in that it transmits signals to other neurons.
Dendrites	A *dendrite* serves as an "input" channel" that receives signals from other neurons.

See Figure 9.11 for an example.

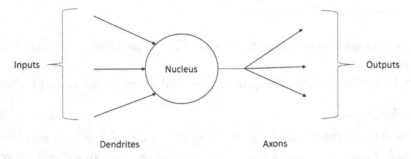

FIGURE 9.11   Abstracted neuron.

Although they may be significant in other applications, we need not include any other elements of a neuron in our abstraction.

How Do We Model Artificial Neural Networks?

Using the model proposed in the prior section, let's see how we can develop an abstraction of a neural network called an ANN. To begin, please recall that there are three major types of neurons, *sensory*, *motor*, and *interneurons*.

One of the main functions of neurons is to respond to sensory input. Figure 9.12 provides a simplified example of how that process works.

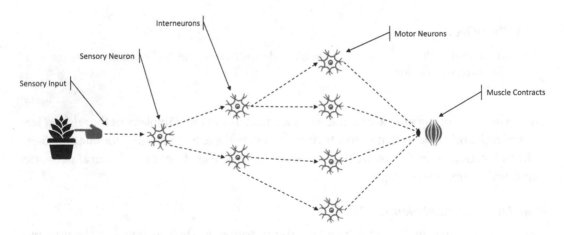

FIGURE 9.12   Response to sensory input.

When we touch something that causes pain, signals propagate along nerves to a sensory neuron, which forwards the event to the appropriate interneurons. Eventually, interneurons trigger specific motor neurons causing individual muscles to contract, relieving our discomfort.

We can model the neural pathways of this example as depicted in Figure 9.13.

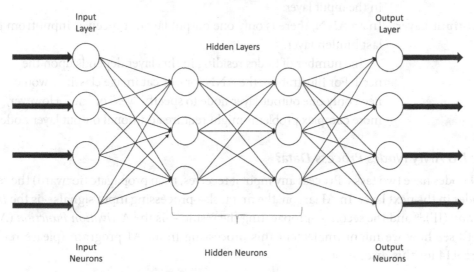

FIGURE 9.13   Abstract Neural Network (ANN).

In ANNs, we call sensory neurons *input nodes*; they reside on the *input layer*. Likewise, we refer to interneurons as *hidden nodes*; they exist in *hidden layers*, and motor neurons are *output nodes* and are part of the *output layer*.

A description of each ANN layer appears below.

Input layer   Nodes residing on the input layer receive data from external sources. Typically, the input layer would contain one node for each data element serving as input to the ANN.

So, for example, if we were writing an ANN to identify images containing cats, each input layer node would receive the value of one pixel.[15] Thus, we would size the input layer based on the number of pixels in the image.

Hidden layers   The function of a hidden layer node is to remove redundant information from the neural network. They receive and process "signals" from input nodes and then pass on the results to either other hidden nodes or directly to output nodes (see below).

Although ANNs may (and usually do) contain more than one hidden layer, no rules exist that specify how many you should use for a given problem domain. Based on my experience, most solutions require two or three.

---

[15] The term pixel refers to the basic picture element of a digital image or screen display. It contains the color and brightness of a single "dot" (point). Please refer to Chapter 5 for more detail.

Unfortunately, the same vagueness exists for determining the number of nodes that should reside within each hidden layer. While trial and error often rules the day, a good guesstimate is that hidden layers should contain less than twice the number of nodes residing in the input layer.

Output Layer   In an ANN, there is only one output layer. It receives input from the last hidden layer.

The number of nodes residing in this layer depends upon the need. For illustration, the ANN for our cat image classifier would need only one output-layer node to specify "yes" or "no." However, more complex problems might require additional output layer nodes.

How Do ANN Nodes Process Data?

ANN nodes have two tasks: Process any input it receives, then propagate (forward) the result to nodes in the next layer. In AI jargon, the first task—processing input signals—is the *Input Function* (IF),[16] and the second—propagating the results—is the *Activation Function* (AF).

Let's see how we might implement this processing in an AI program (please refer to Figure 9.14 for this discussion).

ANN Input Function

ANN nodes may have multiple input and output connections, each containing two attributes: A *value* and a *weight*. The *value* quantity represents actual data which are either direct input (e.g., the value of a pixel received by an input node) or the output generated by another node (i.e., the result of an AF; see below).

Weights[17] represent each node's relative importance in computing a correct result. For example, pixels near image borders might not be as significant (i.e., carry as much *weight*) as those nearer the center (where the cat's likeness likely exists). As we will see, by adjusting their relative weights, ANN nodes "learn" which inputs are consequential.

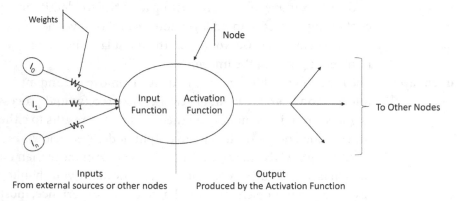

FIGURE 9.14   ANN node processing.

---

[16] This is also called the *net input function*.

[17] In some of the literature, node *weights* equate to *synapses*. For our purposes, I believe extending the metaphor to this extent adds unwarranted complexity.

We calculate the IF using the following formula:

Equation 9.1

$$\sum_{x=0}^{n} W_x \cdot I_x \quad .$$

Don't let the formal symbology intimidate you. When simplified, this formula is simply a *weighted sum* computed as follows:

Equation 9.2

$$f(x) = (W_0 \cdot I_0) + (W_1 \cdot I_1) + \cdots + (W_n \cdot I_n)$$

In other words, we multiply each input's *value* by its *weight* and then sum all the results.[18] (Note that the symbol *f(x)* represents the equation's result.)

Again, using our cat identifier as an example, for each image presented to the ANN, every one of its nodes (i.e., input, hidden, and output) uses this exact equation to calculate the weighted sum of its input.

The following section will discuss how a node uses this computed value as a component of its AF.

ANN Activation Function

An AF computes a node's *output*. The AF uses the result of the IF as input, then performs a selected mathematical operation (see below) to calculate an output *value*. This result is the value the node propagates to the next layer. Executing the AF is the artificial analog of a neuron "firing."

The mathematical operations used in AFs range in complexity depending on the ANN's objectives. One of the simplest is a *binary step function*. We compute it using the formula depicted in Equation 9.3.

Equation 9.3

$$AF = \begin{cases} 1 \text{ if } x \geq 1 \\ 0 \text{ if } x < 1 \end{cases}$$

Again, the formula is far simpler than the symbology makes it appear. Given that *x* represents the output of a node's IF, we interpret Equation 9.3 as follows:

The value of the AF is 1 if the IF is greater than or equal to 1

The value of the AF is 0 if the IF < 1

---

[18] In mathematics, this is called a *dot product*.

As noted previously, there are several types of AFs used in ANNs. Some examples include the following:

- Sigmoid function
- Hyperbolic tangent function
- Softmax function
- Softsign function
- Rectified Linear Unit (ReLU) function
- Exponential Linear Units (ELUs) function

We will not review each of these variants in detail; I mention them solely for completeness. The points to note regarding AFs are as follows:

- They are integral to every node in an ANN
- They transform data into an appropriate set (range) of values
- They serve as input to other nodes

In the next section, we'll show how all the pieces of an ANN work together to form a complete solution.

How Does an ANN Work?

To understand how ANNs function, let's assume we've built one that will determine whether a given digital image contains a cat's likeness. Specifically, the ANN outputs the value 1 if its input image depicts a cat; otherwise, it generates a 0.

Figure 9.15 presents a simplified depiction of the ANN that will serve as our image classifier. It comprises three layers: A three-node input layer, a single hidden layer with two nodes, and an output layer containing one node.

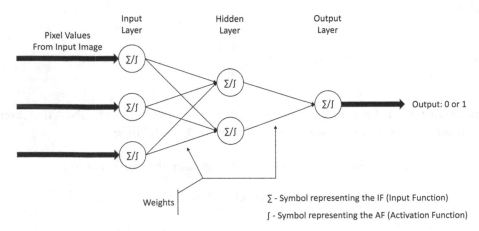

FIGURE 9.15 An ANN in operation.

Each node includes an IF and an AF represented by the symbols Σ and $\int$, respectively. Although the actual values don't appear in the figure, each connection has an associated weight.

The ANN begins processing by "firing" the nodes on the input layer. Specifically, each input-layer node reads its input (i.e., its associated pixel value), then executes its respective IFs and AFs. Next, the two hidden-layer nodes "fire" using the input layer's AF (output) values as input. They, in turn, compute their respective IFs and AFs, the latter serving as input to the single output-layer node. Finally, the AF of the output node indicates whether the ANN identified an image of a cat in the original image.

As I think you'd agree, ANN processing is straightforward. From left to right, nodes in each layer "fire" and pass their results to the next layer. The output node produces either a 1 or a 0, indicating whether it "recognized" a cat's likeness in the input image.

But that description still doesn't explain *how* the ANN works.

Based on this example, it seems we can simply implement the code for the ANN and, *voilà*, we have a working image recognizer. But, alas, it's not that simple. For example, how does the ANN "know" it should identify cats rather than dogs—or telephone poles?

To clarify this issue, we'll need to look more closely at how ANNs use *weights*.

As described above, IFs use an *input* (either a pixel value from the original image or the output of a preceding node's AF) and a *weight* as part of its computation. Thus, *inputs* and *weights* hold equal significance when computing the IF.

We also noted that weights indicate the relative importance of a given input signal. Nonetheless, although it's obvious how the IF receives input values, it's unclear how nodes get their weight values assigned.

Given that weights play such an essential role in an ANN, shouldn't we know how their values get set? I mean, we can't leave that to chance, can we?

Well, it turns out, that's just what we do.

When an ANN begins executing, its weights assume arbitrary values. Thus, in turn, the relative importance of each input is also arbitrary. Consequently, until it can assign appropriate values to its weights, the ANN's output is no better than a random guess. In other words, the ANN is only as accurate as its weights.

So, how does an ANN determine what value it should assign to each of its weights?

It *learns*.

That's the focus of the next section.

How Do ANNs Learn?

In the prior section, we discussed ANNs in general terms. However, to provide a concrete example of how neural networks learn, we need to introduce a specific type of ANN called an Feed-Forward Network (FFN).

We define an FFN as follows:

DEFINITION 4

In a *feed-forward neural network*,[19] nodes do not form cycles, and information flows in one direction.

---

[19] A more complex type of neural network, called a recurrent neural network, contains cycles.

For example, the ANN depicted in Figure 9.15 is an FFN because data propagate from the left (i.e., the input pixels) to the right (i.e., the ANN's output).

As a brief review, we ended the previous section by noting that *weights* are critical to the overall accuracy of the ANN, which led us to the obvious question: What values should we assign them? Surprisingly, the answer was as follows: We don't know.

So how do we address this issue? We allow an FFN to *learn* what values to assign to its *weights* through *training*.

Let's describe how this process works.

Step 1: Gather hundreds (if not thousands) of test images—some containing cats, others not. Label each accordingly.

Step 2: Present each image to the FFN and allow it to compute a result (i.e., *yes* or *no*).

Step 3: Compare the FFN's actual output with the expected result for each image.

Step 4: Compute the extent of the error, if any.

Step 5: Allow each FFN node to adjust its *weights* based on the relative accuracy of the result.

Step 6: Repeat this process until the ANN functions with a high degree of accuracy.

We refer to the error computation referenced in Step 4 as a *Loss Function (LF)*:[20]

DEFINITION 5

A *Loss Function* determines the degree of error (i.e., the "loss") between a neural network's computed output and the expected result.

In other words, the *LF* indicates how inaccurate the FFN's "guess" is from the correct answer.

There are several types of *LFs* typically used in FFNs; some examples appear below.

- Mean Squared Error loss (MSE)

- Mean Squared Logarithmic Error loss (MSLE)

- Mean Absolute Error (MAE)

FFN designers will select the one that best fits the type of network they're designing.[21]

As highlighted in Step 5 above, nodes use the output of the LF to adjust their *weights*. We refer to this process as *backpropagation*.

---

[20] These are also called *Cost Functions*.

[21] A mathematical discussion of loss function is beyond the scope of this book. We will use a remarkably simple loss function in the code presented in the Advanced Section.

DEFINITION 6

Backpropagation[22] is a supervised[23] learning method that allows a neural network to determine the accuracy of its predictions and adjust its *weights* accordingly.

We call this technique *backpropagation* because we propagate the error computed by the LF "backward" through the network allowing each node to adjust its weight individually and thus improve the overall accuracy of the FFN.

See Figure 9.16 for an example.

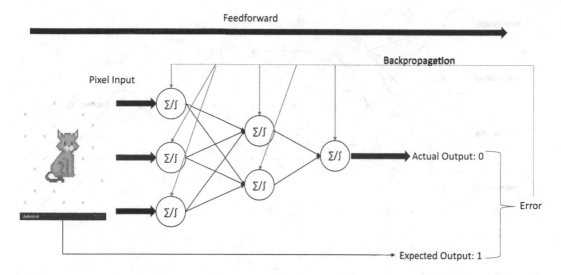

FIGURE 9.16   Backpropagation.

When training completes, we can present random digital images to our FFN, and it will reliably determine which ones contain pictures of cats. Pretty cool.

Other Neural Network Considerations

The examples presented thus far have avoided discussing some of the intricacies associated with implementing neural networks. The sections that follow will "fill in the gaps."

What are Bias Nodes?

One of the most noteworthy features of neural networks is their ability to reveal relationships in an underlying data set. For example, during its training, the FFN for our cat image analyzer uncovered correlations in pixel data common to images of felines. Thus, it "learned" how to classify pictures accordingly.

---

[22] Backpropagation is a portmanteau of the words "backward propagation."

[23] In AI, we call this type of training *supervised learning*. There are types of neural networks that use *unsupervised learning* techniques.

However, there are times when the underlying data don't fit neatly into categories. In such cases, a neural network might need some "assistance" to determine the importance of a data element.

That's where *bias nodes* come into play. They influence data classification in neural networks by setting thresholds for the relative importance of data elements.

Although the mathematical scaffolding to explain bias nodes is beyond the scope of the text, it is a simple matter to include them in a neural network.

Figure 9.17 provides an example.

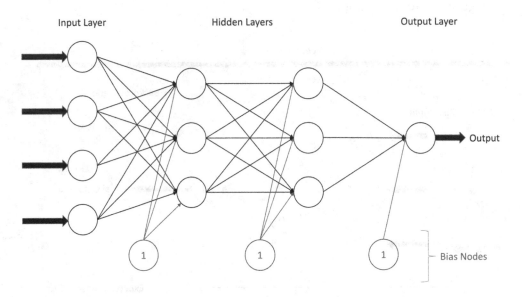

FIGURE 9.17   Bias nodes.

The *value* assigned to bias nodes is usually 1. However, their weights adjust during training like any other node. Thus, the neural network also "learns" the degree to which each bias node should affect thresholds.

What are Epochs?
As we discussed earlier, the process by which ANNs "learn" is as follows:

- Process controlled test data

- Compare actual and expected results

- Compute the error (if any)

- Adjust weights accordingly

However, as depicted in Figure 9.18, training ANN is not a "one-and-done" process. Typically, it requires multiple passes through a data set. We call each iteration an *epoch*.

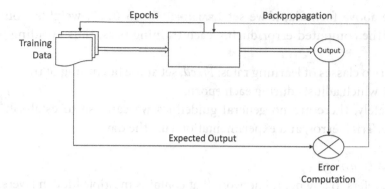

FIGURE 9.18   Training epochs.

DEFINITION 7

An *Epoch* is one complete iteration through an AI training data set.

To improve results, designers usually reorder the data elements during each epoch to ensure the ANN's weights don't become biased by the last few records processed during the previous pass through the data set. That said, there is no assurance whatsoever that executing more epochs will yield a more "intelligent" ANN.

What is Learning Rate?

As the previous sections highlighted, we "teach" ANNs by feeding training data forward and adjusting weights via backpropagation. This process is iterative and ensures that the network improves incrementally.

However, consider what might happen if the training process allowed weights to vary widely during each epoch. Broad oscillations might extend the training period, and worse, nodes might repeatedly "overstep" an optimal value during each pass.

Thus, we can improve the training process by restricting the degree to which weight values may change during each iteration. We control this process by establishing a *learning rate*.

DEFINITION 8

Learning rate[24] is an adjustable parameter that controls the degree that weights may change during each iteration.

When incorporating a learning rate, we calculate weight adjustments as highlighted in Equation 9.4.

Equation 9.4

$$\text{WEIGHT}_{NEW} = \text{WEIGHT}_{OLD} - (\text{LEARNINGRATE} * \text{ERROR})$$

---

[24] In AI parlance, this is an example of a *hyperparameter*, which are adjustable values used to manage the learning process.

Using the above formula, if we set LearningRate to 0.10, weights would adjust by only 10% of the computed error during each training pass, thus avoiding wide swings in values.

There are two classes of learning rates: *Fixed*, set at the beginning of the training phase, and *variable*, which adjusts during each epoch.

Unfortunately, there are no general guidelines we can use to establish an optimal learning rate. Trial, error, and experimentation rule the day.

What is Deep Learning?

The term DL refers to any neural network that contains multiple hidden layers. The design of DL networks ensures that each layer "learns" from the one preceding it. As we add hidden layers, we increase the complexity of the learning process. However, this is true only to a certain extent; eventually, you reach a point of diminishing returns.

WHAT ARE OTHER TYPES OF NEURAL NETWORKS?

ANNs come in many "flavors." The following sections summarize several of the more common designs.

Single-Layer Feed-Forward Network

A single-layer feed-forward network consists of only an input and an output layer. (By convention, we don't count the output layer.) As depicted in Figure 9.19, multiple input-layer nodes connect to a single output layer node, usually generating a single binary result.

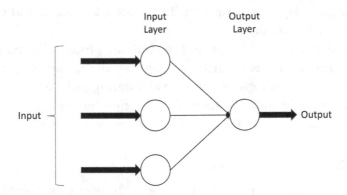

FIGURE 9.19   Single-layer neural network.

Single-layer designs are the oldest and simplest form of neural network. As an aside, for those readers who believe that AI is a recent phenomenon, consider that simple feed-forward networks—often called perceptrons—were introduced by Frank Rosenblatt in 1957.

Multilayer Feed-Forward Network

Multilayer feed-forward networks include one or more "hidden" layers positioned between the input and output layers. See Figure 9.20 for an example.

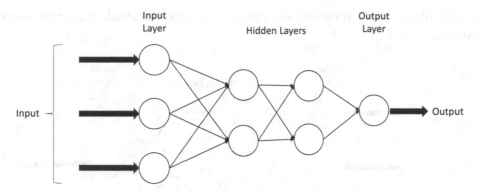

FIGURE 9.20   Multilayer network redux.

As we have already seen, multilayer networks are bidirectional: Input moves "forward," and errors propagate backward (to adjust weights).

Convolutional Neural Networks

Used primarily for image classification, the success of Convolutional Neural Networks (CNN) is the primary reason that the public has become aware of AI and concepts like DL (see above).

The ability of CNNs to classify images and identify objects within images has revolutionized such technologies as robotics, self-driving cars, Optical Character Recognition (ORC), medical diagnostics, security technology, and assistance for the visually impaired.

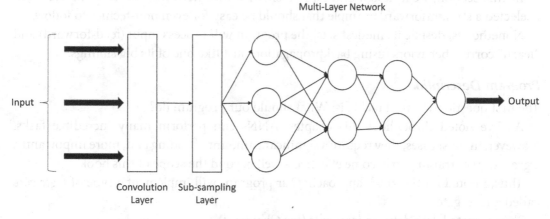

FIGURE 9.21   Simple Convolutional Neural Network.

Unlike FFNs, CNNs don't process images using individual pixels. Instead, they use filters and subsampling layers to "view" images as three-dimensional objects.

See Figure 9.21 for a simplified example of a CNN's design.

Recurrent Neural Networks

Recurrent Neural Networks (RNNs) can predict the next element in sequential data. In this case, sequential data are any series of words, images, numbers, etc. For example, many modern email and SMS[25] programs use RNNs to prompt users with phrase and response suggestions.

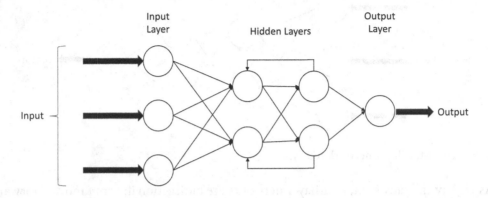

FIGURE 9.22   Simplified Recurrent Neural Network.

As depicted in Figure 9.22, RNNs are like FFNs. However, as the arrows indicate, RNN nodes receive input from succeeding layers.

ADVANCED SECTION

ANN Programming Example

Okay, it's time for some code.

In this section, we'll design and build a small neural network. But don't be alarmed. I selected a straightforward example that should be easy for even non-techies to follow.

Nonetheless, despite its modest size, the program will process input (feed-forward) and "learn" correct behaviors (using backpropagation) just like one of its big siblings.

Program Description

The first question we must tackle is: What should our program do?

As I've noted throughout this chapter, ANNs can perform many incredible tasks. However, in most cases, they require a significant amount of coding and, more importantly, a great deal of training to become effective—well beyond the scope of this book.

Thus, I opted for the KISS[26] approach: Our program will implement a type of *logic gate* called an AND gate.

To get started, let's define a *logic gate* (see Chapter 4).

DEFINITION 9

A *logic gate* is an electronic component that determines its output based on various combinations of its input.

---

[25] The software that supports texting on smartphones. See Chapter 2.

[26] KISS is a common IT acronym that stands for Keep It Simple, Stupid.

Logic gates comprise the basic circuitry of all digital devices. (See Chapter 4.) They function as follows: When signaled,[27] they produce a binary output (e.g., 0 or 1) based on the current value of their inputs.

There are several types of logic gates. However, for our example, we need only consider one: The AND gate.

DEFINITION 10

We define an AND gate as a logic circuit that determines *logical conjunction*.

In this case, *logical conjunction* means that if all its inputs are 1, the gate will output a 1; otherwise, it outputs a 0.

The easiest way to understand how this gate operates is by using a *truth table*.

DEFINITION 11

A *truth table* specifies the correct output for all input combinations.

Table 9.1 depicts a truth table for an AND gate.

TABLE 9.1   Truth Table for an AND Conjunction

Value 1	Value 2	Result
False	False	False
False	True	False
True	False	False
True	True	True

We interpret an AND condition as follows: Both inputs must be TRUE for the result to be TRUE. Otherwise, the result is FALSE.

Logical conjunction is extremely common. For example, consider trying to enter a popular nightclub. Many such establishments require two forms of identification; both must be valid. Thus, if you don't have two, or one is invalid, you'll spend the night elsewhere.

In computer science, we often represent TRUE as the value 1 and FALSE as the value 0. Hence, we can rewrite the logic values as depicted in Table 9.2.

TABLE 9.2   Truth Table Redux

Input 1	Input 2	Output
0	0	0
0	1	0
1	0	0
1	1	1

---

[27] By the system's internal clock.

For our programming example, we will build a neural network that will learn how to function as an AND gate. Thus, we will need to design and develop the code and provide it with appropriate training data.

Let's see how we can do that.

Coding Caveats

Before we review the code, I'd like to comment on the overall approach I used to develop the sample program.

Why Java?	Although numerous languages are suitable for implementing a neural network, I decided to use Java because it's ubiquitous and easily accessible.
Coding Style	When writing code, software professionals have two audiences: The compiler (or interpreter)[28] and other programmers. Developers should write code that functions correctly and is easy for other programmers to comprehend. (We refer to this latter attribute as *readability*.)
	Unfortunately, readability is subjective, and there are raging debates in the industry regarding *coding style*—the presentation guidelines developers should employ when writing code in a specific language. The disputes involve such items as the positioning of syntactical elements such as braces and parentheses, how frequently to include comments, and where one should insert *whitespace* (i.e., blank lines, tabs, and spaces) to enhance readability. For pedagogical clarity, I opted for a presentation style that allows readers to focus on the code's essential aspects.
	For those of you new to software development, you can safely ignore this discussion. However, for readers with some programming experience, I ask you to look past any objections you might have with the coding style I adopted for this example.
Coding Clarity	The example program presented below serves a pedagogical purpose and does not necessarily represent professional programming practices. More to the point, this text is not a Java tutorial, nor is it a discourse on writing efficient code. Thus, in most cases, I opted for clarity rather than cleverness.
	That said, I make no apologies for the approach I've adopted—I don't want readers of this book growing frustrated trying to weave their way through complex language-specific constructs.[29]

---

[28] See Chapter 5.

[29] In addition, I'm trying to minimize the number of unpleasant emails I might receive when some developers read the code.

Comprehension Despite its pedagogical simplicity, the example still embodies a fair amount of complexity. Readers new to coding shouldn't feel concerned if they don't understand every language nuance immediately; this is normal and expected. However, I assure you, if you focus on understanding how the program works at a high level, the details will follow.

Coding Environment I developed the Java code for these examples using the Cygwin programming environment running on Windows 10. In addition, I tested them running directly under Windows as well. Thus, if you type (or copy) the code accurately, the programs will run correctly and generate output identical to the examples.

One important caveat: When you type in the code, DO NOT include the line numbers that appear in the listings. I added them for discussion purposes only. The Java compiler will not treat you kindly if your program file contains them.

Now that we've dispensed with the disclaimers, let's get started.

Program Listing

Listing 9.1 contains the ANN's Java code in its entirety. In the next section, we'll describe how the code functions. Following that, we'll present a sample of the program's output.

```
001 //
002 //   This file contains the Java code for a very
003 //   simple Neural Network.
004 //
005 //   It contains 2 neurons and "learns" how to
006 //   "recognize" an "AND" condition.
007 //
008
009 //   ================================================
010
011 //
012 //   Define the Neuron Class
013 //
014 class Neuron
015 {
016     private double weight = Math.random();
017
018     public double getWeight()
019     {
020             return weight;
021     }
022
023     public void adjWeight( int theError, double theLearningRate,
        int theVectorData )
024     {
025             weight = weight + (theError * theLearningRate * theVectorData);
```

```
026          }
027   }
028
029   //
030   //   Define the NeuralNetClass
031   //
032   public class NeuralNet
033   {
034        //
035        //       Declare Constants
036        //
037        public static final int NUM_NEURONS = 2;
038        public static final double NN_LEARNING_RATE = 0.15;
039
040        //
041        //       Declare Training Data Array
042        //
043        public static final int trainingData[][] = {
044                {0, 0},
045                {1, 0},
046                {0, 1},
047                {1, 1}
048        };
049
050        //
051        //       Declare Expected Results Array
052        //
053        public static final int expectedResults[] = {
054                0,
055                0,
056                0,
057                1
058        };
059
060        //
061        //       Activation - Simple "Step" Function
062        //
063        public static int activationFunction( double ws )
064        {
065                return (ws > 1.0)?  1 : 0;
066        }
067
068        //
069        //   The main() Method Controls Execution
070        //
071        public static void main( String[] args )
072        {
073                int             vectorError;    // Error Amount
074                int             actualResult;   // Actual Result
075                int             expectedResult;         // Expected Result
076                double   sumOfWeights;   // Sum of Weights
077
078                //
079                //       Declare & Initialize Neurons
080                //
081                Neuron[] neurons = new Neuron[NUM_NEURONS];
```

```
082               for( int i = 0; i < NUM_NEURONS; i++ )
083               {
084                       neurons[i] = new Neuron();
085               }
086
087           //
088           // Loop Until Training Completes
089           //
090           boolean anyErrors = true;      // Ensure at least one loop
091           for( int epoch = 1; anyErrors; epoch++ )
092           {
093               anyErrors = false;                  // Hope for the best!
094               System.out.printf( "EPOCH: [%d]\n", epoch );
095
096               //
097               // Loop Through Each Training Vector
098               //
099               for( int tv = 0; tv < NeuralNet.trainingData.length; tv++ )
100               {
101                       //
102                       // Step 1: Compute the Sum of the Weights
103                       //
104                       sumOfWeights = 0.0;
105                       for( int n = 0; n < neurons.length; n++ )// For each
                          neuron
106                       {
107                               sumOfWeights += neurons[n].getWeight()//
                                  Line split

108                               * NeuralNet.trainingData[tv][n];
109                               System.out.printf(
110                               "\tTV: [%d] Neuron:[%d] TRAINING DATA:
                                  [%d] WEIGHT: [%f] SUM: [%f]\n",
111                               tv, n, NeuralNet.trainingData[tv][n],
                                  neurons[n].getWeight(), sumOfWeights );
112                       }
113
114                       //
115                       //    Step 2: Execute the Activation Function
116                       //
117                       actualResult = activationFunction( sumOfWeights );
118
119                       //
120                       //    Step 3: Compute Error
121                       //
122                       expectedResult = expectedResults[tv];
123                       vectorError = expectedResult - actualResult;
124
125                       //
126                       //    Display results
127                       //
128                       System.out.printf(     // Line split for readability
129                       "\t\tActual Result: [%d] vs Expected Result: [%d]
                          Vector Error: [%d]\n\n",
130                       actualResult, expectedResult, vectorError );
131
132                       //
```

```
133                          //      Check for Errors
134                          //
135                          if( vectorError != 0 )
136                          {
137                                  //
138                                  //      Houston, We Have a Problem
139                                  //
140                                  anyErrors = true;
141                          }
142
143                          //
144                          // Step 4: Adjust the Weights of Each Neuron
145                          //
146                          for( int n = 0; n < neurons.length; n++ )
147                          {
148                                  neurons[n].adjWeight(  // Line split for
                                     readability
149                                          vectorError, NN_LEARNING_RATE,
150                                          NeuralNet.trainingData[tv][n] );
151                          }
152                  }
153          }
154   }    // End method main()
155
156 }      // End Class NeuralNet
```

LISTING 9.1   Java Code for Example Neural Network.

Program Description

Before discussing the code properly, we should review some Java language conventions.

- As we will see below, Java programs cannot execute directly. Instead, we must compile them into an acceptable execution format before running them. (See Chapter 5 for more information.)

- As mentioned above, programmers focus on two main objectives: Writing correct code and ensuring that other developers understand what they've written. To assist with the latter, all text following double forward slashes ("//") does not execute and is considered a "comment" written by programmers for other programmers. (When algorithms become complex, it's often difficult to understand the meaning of code written by another programmer. Therefore, developers include comments to help clarify programming logic.)

- Line numbers appear in the listing for discussion purposes only.

- A Java *method* is a group of statements executed as a single block. (See Chapter 5 for more information.)

Okay, now let's move on to the code.

Most Java programs start execution in the MAIN() method; let's begin our discussion at line 71 with its declaration.

On lines 73–76, we declare variables[30] that we will use later in the program. Following that, on lines 81–85, we declare and initialize the neurons the program will use. (We'll discuss their implementation shortly.)

Training begins with lines 90 and 91, where we set up a loop that will iterate over the training set until the ANN "learns" how to function as an AND gate. Then, it repeats this processing until there are no longer any errors (ANYERRORS = FALSE;).

During each epoch, the program will make one complete pass through the training set (line 99) and perform the following processing:

> Step 1: Compute the sum of the weights (lines 104–112)
> Step 2: Execute the AF (line 117)
> Step 3: Determine whether there are any errors and display the results (lines 122–141)
> Step 4: Backpropagation: Adjust the weights of each neuron (lines 146–151)

That completes the discussion of the function MAIN().

Lines 14–27 comprise the declaration of the NEURON CLASS. This class includes two methods:

> GETWEIGHT()   This method returns the neuron's *weight*.
> ADJWEIGHT()   This method adjusts the neuron's weight as part of the backpropagation process (invoked on lines 148–150). Note the use of the NN_LEARNING_RATE value in the computation.

Lines 37–58 declare the learning rate and the training data vectors. Finally, lines 63–66 contain the declaration of the AF. For this program, we are using a simple step function.

Program Execution

Now that we have a sense of how the program works, let's see it in action.

As mentioned previously (in Chapter 5), two tasks are required to run a Java program. First, you must compile it; the command to do that is as follows:

```
JAVAC NEURALNET.JAVA
```

If the compiler didn't encounter any errors, we execute the program using the following command:

```
JAVA NEURALNET
```

---

[30] See the discussion regarding "lockers" appearing in Chapter 4.

Listing 9.2 presents a sample execution of our program.

```
$ JAVA NEURALNET
EPOCH: [1]
        TV: [0] NEURON:[0] TRAINING DATA: [0] WEIGHT: [0.102437] SUM: [0.000000]
        TV: [0] NEURON:[1] TRAINING DATA: [0] WEIGHT: [0.038734] SUM: [0.000000]
            ACTUAL RESULT: [0] VS EXPECTED RESULT: [0] VECTOR ERROR: [0]

        TV: [1] NEURON:[0] TRAINING DATA: [1] WEIGHT: [0.102437] SUM: [0.102437]
        TV: [1] NEURON:[1] TRAINING DATA: [0] WEIGHT: [0.038734] SUM: [0.102437]
            ACTUAL RESULT: [0] VS EXPECTED RESULT: [0] VECTOR ERROR: [0]

        TV: [2] NEURON:[0] TRAINING DATA: [0] WEIGHT: [0.102437] SUM: [0.000000]
        TV: [2] NEURON:[1] TRAINING DATA: [1] WEIGHT: [0.038734] SUM: [0.038734]
            ACTUAL RESULT: [0] VS EXPECTED RESULT: [0] VECTOR ERROR: [0]

        TV: [3] NEURON:[0] TRAINING DATA: [1] WEIGHT: [0.102437] SUM: [0.102437]
        TV: [3] NEURON:[1] TRAINING DATA: [1] WEIGHT: [0.038734] SUM: [0.141171]
            ACTUAL RESULT: [0] VS EXPECTED RESULT: [1] VECTOR ERROR: [1]

EPOCH: [2]
        TV: [0] NEURON:[0] TRAINING DATA: [0] WEIGHT: [0.252437] SUM: [0.000000]
        TV: [0] NEURON:[1] TRAINING DATA: [0] WEIGHT: [0.188734] SUM: [0.000000]
            ACTUAL RESULT: [0] VS EXPECTED RESULT: [0] VECTOR ERROR: [0]

        TV: [1] NEURON:[0] TRAINING DATA: [1] WEIGHT: [0.252437] SUM: [0.252437]
        TV: [1] NEURON:[1] TRAINING DATA: [0] WEIGHT: [0.188734] SUM: [0.252437]
            ACTUAL RESULT: [0] VS EXPECTED RESULT: [0] VECTOR ERROR: [0]

        TV: [2] NEURON:[0] TRAINING DATA: [0] WEIGHT: [0.252437] SUM: [0.000000]
        TV: [2] NEURON:[1] TRAINING DATA: [1] WEIGHT: [0.188734] SUM: [0.188734]
            ACTUAL RESULT: [0] VS EXPECTED RESULT: [0] VECTOR ERROR: [0]

        TV: [3] NEURON:[0] TRAINING DATA: [1] WEIGHT: [0.252437] SUM: [0.252437]
        TV: [3] NEURON:[1] TRAINING DATA: [1] WEIGHT: [0.188734] SUM: [0.441171]
            ACTUAL RESULT: [0] VS EXPECTED RESULT: [1] VECTOR ERROR: [1]

EPOCH: [3]
        TV: [0] NEURON:[0] TRAINING DATA: [0] WEIGHT: [0.402437] SUM: [0.000000]
        TV: [0] NEURON:[1] TRAINING DATA: [0] WEIGHT: [0.338734] SUM: [0.000000]
            ACTUAL RESULT: [0] VS EXPECTED RESULT: [0] VECTOR ERROR: [0]

        TV: [1] NEURON:[0] TRAINING DATA: [1] WEIGHT: [0.402437] SUM: [0.402437]
        TV: [1] NEURON:[1] TRAINING DATA: [0] WEIGHT: [0.338734] SUM: [0.402437]
            ACTUAL RESULT: [0] VS EXPECTED RESULT: [0] VECTOR ERROR: [0]

        TV: [2] NEURON:[0] TRAINING DATA: [0] WEIGHT: [0.402437] SUM: [0.000000]
        TV: [2] NEURON:[1] TRAINING DATA: [1] WEIGHT: [0.338734] SUM: [0.338734]
            ACTUAL RESULT: [0] VS EXPECTED RESULT: [0] VECTOR ERROR: [0]

        TV: [3] NEURON:[0] TRAINING DATA: [1] WEIGHT: [0.402437] SUM: [0.402437]
        TV: [3] NEURON:[1] TRAINING DATA: [1] WEIGHT: [0.338734] SUM: [0.741171]
            ACTUAL RESULT: [0] VS EXPECTED RESULT: [1] VECTOR ERROR: [1]

EPOCH: [4]
        TV: [0] NEURON:[0] TRAINING DATA: [0] WEIGHT: [0.552437] SUM: [0.000000]
        TV: [0] NEURON:[1] TRAINING DATA: [0] WEIGHT: [0.488734] SUM: [0.000000]
            ACTUAL RESULT: [0] VS EXPECTED RESULT: [0] VECTOR ERROR: [0]
```

```
TV: [1] NEURON:[0] TRAINING DATA: [1] WEIGHT: [0.552437] SUM: [0.552437]
TV: [1] NEURON:[1] TRAINING DATA: [0] WEIGHT: [0.488734] SUM: [0.552437]
        ACTUAL RESULT: [0] VS EXPECTED RESULT: [0] VECTOR ERROR: [0]

TV: [2] NEURON:[0] TRAINING DATA: [0] WEIGHT: [0.552437] SUM: [0.000000]
TV: [2] NEURON:[1] TRAINING DATA: [1] WEIGHT: [0.488734] SUM: [0.488734]
        ACTUAL RESULT: [0] VS EXPECTED RESULT: [0] VECTOR ERROR: [0]

TV: [3] NEURON:[0] TRAINING DATA: [1] WEIGHT: [0.552437] SUM: [0.552437]
TV: [3] NEURON:[1] TRAINING DATA: [1] WEIGHT: [0.488734] SUM: [1.041171]
        ACTUAL RESULT: [1] VS EXPECTED RESULT: [1] VECTOR ERROR: [0]
```

LISTING 9.2   Sample Program Output.

Note that, for this particular execution, the program required four epochs to "learn" the correct behavior.

Program Limitations

For completeness, I should note some of the many limitations of the example program.

- The code is simple and not professional caliber by any stretch of the imagination.

- The program's design makes no provisions to store (and later retrieve) its weights after the training phase. That is, as implemented, the program must undergo a training phase during each execution.

- ANNs usually benefit from the inclusion of one or more hidden layers.

- A professional implementation would use a more sophisticated AF.

- A professional design would ensure a more generic NEURON class that could potentially serve the needs of other ANN implementations.

- Training usually occurs using data external to the program.

The above notwithstanding, the program highlights the many features and components of a neural network.

SUMMARY

We've certainly covered a lot of materials in this chapter; Let's summarize what we've learned.

- Artificial neurons are abstractions of biological neurons

- A collection of neurons function as an ANN

- ANNs undergo training epochs to uncover relationships in data sets

- Neural networks come in many forms and can solve various types of problems

CHAPTER 10

What Is Quantum Computing?

I think I can safely say that nobody understands quantum mechanics.

RICHARD FEYNMAN

Google claims its quantum computer can do the impossible in 200 seconds.

AS REPORTED BY NUMEROUS MEDIA OUTLETS

If you aren't confused by quantum mechanics, you haven't really understood it.

NIELS BOHR

INTRODUCTION

Quantum Computing (QC) is undoubtedly one of the most exciting developments in computer science. Like artificial intelligence,[1] QC leverages nature—but with a dramatic difference: It doesn't just *model* the physical world; it *harnesses* the properties of subatomic particles. The underlying science is called Quantum Mechanics (QM), which describes the fundamental properties of all matter and energy.

QC harnesses subatomic particles in such a way as to enable computations. That is, by manipulating the state of particles—like electrons—a quantum computer can execute multiple concurrent calculations. Then, when the operations complete, the system "measures" the execution state to ascertain the result. This idea may sound crazy, but as we'll see, it really works.

Some readers might argue that this is nothing new because integrated circuits (i.e., "computer chips"), which form the basis of all digital electronics,[2] rely on our understanding of QM. For example, consider that remarkable device we spend a good portion of our day staring at—the smartphone. It comprises billions of transistors and semiconductor circuits that only function because of science's ability to harness QM. Moreover, it likely includes a digital camera whose sensor relies on the photoelectric effects of light.[3]

---

[1] Discussed in Chapter 9.
[2] See Chapter 4.
[3] Einstein won a Nobel Prize for this idea.

DOI: 10.1201/9781003143437-10

The difference, however, is that the electronic components in use today process data digitally. At any moment in time, every "bit"[4] of information is in a single binary state that may assume only one of two discrete values: 0 or 1. As we'll soon see, QC elements may be in multiple states simultaneously.

But we're getting ahead of ourselves.

Before we can understand quantum computers, we need to take a brief sojourn into the world of QM. So come on, hop on the train. I promise you a fascinating ride.

WHAT IS QUANTUM MECHANICS?

QM is a scientific theory describing the behavior of atoms and subatomic particles. Specifically, QM's precise models and formulas are the building blocks for many other disciplines (e.g., quantum field theory and quantum information theory).

Regardless of whether we're conscious of it, we interact with QM every moment of our lives. Specifically, every molecule—indeed every atom—that comprises your body obeys its properties.

Though there are some gaps in science's understanding of the subatomic world, QM is today's most successful theory of nature. In fact, there have been countless experiments confirming the accuracy of the QM model.

Despite an incomplete understanding of its fundamental nature, science has developed technologies that have harnessed QM principles to shape the macro world. Some examples appear below.

Computers	All electronic devices are composed of transistors, which rely on silicon semiconductors whose behaviors we understand and harness using QM.
Lasers	Lasers have found widespread uses, including digital storage (CDs and DVDs[5]), communication mediums (e.g., fiber optics), and medical science (e.g., cosmetic surgery and kidney stone removal). None of which would be possible without QM.
GPS	As we discovered in Chapter 3, GPS relies on a network of satellites, each of which depends upon the precision of internal atomic clocks made possible by QM to compute its precise location.
Digital Cameras	The proliferation of digital cameras results from QM technology designed into their sensors.

WHAT ARE THE PRINCIPLES OF QUANTUM MECHANICS?

The focus of QM is to understand the principles of matter and light at the nanoscopic level. Specifically, it attempts to explain the behaviors of the building blocks of nature: Molecules, atoms, subatomic particles such as protons and electrons, and elementary particles such as *leptons* and *quarks*.

---

[4] Please recall that a "bit" is a *binary digit*.

[5] Want proof that technology moves fast? Consider that laser-based discs were invented and sunsetted in less than a lifetime.

To understand QC, we need a conceptual understanding of some QM principles. Before we start, however, I feel compelled to share several caveats:

- You are not reading a physics textbook. Thus, we will review only the minimum set of ideas and principles of QM that we'll need to understand QC.

- We will keep the discussions at a conceptual level: No formulas and no math.

Enough with the disclaimers; let's begin our journey by describing two of QM's most fundamental principles.

What is Wave-Particle Duality?

During the formative years of physics, scientists believed that matter comprised particles and light propagated as waves. However, one of the most historically significant scientific breakthroughs occurred in the early 1900s when preeminent physicists Max Planck and Albert Einstein discovered the particle nature of light that we now know as *photons*.

The wave-particle duality states that light[6] can behave like both waves and particles. Let's examine the implications of that assertion (see Figure 10.1).

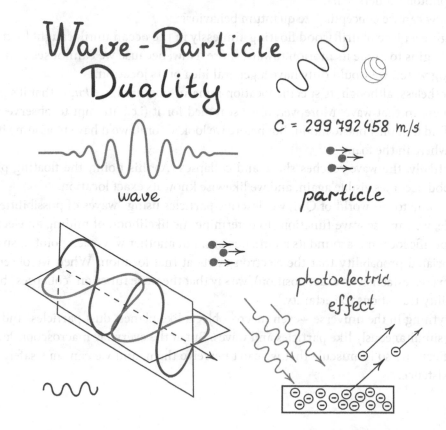

FIGURE 10.1   Wave-particle duality.

---

[6] Technically, all electromagnetic radiation shares this duality; however, that discussion is well beyond the scope of this text.

In our everyday macroscopic world, we experience both wave-like and particle-like behaviors. Examples of waves include the patterns you can make in water when you toss a pebble in a lake or the invisible ripples propagating through the air when we sound a car's horn.

We also experience particle-like behavior with macro-objects, such as the flight of a well-struck baseball as it exits the park or the trajectory of an arrow as it races toward its target.

The point is that waves and particles appear discrete in the everyday world. But this is not so in the world of QM.

To highlight this "weirdness," consider a light bulb controlled by an extremely precise dimmer switch and encircled by a group of people with such exceptional eyesight that each person can see individual photons. We initiate the experiment by flipping the switch to the "on" position, at which point photons emitted by the bulb travel as waves in all directions, and everyone sees the light.

Now, we begin dimming the light, which reduces the number of photons emanating from the bulb. Initially, there are enough photons produced that everyone still sees the light. Eventually, however, we can adjust the dimmer switch to the point that just a few photons radiate from the bulb. At that point, some individuals see the light (as an individual photon); others don't.

So, how can we conceptualize quantum behavior?

Imagine a piece of driftwood floating aimlessly in the ocean until, caught by the tide, a wave begins to guide its motion toward shore. Now, because we cannot see it amid the churning water, we would only have a general idea of its location.

Nonetheless, although its specific location remains obscured, we *know* that it's floating somewhere in that wave. Moreover, if we searched for it (i.e., attempt to observe[7] it), we would find it in only one location. But before we looked for it, we'd have to assume it could be anywhere in the foam.

Eventually, the wave reaches shore and collapses. At this point, the floating piece of driftwood becomes visible again, and we likewise know its exact location.

Returning to the world of QM, we describe particles using "waves of possibilities." For example, we can use wave functions to determine the likelihood of finding an electron at some specific location[8] around its atom's nucleus. Put another way, each point in space has an associated probability that the electron exists at that location. When we observe the electron (i.e., establish its exact position), we say that the wave function "collapses" because probability transitions to certainty.[9]

Everything in the universe—even macro-objects like planes, dust particles, and cats—behave simultaneously like particles and waves. But at the everyday macroscopic level, the wave effects are so minuscule that we can't perceive them, and we can thus safely ignore their existence.

---

[7] In this context, we will use the terms *measure* and *observe* interchangeably.
[8] i.e., its energy state.
[9] In reality, there is still some uncertainty.

However, as we'll see, this is not the case with quantum particles. Indeed, QC actually *exploits* this particle-wave duality.

What is the Uncertainty Principle?

You may be familiar with the Heisenberg uncertainty principle or, more simply, the uncertainty principle, which loosely states that you cannot simultaneously know the precise location and the exact momentum of an object.

Before we dive into the uncertainty principle pool, let's define *velocity*.

DEFINITION 1

Velocity is a *vector* incorporating both the speed and direction of an object.

We can define a *vector* as follows:

DEFINITION 2

A *vector* is a quantity representing both magnitude and direction.

Thus, velocity is the speed at which an object travels in a specific direction. For example, when driving a car, if you were to maintain a constant speed but change direction (i.e., turn the steering wheel), you'd alter the vehicle's velocity. You'd also change the car's velocity if you were to press down on the accelerator while holding the steering wheel steady.

Given the above, we can define the uncertainty principle as follows:

DEFINITION 3

The *uncertainty principle* holds that we cannot accurately measure certain pairs of attributes (e.g., position and momentum) of an object.

To help clarify this concept, consider an analogy proposed by the eminent physicist David Bohm.[10] Let's say you want to determine a car's exact location and how fast it's traveling. However, the only measuring device at your disposal is a camera. (Seems strange, I know, but just go with me on this.)

You take your first picture using an extended exposure, let's say one second. The resulting image appears blurred. Nonetheless, you can estimate how long it took the car to travel the distance across the visual field of the lens during the exposure period. With some simple math, you can approximate its speed. However, you don't know its location.

---

[10] As suggested by my friend, Dr. Michael Bardash.

Now, let's repeat the experiment, but we'll use a faster shutter speed this time. As a result, the image is sharper, and the car does not appear to be moving. Thus, you can estimate its position, but you can no longer compute its speed.

With that conceptual understanding in mind, let's return to the question: Why is it impossible to measure a subatomic particle's momentum and position simultaneously?

We can address this issue using another example. Consider trying to determine the location of an electron using a laser. For this process to work, a photon of light must strike the electron and "rebound" to the measuring device, at which point, using simple math, we can compute the electron's position. However, photons have momentum; thus, they alter the electron's velocity upon impact.

Why does this seem different in the macro world of everyday experience?

Well, consider a police officer using a *lidar* gun—a laser-based speed detector. When the photons strike our car, the change in momentum is so infinitesimally small that we can safely ignore it. (But unfortunately, we can't disregard any subsequent speeding ticket.)

What is Superposition?

I'm sure that most of us have tossed a pebble into a pond and watched the waves radiate outward from the point it enters the water. Figure 10.2 depicts an example.

FIGURE 10.2   Pebble in a pond.

Now imagine that you tossed several pebbles so that they struck the water simultaneously. As depicted in Figure 10.3, we would see waves radiating from each pebble's point of entry and then begin to overlap, creating a much more complex pattern.

FIGURE 10.3   Overlapping waves.

When this occurs, we would say that the waves are in a *superposition*, which we define as follows:

DEFINITION 4

Superposition combines two or more states to form a new state.

So, what does this mean in the context of QM?

The waves in Figure 10.3 are physical, resulting from the movement of water. However, in QM, waves are more abstract, and we represent them mathematically. That is, waves are a set of *equations* that describe an object's *probabilities*.

So, as discussed above, we can use wave probability functions to determine the prospect of an electron existing at a specific location and moment in time. Stated another way, QM wave functions don't predict a particle's movement *through* space; they compute the probability of the particle appearing at a particular position *in* space.

When an electron (or any other subatomic particle) is in *superposition*, we can say that each of its potential states is a valid outcome. Thus, we can think that an electron simultaneously resides in a cloud of locations. However, it's not until we observe (measure) the particle that we know its precise location.

Another example may help.

Let's think of an electron as a tiny clear ball that will display a particular color—either red or green—when we point a laser at it. However, until we observe it (i.e., hit it with a laser), it remains "clear," and we say it's in a superposition of both the red and green states.

Though it may seem strange, superposition is not a new concept. Please recall this simple equation from high school algebra:[11]

$$x^2 = 25 \tag{10.1}$$

The solution to this equation is either 5 or −5.[12] Both values are equally correct. It's not until we select one that we have a specific answer.

We can think of the probabilities embodied in wave functions similarly. All results are possible until we observe the particle and determine its actual state.

We will describe how superposition supports QC later in this chapter.

What is Entanglement?

In everyday life, we commonly derive information about one object when observing another. For example, let's say you received a pair of gloves as a birthday present. If, after opening the box, you remove the first glove and note that it's configured for a right hand, it would be fair to assume that the second one is for the left hand. So, we would say that the gloves are *correlated*.[13]

Similarly, subatomic particles can become so strongly correlated that we can describe them using the identical wave function.

We call this arrangement *entanglement*.[14]

DEFINITION 5

Quantum entanglement occurs when multiple particles interact so strongly that we cannot independently describe their states (properties).

Entanglement describes the *superposition* of multiple quantum particles. As mentioned above, the properties of individual particles are uncertain. However, if two electrons are entangled, their properties are highly predictable when measured together (Figure 10.4).

WHAT IS QUANTUM COMPUTING?

Now that we understand some of the principles of QM, let's see how we can harness its properties to create quantum computers. We'll begin our discussion by describing the most fundamental unit of information in a quantum computer: a *qubit*.

---

[11] I know, I lied when I said there would be no math.
[12] Recall that when you multiply two negative numbers, the result is a positive number.
[13] Note that this isn't a 100 percent true: Manufacturing issues or packing oversights could result in a box containing two left-handed or two right-handed gloves.
[14] For our discussion, we can ignore how particles become entangled.

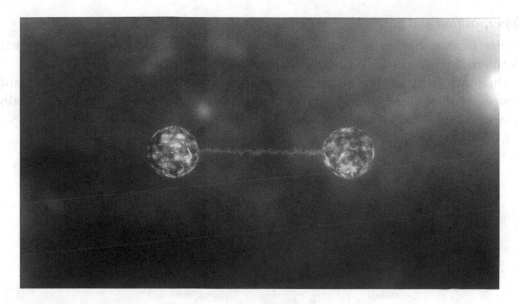

FIGURE 10.4   Quantum entanglement—Conceptual image.

What is a Qubit?

In Chapter 5, we noted that the basic unit of information in a digital computer is a *bit* and that each bit may hold only one of two discrete values: 0 or 1.

We refer to the basic unit of information in a quantum computer as a *qubit*.[15] However, a qubit differs from its traditional counterpart as follows:

> **DEFINITION 6**
>
> A *qubit* can represent the values 0, 1, or some combination of both 0 and 1 in *superposition*.

Because it holds values in superposition, a qubit can represent both the 0 and 1 states simultaneously, with a certain probability of the value being 0 and a certain probability of it being 1. We'll soon see how this superposition of values can dramatically alter how we represent and process data.

Quantum computer designers achieve qubit superposition using lasers and microwaves. Although the technical implementation is beyond the scope of this text, the key takeaway is that while qubits remain in superposition, a quantum computer can execute a vast number of calculations simultaneously. QCs can thus solve problems exponentially faster than traditional digital computers by leveraging this parallel processing.[16]

When execution completes, the quantum computer measures (observes) the qubits. At that point, the quantum state of each qubit "collapses" to either a 0 or 1, yielding the result.

---

[15] Pronounced "que-bit."

[16] Unfortunately, as we will see, the types of problems a quantum computer can solve are limited.

Superposition and Entanglement Redux

Earlier in this chapter, we kept our discussions regarding superposition conceptual. However, to move forward, we need to step back and refine this abstraction a bit.

Quantum particles, like electrons, have many properties like *mass*, *position*, and *charge*. Another common attribute is *angular momentum*,[17] which physicists usually refer to as *spin*.

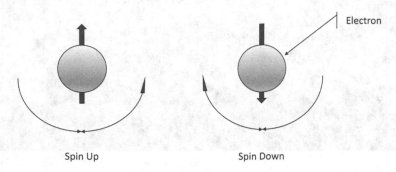

FIGURE 10.5   Particle spin.

As depicted in Figure 10.5, we can envision a particle's spin as either "up" or "down." Given that representation, we can assign values to the spin as we do for bits in a digital computer:

Spin Up = 1
Spin Down = 0

As noted previously, quantum particles can assume a superposition of states. Thus, we can represent a superposition of spin up and spin down as depicted in Figure 10.6.

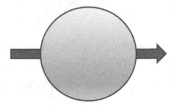

FIGURE 10.6   Electron in superposition.

However, one qubit is quite limiting. Therefore, to execute programs of any reasonable complexity, we need to combine many qubits together and allow them to interact.

As depicted in Figure 10.7, we can do that because quantum spin creates a small magnetic field in its vicinity.

We can change a particle's spin by applying an oscillating magnetic field. Using an appropriate frequency, we can set the state to either a 0 or 1.[18]

---

[17] *Spin* is a very abstract quantum attribute, and its exact definition is well beyond the scope of this text.
[18] The details of how this works is not pertinent to this discussion.

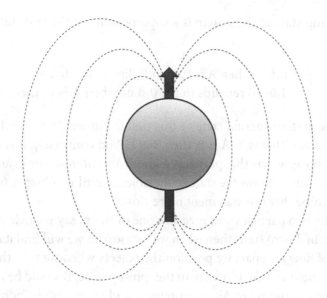

FIGURE 10.7 Magnetic field.

However, the energy field produced by one particle can affect the energy of another one. Thus, if more than one particle is nearby, the total energy also depends on the spin of the other objects.

So, what does this all mean?

Time for an example. Consider two particles, A and B. Let's assume using a magnetic field that we set the spin states of both A and B to 0 (i.e., spin down). We then place object A into a superposition of the values 0 and 1.

As represented in Figure 10.8, we can now describe this system as follows: Particle A is in a superposition of states (i.e., both spin up and spin down), and particle B is in the 0 state (i.e., spin down).

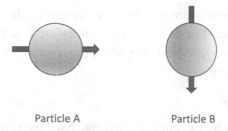

Particle A   Particle B

FIGURE 10.8 Initial state.

Now, let's apply a magnetic field to this system to change particle B's state. You're likely expecting B to flip from the 0 state (i.e., spin down) to the 1 state (i.e., spin up). However, what happens is a lot stranger than that.

Because A is in superposition, and its magnetic field affects B, B both flips and doesn't flip. That is, B enters its own state of superposition.

Thus, the resulting state of the system is a superposition of the two states 0,1 and 1,0 as follows:

> **0,1**   When A is 0, then B flips to the 1 state
> **1,0**   B remains in the 0 state when A is in the 1 state

We don't know the system's actual state at this point. But we do know that the values of the objects are opposite. That is, if A is 0, then B is 1. And conversely, if A is 1, then B is 0.

As highlighted above, we say that particles A and B are *entangled* or in an *entangled state*. However, we don't—can't—know the state of the objects until we observe (measure) them.

We need to examine that last statement more closely.

Let's separate the two particles and measure one of them, say particle A. If we discover that A is in the 0 (spin down) state, then when we measure B, we will find it in the 1 (spin up) state—regardless of how far apart we position the objects when we take the measurement. The opposite would hold as well: If A were in the spin-up state, B would be in the spin-down state. It's as if B "senses" the act of A's measurement and immediately "adjusts" its value.

As strange as this behavior may seem,[19] this is how QM works. Moreover, physicists have conducted countless empirical tests to confirm this behavior. It's *real*.

In terms of QC, we have a system in which two entangled qubits simultaneously have no value yet hold distinctly opposite values. Moreover, there is a probability associated with each object's spin state. For example, 75% spin up and 25% spin down. Thus, as we'll see in the Advanced Section, we can leverage this paradigm to write programs that simultaneously compute each result and then select the correct one when the program completes.

Consider the power of this paradigm: The more entangled particles, the more entangled states. The more entangled states, the more solution paths you can follow simultaneously.

QC power grows exponentially as you add qubits. Harnessing such potential is the Holy Grail of QC research. However, the tricky bit is finding a practical way to exploit this processing paradigm because, as we'll discover in the next section, qubit states are incredibly fragile.

Note that this model runs counter to how we interpret values using traditional digital components: Bits are either 0 or 1. That is, bit values are binary and are never ambiguous, and by comparison, conventional computer programs are far more pedestrian in their approach to problem-solving.

How Fragile are Qubits?

Let me begin this section by categorically stating that quantum computers exist despite the implementation difficulties. Although they are not mainstream yet, they are tangible, operational machines, not just conceptual models.

But because this is the salad days of this emerging technology, researchers are exploring many unique designs. So, unlike digital computers, there is no "standard" approach to constructing a QC.

Researchers use several technologies to implement qubits. However, one problem common in all current designs is that qubits are *fragile*. Entanglement is challenging to achieve

---

[19] Even Einstein referred to this phenomenon as "spooky action at a distance."

and maintain. Unfortunately, even the merest of vibration or the tiniest variation in temperature can cause qubits to lose their states before completing a computation. Scientists refer to this issue as *decoherence*.

Thus, to isolate qubits from the external environment, QCs require vacuum chambers and supercooled hardware with temperatures approaching *absolute zero.*

DEFINITION 7

Measured using the *Kelvin scale*, science defines *absolute zero* as the complete absence of heat and motion. Thought to be the coldest temperature possible, it's equivalent to −273.15° Celsius and −459.67° Fahrenheit.

Because of this instability, quantum computers are complicated to design, engineer, and build and often decohere before programs of any significant complexity can complete successfully. Until researchers address these issues, it's unlikely that quantum computers will become commonplace.

How Powerful are Quantum Computers?

As we will see, although impressively powerful, quantum computers are not well-suited to address typical mainstream computing problems and will therefore not replace traditional computers for most applications. Instead, because we can place qubits into superposition, QCs excel at applications that have many variables and many potential outcomes.

To begin our discussion of the power of QC, please recall that a single qubit can hold multiple values (0 and 1) simultaneously. In contrast, a bit in a traditional digital computer is either in the 0 or 1 state. Consequently, it requires a single qubit to represent all the possible values contained in two bits.

Extending this model, two qubits in superposition can represent four states concurrently: 0-0, 0-1, 1-0, and 1-1. We would need four bits to represent the four combinations simultaneously. Similarly, three qubits are equivalent to eight bits, four qubits would require sixteen bits, and so on.

Note that we need to double the number of bits with the addition of each qubit. In general, n qubits would require 2^n digital bits to represent each possible state.

Now, given that model, consider the following:

- 50 qubits require 2^{50} ($\approx 10^{15}$) bits—which is about a *petabyte*.

- 70 qubits require 2^{70} ($\approx 10^{21}$) bits—about a *zettabyte*. A quantum computer of this size, if fully exploited, could perform calculations that are otherwise impossible to compute using every traditional computer.

- A quantum computer containing 300 qubits would be the equivalent of 2^{300} ($\approx 10^{90}$) bits. This value exceeds the estimated number of particles existing in the known universe.

Hopefully, these examples highlight the enormous computational complexity that is the promise of QC.

Quantum Supremacy

One of the measures of the power of QC is *Quantum Supremacy* (QS).

DEFINITION 8

Quantum supremacy will be the point at which quantum computers can perform calculations that are beyond the capabilities of the most powerful digital computers.

As of this writing, there is a debate among experts regarding whether the industry has achieved QS. Nonetheless, until researchers can harness that power to be of practical value, such claims are little more than high-tech hot air.

How Accurate are Quantum Computers?

It might be difficult to accept, but computers are not perfect. On the contrary, they are mechanical devices and are thus subject to failure. So, for example, although the likelihood is minuscule, there is a nonzero probability that your desktop, laptop, or smartphone may "flip a bit." However, because, as a rule, today's digital devices are so remarkably dependable, we usually don't even consider such a possibility.

The reality of imperfection also holds for quantum computers—but more so. QCs don't always compute the correct/best answer. Specifically, because of the current state of the technology, it's challenging to hold qubits in superposition for extended periods. Thus, the more complex the problem, the longer the execution time and the higher the probability that a quantum computer will not generate the best/correct result.

Consequently, programmers usually execute a quantum algorithm multiple times to ensure computational accuracy.

WHAT ARE SOME USES OF QUANTUM COMPUTERS?

There is always vast amounts of hype and hysteria surrounding any emerging technology. QC is no exception. So, the only real question is whether QC will live up to its extraordinary expectations.

Let's begin by stating that quantum computers will not replace mainstream digital computers any time soon. Specialized hardware requirements aside, the types of problems quantum computers are good at solving (see below) are not your everyday applications. Thus, your desktop, laptop, and smartphone are in no danger of obsolescence.

However, as noted above, as the number of variables and potential outcomes for a problem domain increase, the more likely it becomes that a quantum computer will outperform its traditional counterparts.

To that end, the following sections present the types of applications where QC excels.

Cryptography

Where would the world be without digital cryptography? We couldn't authenticate our identities, perform online banking, exchange secure messages, ensure data privacy, trade cryptocurrencies, etc. (See Chapter 8 for more information.)

The crypto solutions in use today rely on the fact that certain computations (e.g., integer factorization) require an enormous amount of processing power to "undo." So, for example, once we encrypt a password using modern cryptographic algorithms, it's highly improbable that a hacker can "reverse engineer" it even using the most powerful digital computers.

That is not the case with quantum computers. On the contrary, they have the power to crack codes in minutes that would take traditional computers over 10,000 years. Thus, when quantum computers do become mainstream, the IT industry will have no choice but to revamp the current approach to digital cryptography.

Quantum Simulation

At the opening of this chapter, we introduced the world of QM and hinted at the wonder and complexity of nature's design at the subatomic level. Given QC's power and ability to perform complex calculations, they are well-suited to model quantum systems that would otherwise overwhelm or remain beyond the scope of classical computers.

The irony is difficult to overlook: We can use quantum states in quantum computers to model quantum states in Nature. How cool is that?

Optimization

One of the most challenging tasks in classical computing involves *optimization*, which we define as identifying the best solution given many variables, choices, and constraints.

One of the classic examples of this type of algorithm is the traveling salesperson problem (Figure 10.9). We can describe it as follows:

> Given a list of cities and their relative distances, compute the shortest route that visits all locations and begins and ends in the same place.

FIGURE 10.9   Traveling salesperson problem.

Note that the more cities we include in the salesperson's travel itinerary, the more possible solutions we must consider.

Unfortunately, this class of problem can quickly overwhelm classical computers because the solution requires an exhaustive search. That is, traditional approaches must compute every path before selecting the optimal route.

Quantum computers approach the problem differently. Because of superposition, they can examine each path simultaneously and determine an optimal route in just a fraction of the time.

Please note that this is but one example of an optimization problem; there are many others (as we'll explore in the Advanced Section).

For example, most corporate executives want to optimize many interdependent aspects of their businesses: Costs, production times, delivery schedules, product quality, supply logistics, etc. However, the combinations and permutations quickly become overwhelming using digital computers.

In contrast, QC promises to arrive at such solutions previously considered impossible using traditional methodologies.

Machine Learning

Artificial intelligence (see Chapter 9) has revolutionized and will continue to revolutionize how humans interact with machines. However, AI solutions require training, and training relies on learning models.

Researchers are now exploring how quantum computers can reduce the "learning curve" of AI solutions.

Searching Algorithms

Although extensive research has optimized how classical computers search for data, it's still a relatively expensive process. However, because they can explore multiple paths concurrently, quantum computers can dramatically reduce the time required to locate and process information.

ADVANCED SECTION

A Quantum Computing Example

It's time to put all our newfound understanding of QM to use by reviewing a simple albeit contrived example that highlights the differences between classical and QC.

Assume we manage a freight company specializing in moving hazardous cargo, and for driver and public safety, we need to segregate loads. Specifically, some types of products are so dangerous in combination that we can't ship them on the same truck.

Nonetheless, because we are a business, we want to manage costs. Thus, we want to minimize the number of trucks and empty cargo space in their respective trailers while ensuring that we don't comingle mutually hazardous cargo.

Let's suppose our first shipment contains only three products: A, B, and C. When we review the warning labels, we discover that:

- A and B are safe to ship together
- A and C are too hazardous to ship together
- B and C are too hazardous to ship together

Given the above restrictions, we want to maximize safety while minimizing the number of trucks required to complete the shipments.

Obviously, this example is trivial enough to work out with little more than a pencil and paper. Nonetheless, let's see how we might solve it using a quantum computer.

Let's label our trucks T_0,[20] T_1, T_2, ... T_n. Because we have only three products to ship, we'll need at most three trucks. However, after a moment's reflection, we realize that we'll only need two: T_1 and T_2.

Given that we have three products to ship and two trucks from which to choose, we can compute the total number of combinations as follows:

2 * 2 * 2 = 8

As illustrated in Table 10.1, we can represent the combinations using classical *bits*.

TABLE 10.1 Product Shipping Choices

Product A	Product B	Product C
0	0	0
0	0	1
0	1	0
0	1	1
1	0	0
1	0	1
1	1	0
1	1	1

The 0s and 1s represent the trucks T_0 and T_1, respectively. Thus, the values appearing in Row 1 (0, 0, 0) indicate that all products would ship via Truck T_0. Row 2 suggests that Products A and B would travel in Truck T_0, and Product C would roll out on Truck T_1.

Please note that Table 10.1 contains all product/truck combinations, not just valid ones. For example, Row 1 is not viable because of the constraint specifying that Product C cannot ship on the same truck with either Products A or B. Thus, we need a way to grade or weigh each choice so we can select one that's optimal.

---

[20] Please recall that in computer science, we always start counting at 0.

Because of this example's simplicity, we might opt to grade each row using 0s and 1s: If the option is viable, it gets a 1; if not, we assign it a 0.

However, as the numbers of products, trucks, and constraints expand, that approach becomes increasingly untenable. So instead, we should develop a formulaic method that allows us to *compute* grades for each option.

One way we can achieve this is to establish a simple scoring system that calculates values based on safe/unsafe combinations. For example, we know that Products A and B may ship in the same truck; thus, we can assign that product combination the value 1. On the other hand, for unsafe groupings (e.g., Products A and C), we can use a value of −1. Also, if a product ships alone, which is valid, we will assign that option a value of 0.

Given this approach, we can assign grades to Row 1 of Table 10.1 (i.e., all products ship in Truck T_0) as depicted in Table 10.2:

TABLE 10.2   Row 1 Grades

Product Combination	Grade
Products A and B	1
Products A and C	−1
Products B and C	−1
Total Grade	−1

Extending this idea, we can compute grades for all the other rows and add a "grade" column to Table 10.1; Table 10.3 presents the result.

TABLE 10.3   Graded Options

Product A	Product B	Product C	Grade
0	0	0	−1
0	0	1	1
0	1	0	−1
0	1	1	−1
1	0	0	−1
1	0	1	−1
1	1	0	1
1	1	1	−1

After reviewing the results, we can quickly determine that there are two valid shipping options:

- Ship Products A and B on Truck T_0 and ship Product C on Truck T_1 (Row 2)

- Ship Products A and B on Truck T_1 and ship Product C on Truck T_0 (Row 7)

As you may have already noted, these two options are variations of the same theme: Ship Products A and B together; Product C ships alone.

At the risk of appearing repetitive, it was a trivial matter to determine the most appropriate shipping combinations in this example. But consider how quickly the complexity would increase as you add products, trucks, and additional constraints.

For example, what if Product A couldn't ship with both Products B and C together but could reside in the same truck with either one of them individually. In addition, the solution might need to address other concerns like destinations, driver schedules, customer delivery requirements, and the cost of partially empty containers.

As you might expect, the number of combinations quickly grows beyond the practicality of arriving at a solution manually. Moreover, because they must conduct an exhaustive search of all outcomes, the computations might also become infeasible for traditional automated solutions. That's because bits can hold only one value (0 or 1) at a time, and the combination of three bits can represent only one of the eight options at any moment (e.g., 1,0,1). Thus, a classically designed computer program must iterate through all combinations—one at a time—to compute the grades and determine the best choices.

Can we do better?

Enter quantum computers.

As we noted earlier, qubits can enter a state of superposition and can thus represent all eight combinations *simultaneously*. As a result, an algorithm specifically designed for a quantum computer will calculate the scores for all eight options concurrently.

To accomplish this, quantum computer programmers must:

- Establish a superposition of qubits representing all possible solutions. That means creating a superposition of all eight product/truck combinations noted above.

- Execute a QC-designed algorithm that calculates results using qubits. In our example, that means simultaneously computing the grade for each option.

- When processing completes, measure the states of the qubits.

If this solution approach appears "peculiar" from the other programming examples appearing in this book, it's because it is. Quantum computers process data *differently*; thus, developers must alter their programming approach to harness their power.

Quantum computers can really "strut their stuff" when you need to compute a result based on many variables, options, and constraints. In such cases, the effort required to establish the superposition of the qubits is more than offset by the comparatively short execution time.

SUMMARY

In this chapter, we dipped our toes into the vast subatomic ocean called QM. We introduced concepts such as wave-particle duality, the uncertainty principle, superposition, and entanglement.

We then discussed how the principles of QM serve as the foundation for QC. We explained that qubits serve as the basic unit of data in a quantum computer and that, by harnessing entanglement and superposition, they can compute multiple solution paths concurrently. We also compared the power of QC to that of classical solutions.

Finally, we observed that although quantum computers might suffer from a limitation in scope, they nonetheless hold the promise of almost unlimited power.

CHAPTER 11

What's Next?

The best way to predict the future ... is to invent it.

ALAN KAY

Technology is anything invented after you were born. Everything else is just stuff.

ALAN KAY

INTRODUCTION

Margret Atwood famously said, "People use technology only to mean digital technology. Technology is actually everything we make." To underscore her point, one must look no further than disciplines such as medicine, physics, and material sciences to see that technology is advancing so rapidly and so broadly that it has become challenging to remain current.

Nonetheless, in keeping with the focus of this book, the following sections will provide a glimpse at some exciting advances in digital technology that are peeking over the electronic horizon.

WHAT IS IoT?

As most readers of this book know, the Internet has connected the world in ways we hadn't even thought of a few years ago. We can work, chat, compose music, and play games with folks worldwide as if they were sitting in the same room.

But that's only the beginning.

You might be familiar with smart home technology—the ability to automate lights, thermostats, alarms, sprinkler systems, etc. But what about coffeepots, cars, refrigerators, toasters, alarm clocks, activity trackers, and, well, everything else.

The next level of interconnectivity, called the Internet of Things (IoT), is in its nascent stages.[1]

---

[1] As of the time of this writing.

DOI: 10.1201/9781003143437-11

DEFINITION 1

The Internet of Things is a developing technology that embeds physical objects with digital sensors and software, allowing them to connect, communicate, and interoperate with other "intelligent" devices and systems via the Internet or local networks.

With IoT, every digital device will eventually be able to communicate with each other. Consider the following examples.

- In addition to waking you at the appropriate time, your alarm clock could signal your coffee maker to begin a brew cycle, start your shower so the water would be warm, and, after querying your calendar, send your car's navigation system the location of your first stop.

- Your refrigerator could automatically place electronic orders with your grocery store.

- An intelligent traffic system could reduce congestion by automatically rerouting cars via their navigation systems.

- IoT devices could monitor cardiac patients' heart and respiratory rates, allowing their doctors to adjust their pacemakers in real time.

Below are some other advanced uses of IoT.

Asset Tracking	IoT can track products from "cradle to grave."
Device Monitoring	Smart monitors can provide status on components such as pipeline valves, electrical junctions, and machine parts.
Smart IDs	Using IoT-enabled badges, organizations can identify and monitor the location of all personnel in sensitive facilities.
Fleet Status	While humans still drive trucks (see below), IoT can provide transportation companies with real-time monitoring of vehicles and driver performance.

Is IoT a good thing? Of course, it can be—if controlled and used appropriately.

Is there a downside? Yes. I know I'm harping, but so long as humans reside on this planet, one or more of them will determine how to exploit IoT's power for illegitimate purposes.

ANYTHING AS A SERVICE

Most folks have become comfortable with the notion of cloud computing (see Chapter 7). Many of us use software applications that don't reside on our personal computing devices—they're located somewhere "on the Web." Many of us also store data on "cloud drives," so it is accessible from anywhere in the world via an Internet connection.

Anything as a Service (XaaS) is the next logical step, extending this idea to its extreme.

DEFINITION 2

Anything as a Service refers to the ability of users to acquire all computing services—hardware, software, data, etc.—from a remote location via an Internet connection.

In short, XaaS allows you to relocate everything that currently resides on your desktop, laptop, or smartphone onto a "cloud" service.[2] Then, you direct your local platform to the appropriate location whenever you need to use it. In effect, your personal computer becomes a portal, allowing you a "view" into the remote computing world.

This processing model has many advantages. For example, users no longer need to concern themselves with such mundane issues as hardware and network outages, data backup and recovery, and system security. Instead, your XaaS provider assumes those responsibilities.

However, as with any human innovation, XaaS has some downsides; I've noted a few below.

Vendor Dependence	Once you've selected a XaaS service, changing providers might become difficult or cost prohibitive.
Security	You must rely on your provider's integrity and professional capabilities to ensure the safety and integrity of your data. I should note that this might be an advantage for users if they select reputable providers who take that responsibility seriously.
Costs	Although we may benefit from economies of scale, the costs associated with XaaS may be beyond the means for some user communities.

The above notwithstanding, XaaS will likely become the *de facto* computing model of the future.

TRANSPORTATION AS A SERVICE

Most of us understand that self-driving vehicles are *fait accompli*. Soon every passenger—including the nominal driver—will be able to enjoy a movie, a quick nap, or read the news on a smartphone while self-driving cars safely deliver them to their intended destinations.

To extend this idea, the day will come when we no longer need to own vehicles. Instead, we'll subscribe to a service that allows us to "summon" a car whenever we need one. Then, after we complete our trip, we'll dispatch it back to its garage while it awaits a page from the next customer.

---

[2] The early versions of Google's Chromebook pioneered this idea.

HUMAN AUGMENTATION

The phrase, *human augmentation*, sounds like a plot in a horror movie or the evil plan of some demented doctor in a science fiction novel. But, though still controversial, it is much more benign than it sounds.

> **DEFINITION 3**
>
> *Human augmentation* is the practice of enhancing human abilities using various types of technology.

Human augmentation can take many forms:

- AI-based image analysis can enhance the effectiveness of ophthalmologists when diagnosing eye disorders

- Digital-based medical implants can help patients overcome physical disabilities

- Computer-assisted training programs used by professional athletes

Although some critics consider these practices controversial, human augmentation has become the norm since the advent of the crutch and the introduction of the first set of corrective lenses to improve eyesight. This trend will continue to gain momentum with each innovation in technology. The desire for personal improvement and lifestyle enhancement is an innate human trait and desire.

We, as a society, must determine where to set the boundaries—if any.

METAVERSES AND EXTREME VIRTUALIZATION

As has been famously stated, necessity is the mother of invention.

We experienced that reality during the COVID-19 pandemic when businesses had to adopt and adapt to remote working arrangements. Overnight, offices became virtual, meetings took place using Web-based conferencing platforms, and even the most extreme technophobes quickly became conversant with email, texting, and chat services.

This trend will only increase as society continues to embrace *metaverses*.

> **DEFINITION 4**
>
> A *metaverse* is a digital-based virtual world shareable by many concurrent users via the Internet.

Made common in the world of gaming, metaverses have achieved a "life-like" feel through the integration of technological advances in Virtual Reality (VR) and Augmented Reality (AR). When "entering" a metaverse, users experience an enhanced version of reality or immerse themselves in a newly constructed virtual world limited only by the imagination of its human creators.

ROBOTS AND JOBS

Most readers will not be shocked or surprised by the title of this section. Robots have crept their way into our everyday lives and are now commonplace: They build our cars, dust our floors, and even serve as waiters in restaurants.

As AI technology advances, so will the trend in having robots perform the mundanities of everyday life. Soon, robots will:

- Deliver mail

- Replace fast-food workers and line cooks

- Serve as librarians

- Drive our cars and deliver our goods

- Function as proofreaders and editors (Yikes! I hope my publisher doesn't read this!)

There are many predictions about the effect robots will have on society and the human condition. Some are promising; others are dire.

As with all changes, it's probably a little of both. It suffices to say that society will establish boundaries, like all technological innovations.

THE END OF PROGRAMMING?

Software programming is labor-intensive and is thus costly to produce. As a result, for decades, the IT industry has tried to develop methodologies that will reduce—or even eliminate—the need for application developers.

To that end, a research group called Open-AI is experimenting with a coding model called Codex that can generate Python[3] code from instructions specified in English. Although the concept is still in the preliminary stages of development, Codex holds the promise of allowing the average computer user to create simple programs using plain language.

SUMMARY

As many folks are fond of saying, the future is now. To that end, this chapter presented some exciting, innovative technologies such as XaaS, new programming paradigms, robotics, IoT, and Transportation as a service.

---

[3] Python is a popular programming language.

Glossary of Terms

Absolute zero: Measured using the Kelvin scale, science defines *absolute zero* as the complete absence of heat and motion. Thought to be the coldest temperature possible, it's equivalent to $-273.15°$ Celsius and $-459.67°$ Fahrenheit.

Abstraction: An *abstraction* distills a problem domain's essential and relevant attributes to simplify its representation.

AC: *Accumulator*—A special-purpose register within the CPU.

ADC: See *analog-to-digital converter*.

AF: AF is the *activation function* in a neural network.

A-GPS: Assisted GPS or augmented GPS.

AI: See *artificial intelligence*.

Algorithm: An *algorithm* is a solution methodology suitable for implementation on a computer (i.e., using software).

ALU: Arithmetic/logic unit.

Amplitude: *Amplitude* is a measure of a wave's energy.

Analog communication: *Analog communication* uses a continuous signal that varies in frequency or amplitude. The human voice is an excellent example of an analog signal.

Analog-to-digital converter: An *Analog-to-Digital Converter* (ADC) samples audio signals (e.g., music) and converts each sample into a numerical value.

AND gate: We define an *AND gate* as a logic circuit that determines logical conjunction.

ANN: Artificial Neural Network.

Application: An *application* is a finite arrangement of instructions packaged as one or more programs that, when executed, use data to accomplish a specific set of tasks within a targeted computing environment.

AR: Augmented reality.

Artificial intelligence: *Artificial intelligence* is a machine's ability to simulate the cognitive capabilities of human beings.

ASCII: American Standard Code for Information Interchange.

ATM: Automated teller machine.

Atomic clock: An *atomic clock* measures time by tracking the oscillation of atoms.

Authentication: *Authentication* is the process of determining your identity.

Authorization: *Authorization is the process of establishing the limits on what system resources individual users may access.*

Backbone: A *backbone* is a network connection that interconnects (joins) multiple network segments.

Backpropagation: *Backpropagation* is a supervised learning method that allows a neural network to determine the accuracy of its predictions and adjust its weights accordingly.

Backtracking: *Backtracking* is a programming method whereby processing continues along a given "path" in search of a solution. At each "fork in the road," the program "guesses" which "path" it should follow. If this choice proves unsuccessful, the program "backs up" (i.e., returns to) a prior choice and selects an alternate "path."

Band: Frequency band. See also *channel*.

Base station: See *cell site*.

Binary digit: *Binary digits* are the 0s and 1s of electronic data.

BIOS: Basic Input/Output System. See *Firmware*.

Bit: See *binary digit*.

Bitcoin miner: A *Bitcoin miner* is a Bitcoin participant who creates new Bitcoin.

Bitcoin mining: The creation of new Bitcoin.

Broadcast: *Broadcast* is a one-way communication system wherein a single transmitter sends information to many recipients.

Bus: See *computer bus*.

Byte: In computers, a *byte* is a group of 8 bits.

CAN: Campus Area Network (also called a corporate area network).

CDSM: Code Division Multiple access

Cell network: A *cell network* comprises a set of cell sites spanning a broad geographic area (e.g., a city)

Cell phone: A *cell phone* is a portable device that allows users to connect to the traditional, public (switched) telephone network to initiate and receive calls.

Cell site: A *cell site* comprises a tower (hosting the antennas) and a small structure or building that hosts the necessary electronics enabling the site to connect to the mobile carrier's network.

Cellular network: A *cellular network* is a set of interconnected stations (called *cells*) that use radio-based technologies (i.e., wireless connectivity) to communicate with mobile phones.

Channel: A *channel* is a specific frequency within a band.

CHF: See *Cryptographic Hash Function*.

Client-server model: The *client-server model* is a communications framework that pairs a service requestor with a service provider via a network connection. The requestor is the client; the provider is the server.

Cloud computing: *Cloud computing* uses remote (off-site) hardware and software computing services such as servers, storage, applications, and databases.

CNN: Convolutional Neural Network.

Compilation: *Compilation* is the process of translating a computer program written in one language (called the source language) into another language (called the target language).

Computer algorithm: See *algorithm*.

Computer bus: A *bus* facilitates the transport of data among connected components.

Computer memory: See *Memory*.

Computer programming: *Computer programming* is a set of tasks and procedures conducted by software developers that, when completed, generate a set of executable instructions that achieve a specific result.

Context: Context is the execution state of a process.

Control channel: A *control channel* allows cell phones to complete many administrative tasks such as logging onto the network, call initiation, and voice channel assignment.

Corporate area network: See *CAN*.

CPU: Central Processing Unit.

CRC: Cyclic Redundancy Check.

Cryptocurrency: *Cryptocurrency* is a monetary system with no central authority or issuing agency but instead uses a distributed, decentralized design to track transactions and create new monetary units.

Cryptographic Hash Function: A *Cryptographic Hash Function* is a mathematical computation applied to a series of bytes (often called the "message") that generate a unique value called the hash.

CU: Control unit.

Cycle: A *cycle* is one repetition of a wave.

DAC: See *Digital-to-Analog Converter*.

Darknet: A d*arknet* is a private, layered network that restricts accessibility to select groups or individuals.

Dark web: The *dark web* (or darknet) is a subset of the deep web that requires specialized software, custom configurations, and explicit authorization to access any of its servers.

Data structure: A *data structure* is a formalized arrangement of binary digits (0s and 1s).

DAW: Digital Audio Workstations.

Deep web: The *deep web* comprises all unindexed servers connected to the Internet.

Digital currency: *Digital currency* is money that is available only in an electronic form.

Digital information: *Digital information* is data that we can represent as a series of 1s and 0s. So, for example, every file on your smartphone or computer—emails, songs, pictures, etc.—contains only 1s and 0s.

Digital-to-analog converter: A *digital-to-analog converter* transforms digital values (1s and 0s) into an analog signal suitable for playback through an amplifier and speakers

Digitization: We define digitization as the process of converting data into a binary representation that consists solely of 1s and 0s.

DL: Deep Learning.

DLT: Distributed Ledger Technology.

DNS: Domain Name System

DoD: The United States Department of Defense.

Duplex communication: A *duplex communication* system allows communicating parties to exchange messages in both directions. (See *full duplex* and *half duplex*.)

Electronic Serial Number: See *ESN*.

Entanglement: See quantum entanglement.

Ephemeris: An *ephemeris* is a compilation of tables (often called an astronomical almanac) that specify the orbits of satellites (both natural and artificial).

Epoch: An *epoch* is one complete iteration through an AI training data set.

EPROM: Erasable ROM.

EEPROM: Electrically Erasable ROM.

ESN: Electronic serial number (for CDMA-based cell phones).

Ethernet: *Ethernet* is a network protocol that packages, manages, and controls data transmission over LAN connections.

Everything as a service: *Everything as a service* refers to the ability of users to acquire all computing services—hardware, software, data, etc.—from a remote location via an Internet connection.

Execution state: See *context*.

Expansion slot: An *expansion slot* is an electronic "socket" into which you can insert optional components.

Extranet: *Extranets* are like *intranets* in that they remain under the control of a single organization. However, they allow limited access to external entities and users

Feed-forward neural network: In a *feed-forward neural network*, the nodes do not form cycles, and information flows in one direction.

FFN: See *Feed-Forward Neural Network*.

Firmware: *Firmware* is software integrated into the hardware that controls the operation of the underlying circuitry.

FPU: Floating-Point Unit.

Frequency: Cycles per second.

Frequency band: A *frequency band* is a predefined range of frequencies with specific upper and lower limits.

Full duplex: With *full-duplex* communication, each communicating entity uses two channels: One for sending and one for receiving.

FTP: File Transfer Protocol

Gateway: A *gateway* is a network node that allows access to other networks (e.g., the Internet).

Genesis block: A *genesis block* is the initial block (Block 0) of a blockchain.

Geographic Information System: See *GIS*.

Gigahertz: A *gigahertz* is 1 billion cycles (hertz) per second.

GIS: A *GIS*, or *Geographic Information System*, functions as a data framework that allows computer-based applications to store, retrieve, and otherwise manipulate spatial and geographic-related information.

GPS: Global Positioning Systems.

GPS receiver: A *GPS receiver* processes radio signals transmitted by orbiting GPS satellites

GSM: Global System for Mobile Communication

GUI: Graphical User Interface.

Hacker: A *hacker* is an individual or organization that attempts to gain unlawful access to other individuals' or organizations' computer systems and data.

Half duplex: In *half-duplex* systems, communicating entities share the same channel.

HAN: Home Area Network.

Hard boot: Applying power to a system. See *soft boot*.

Hardware register: See *register*.

Hash function: A *hash function* is a "one-way" formula that returns a unique, one-way, fixed-length value for a given input.

Heisenberg uncertainty principle: The *uncertainty principle* holds that we cannot accurately measure pairs of attributes (e.g., position and velocity) of an object.

Hertz: *Hertz* is a measure of frequency; 1 hertz is one cycle per second.

HTTP: Hypertext Transfer Protocol

HTTPS: Hypertext Transfer Protocol Secure

Human augmentation: *Human augmentation* is the practice of enhancing human abilities using various forms of technology.

Hyperparameter: *Hyperparameters* are adjustable values used to manage the learning process.

IaaS: Infrastructure as a service.

IF: *Input Function* for a node in a neural network.

IMAP: Internet Messaging Access Protocol

IMEI: International Mobile Equipment Identity (for GSM-based cell phones).

Internet of Things: The *Internet of Things* is a developing technology that embeds physical objects with digital sensors and software, allowing them to connect, communicate, and interoperate with other "intelligent" devices and systems via the Internet or local networks.

Interpreter: An *interpreter* is a software application that executes instructions without requiring compilation.

Inter-process communication: *Inter-process communication* is a software service that allows processes to exchange data

Intranet: An *intranet* is one or more interconnected networks controlled by one organization for the benefit of its users

IoT: See *Internet of Things*.

IP: Internet Protocol. See also *TCP/IP*.

IPC: See *Inter-Process Communication*.

IR: Instruction Register.

ISP: Internet Service Provider.

JVM: Java Virtual Machine. See also *VM*.

Kilohertz: A kilohertz is 1,000 cycles (hertz) per second.

LAN: Local Area Network.

Learning rate: *Learning rate* is an adjustable parameter that controls the degree that weights may change during each iteration.

LF: See *Loss Function*.

Logic gate: A *logic gate* determines its binary output based on various combinations of its input.

Loss Function: A *Loss Function* determines the degree of error (i.e., the "loss") between a neural network's computed output and the expected result.

MAC address: Media Access Control address.

Mail delivery agent: A *mail delivery agent* is a software component that functions as an email user's inbox.

Mail transfer agent: A *mail transfer agent* is a software component that sends email messages from senders to recipients.

Mail user agent: A *mail user agent* is an application that allows users to compose and send emails (e.g., Outlook, Gmail, etc.)

Malware: *Malware* is any software written for malicious purposes.

MAN: Metropolitan Area Network.

MAR: Memory Address Register.

MC: Memory Controller.

MDA: See *Mail Delivery Agent.*

MDR: Memory Data Register.

Megahertz: A *megahertz* is 1 million cycles (hertz) per second.

Memory: *Memory* is the primary storage location for all instructions and data currently executing within a computer.

MEO: Medium Earth Orbit.

Metaverse: A *metaverse* is a digital-based virtual world shareable by many concurrent users via the Internet.

MIME: Multipurpose Internet Mail Extensions

MIN: A *MIN*—mobile identification number—is a cell phone's telephone number.

Miner: See *Bitcoin miner.*

Mining: See *Bitcoin mining.*

ML: Machine Learning.

MMS: Multimedia Messaging Service—text messaging.

MMSC: Multimedia Messaging Service Center—helps cell networks send MMS attachments such as photos or videos.

Mobile identification number: See *MIN.*

Mobile network: *See* cell network.

Modem: A MOdulator-DEModulator.

Motherboard: The *motherboard* is the primary piece of circuitry for most electronic devices

MPEG-4: Moving Picture Experts Group (All Inclusive and Interactive)

MP4: See MPEG-4

MTA: See *Mail Transfer Agent.*

MTSO: Mobile Telephone Switching Office.

MUA: See *Mail User Agent.*

NAVSTAR: Navigation System with Timing and Ranging.

Network: A *network* comprises two or more systems (called *nodes* in network terminology) that exchange data via wired or wireless communication technologies.

Network gateway: See *gateway*.

Networking: *Networking* is the ability to connect two or more electronic devices with the express intent to share data or computing resources.

Network protocol: A *network protocol* establishes the rules, procedures, and formats that allow electronic components to exchange data securely, efficiently, and reliably.

NIC: Network Interface Controller.

NLP: Natural Language Processing.

Node: A *node* is any physical device that can forward or consume transmitted data via a network.

Nonce: Number used once.

OCR: Optical Character Recognition

Operating system: An *operating system* oversees and controls access to all system resources (both hardware and software) and manages the execution of all application programs.

OS: See *Operating System*.

OTP: One-Time PIN.

OUI: Organizational Unique Identifier. See also *MAC address*.

PaaS: Platform as a Service.

PAN: Personal Area Network.

PC: Program Counter.

Personally identifiable information: *Personally Identifiable Information* (PII) is data that identify a specific individual.

Photon: A *photon* is the quantization of light energy into discrete packets.

Piconet: When connected, a group of Bluetooth devices from a *piconet*.

PII: See *personally identifiable information*.

Pixel: The term *pixel* refers to the fundamental picture element of a digital image or screen display. It contains the color and brightness of a single "dot" (point).

PK: Public Key.

POP3: Post Office Protocol 3 (Version 3).

Portal: A *portal* serves as a controlled entry point into a network.

POTS: Plain Old Telephone System (i.e., landlines)

PoW: Proof of Work.

PPS: Precise Positioning Service.

Process: A *process* is the running image of a program as it executes in memory. See also, *program*.

Program: A *program* is an ordered collection of computer instructions contained in a file. See also, *process*.

Programming language: A *programming language* is a formalized set of general-purpose instructions that produce a precise result when combined and executed in a specific arrangement.

Protocol: See *network protocol*.

Pseudocode: *Pseudocode* allows developers to describe programming logic using human-readable constructs without becoming mired in a specific language's syntactic details.

Public-key encryption: *Public-key encryption* is a cryptographic technique that requires two keys: A public key and a private key.

QC: Quantum Computing.

QM: Quantum Mechanics.

QS: See *Quantum Supremacy*.

Quantum entanglement: *Quantum entanglement* occurs when multiple particles interact so strongly that we cannot independently describe their states (properties).

Quantum supremacy: *Quantum supremacy* is when quantum computers can perform calculations that are beyond the capabilities of the most powerful digital computers.

Qubit: A *qubit* can represent the values 0, 1, or some combination of both 0 and 1 in a superposition.

RAM: Random-Access Memory.

Register: A *register* is a high-speed memory repository within the CPU.

RFC: Request For Comment.

RL: Reinforcement Learning.

RNN: Recurrent Neural Network.

ROM: Read-Only Memory.

RTMP: Real-Time Messaging Protocol

SaaS: Software as a Service.

Search engine: A *search engine* is a software application comprising two main parts: A cataloging component that scans the Web, indexing every data element found on every website, and a searching component that, based on user queries, displays the URLs of previously indexed websites.

SFTP: Secure File Transfer Protocol

SID: System IDentification number uniquely identifies a specific cell phone network.

Simple Mail Transfer Protocol: Simple Mail Transfer Protocol (SMTP).

SK: Secret key.

Smartphone: A *smartphone* is a mobile electric device that provides functionality beyond basic cell phone capabilities. Examples include email, movie streaming, videoconferencing, interactive games, and payment services.

SMS: Short Message Service—the primary form of texting

SMTP: Simple Mail Transfer Protocol.

Soft boot: Restarting the operating system. See *hard boot*.

Software: *Software* is an organized arrangement of data and instructions that, when executed, direct the operations of the underlying hardware to accomplish a particular purpose.

Spam: *Spam* refers to unwanted electronic junk mail. It derives its name from a 1970s Monty Python's Flying Circus comedy skit set in a restaurant wherein the characters repeatedly recite the word "spam."

SPS: Standard Positioning Service.

Superposition: *Superposition* combines two or more states to form a new state.

System identification number: See *SID*.

TCP: Transmission Control Protocol. See also *TCP/IP*.

TCP/IP: Transmission Control Protocol/Internet Protocol.

Technology: *Technology* is the purposeful adaptation of science and knowledge by humans to benefit other human beings.

Terahertz: A *terahertz* is 1 trillion cycles (hertz) per second.

Time To First Fix: *Time To First Fix* is the time a GPS receiver requires to calculate an initial fix.

Topology: *Topology* characterizes the organization and hierarchy of the nodes residing on a network.

ToS: Terms of Service.

Traveling salesperson problem: Given a list of cities and their relative distances, compute the shortest route that visits all locations and begins and ends in the same place.

Trilateration: *Trilateration* is a process that relies on geometry to compute a specific location based on measuring distances from known points.

Truth table: A *truth table* specifies the correct output for all input combinations.

TTFF: See *Time to First Fix*.

TTSF: Time to Subsequent Fix.

Uncertainty principle: See *Heisenberg uncertainty principle*.

URL: Uniform Resource Locator.

USB: Universal Serial Bus.

Vector: A *vector* is a quantity representing both magnitude and direction.

Velocity: *Velocity* is a *vector* incorporating both the speed and direction of an object.

Vendor-assigned address: Part of a MAC address. See also *MAC address*.

Virtual machine: A *virtual machine* is a software representation of a computer system that emulates hardware functionality.

VM: See *Virtual Machine*. See also *JVM*.

VOIP: *Voice Over IP*—Computer-based telephony.

VPN: Virtual Private Network.

VR: Virtual Reality.

Wave cycle: See *cycle*.

Wavelength: We define *wavelength* as the distance between two successive peaks in a wave.

XaaS: See *Anything as a Service*.

Reading List

CHAPTER 1—INTRODUCTION

On the history of computing:

- Ceruzzi, P.E. (2003). *A History of Modern Computing*, Second Edition. The MIT Press.
- Williams, M.R. (1997). *A History of Computing Technology*, Second Edition. Wiley-IEEE Computer Society.
- Ifrah, G. (2001). *The Universal History of Computing: From the Abacus to the Quantum Computer*. Wiley.

CHAPTER 2—HOW DO CELL PHONES WORK?

- Horst, H.; Miller, D. (2006). *The Cell Phone: An Anthropology of Communication*. Routledge.
- Aschoff, N. (2020). *The Smartphone Society: Technology, Power, and Resistance in the New Gilded Age*. Beacon Press.

CHAPTER 3—HOW DOES GPS WORK?

- Bhatta, B. (2011). *Global Navigation Satellite Systems: Insights into GPS, GLONASS, Galileo, Compass, and Others*. CRC Press.
- Kaplan, E.D. (2017). *Understanding GPS/GNSS: Principles and Applications*, Third Edition (Gnss Technology and Applications Series). Artech House.

CHAPTER 4—HOW DOES COMPUTER HARDWARE WORK?

- Bowman, C.F. (2002). *How Things Work: The Computer Science Edition*. CRC Press.
- Hsu, J.Y. (2001). *Computer Architecture Software Aspects, Coding, and Hardware*. CRC press.
- Patterson, D.A.; Hennessy, J.L. (2013). *Computer Organization and Design (MIPS Edition)*, Sixth Edition. Morgan Kaufmann.
- Dumas II, J.D. (2017). *Computer Architecture Fundamentals and Principles of Computer Design*, Second Edition. CRC Press.

CHAPTER 5—WHAT IS SOFTWARE?

- Bowman, C.F. (2002) *How Things Work: The Computer Science Edition*. CRC Press.
- Bowman, C. F. (1994). *Algorithms and Data Structures: An Approach in C*. Oxford University Press.

- Chemuturi, M. (2018). *Computer Programming for Beginners: A Step-By-Step Guide*. Chapman and Hall/CRC.
- Thomas, D.; Hunt, A. (2019). *The Pragmatic Programmer: Your Journey To Mastery*, Second Edition. Addison-Wesley Professional.
- Althoff, C. (2017). *The Self-Taught Programmer: The Definitive Guide to Programming Professionally*. Self-Taught Media.
- Louridas, P. (2020). *Algorithms*. The MIT Press.

CHAPTER 6—HOW DO COMPUTERS COMMUNICATE?

- Bowman, C.F. (2002). *How Things Work: The Computer Science Edition*. CRC Press.
- Hura, G.S.; Singhal, M. (2001). *Data and Computer Communications: Networking and Internetworking*. CRC Press.
- Morreale, P.A.; Anderson, J.M. (2015). *Software Defined Networking Design and Deployment*. CRC Press.
- Ross, K.W.; Kurose, J.F. (2017). *Computer Networking: A Top-Down Approach*, Sixth Edition. Pearson India.

CHAPTER 7—HOW DOES THE INTERNET WORK?

- Bowman, C.F. (2002). *How Things Work: The Computer Science Edition*. CRC Press.
- Comer, D.E. (2018). *The Internet Book: Everything You Need to Know about Computer Networking and How the Internet Works*. Chapman and Hall/CRC.
- Knodel, M. (2020). *How the Internet Really Works: An Illustrated Guide to Protocols, Privacy, Censorship, and Governance*. No Starch Press.

CHAPTER 8—HOW DO CRYPTOCURRENCIES WORK?

- Haynes, A.; Yeoh, P. (2020). *Cryptocurrencies and Cryptoassets: Regulatory and Legal Issues*. Routledge.
- Chowdhury, N. (2019). *Inside Blockchain, Bitcoin, and Cryptocurrencies*. Auerbach Publications.
- Seymour, R.B. (2021). *The Blockchain Future*. Independently published.

CHAPTER 9—WHAT IS ARTIFICIAL INTELLIGENCE?

- Bhargava, C.; Sharma, P.K. (2021). *Artificial Intelligence: Fundamentals and Applications*. CRC Press.
- Norvig, P.; Russell, S. (2021). *Artificial Intelligence: A Modern Approach*, Fourth Edition. Pearson.

CHAPTER 10—WHAT IS QUANTUM COMPUTING?

- Chen, G; et al. (2007). *Quantum Computing Devices: Principles, Designs, and Analysis*. Routledge.
- Bernhardt, C. (2020). *Quantum Computing for Everyone*, Reprint Edition. The MIT Press.

CHAPTER 11—WHAT'S NEXT?

- Blair, M. (2022). *Metaverse for Beginners*. Independently published.
- Verschraegen, G.; et al. (2019). *Imagined Futures in Science, Technology, and Society*. Routledge.

Index

Note: Locators in *italics* represent figures and **bold** indicate tables in the text.

Printed in the United States
by Baker & Taylor Publisher Services

Printed in the United States
by Baker & Taylor Publisher Services